READER

In light-hearted, nostalgic reminiscences in Hail, Hail to U City High, *Alan Spector has obviously found in his own high school in the mid-sixties the recipe for a good school...the memories of those "days we spent with you" are still dear and vividly recaptured in this book.*

Wallace G. Klein
University City High School Historian and Alumni Coordinator
University City High School Class of '40; Faculty '54-'83

It's been almost a half century since the nation's baby boomers entered their formative high school years. Alan Spector brings their memories alive again through the eyes of his suburban Missouri classmates of University City '64. It's all there—the classes (including scary drivers' education movies), the crushes (usually without sex), and the calamities (the JFK assassination, the Vietnam War). Spector captures the boomers' key moments, from rushing home for The Three Stooges *to avoiding the draft by gaining weight, then follows his colorful classmates for four decades in a fast-moving, personal read on a generation.*

Ted Gest
President—Criminal Justice Journalists
Author—*Crime & Politics*
University City High School Class of '64

Few public high schools in America can equal (University City's) high level of academic achievement and comparable success with its extra-curricular programs such as theatre, music, athletics, and public service. Alan Spector has effectively captured the essence of what it was like to grow up in such a place and why we should strive to spread its example.

Ken Holtzman
Former Major League Baseball Pitcher
University City High School Class of '63

Al's storytelling drew me in and made me feel part of his class and their close relationships. Everyone reading Hail, Hail to U City High *will be able to relate their own friendships to those of Al's classmates.*

Judith Van Ginkel, PhD
President—Every Child Succeeds
Author—*Life Begins and Ends with Girlfriends*
Stonewall Jackson High School (West Virginia) Class of '58

Don't ever underestimate the power a teacher has on their students. Alan's book reminds us how all it takes is for one teacher to make a difference in the life of their students. It doesn't matter what era you grew up in, your teachers leave lasting memories.

Brad Cohen
Author—*Front of the Class: How Tourette Syndrome
Made Me the Teacher I Never Had*
Parkway Central High School (Missouri) Class of '92

Snapshots of high school memories as viewed through the lens of the distant future. A chance to relive a treasure trove of fascinating stories.

Lester Horwitz
Pulitzer Prize-Nominated Author—*The Longest Raid of the Civil War*
Hughes High School (Ohio) Class of '49

Anyone who has ever been part of a group of people who meant so much to each other that their friendship overcomes time and distance will thoroughly enjoy Al Spector's book.

Ken Fouts
Director—NBC Sports (retired)
Bellevue High School (Nebraska) Class of '59

Following his first book, Baseball: Never Too Old to Play the Game, *Alan Spector has hit a home run. In* Hail, Hail to U City High, *Al looks to the future of his high school class (1964) of baby boomers as they move into a new phase of their lives. And he rightfully focuses on two things — their personal fitness and the importance of pursuing the passions of their youth. Their stories and his hopes for his classmates are really about all of us.*

Logan Franklin
Author—*Living a Fitness Lifestyle and Gray Iron:*
A Fitness Guide for Senior Men and Women
San Ramon Valley Union High School (California) Class of '56

Alan Spector has taken his high school graduating class of 1964 on a wonderful journey back to their sweet youth. This lively part chronicle, part memoir...is a testament both to Alan's diligent research and the vivid memories he has captured. Reading the book is a rekindling experience. It is also a bittersweet journey that chronicles the loss of youth and the loss of fellow classmates who have passed on. The book is special, much like University City High School.

Robert Berkowitz
Rutgers University History Teacher; Historical Novelist
West Orange Mountain High School (New Jersey) Class of '65

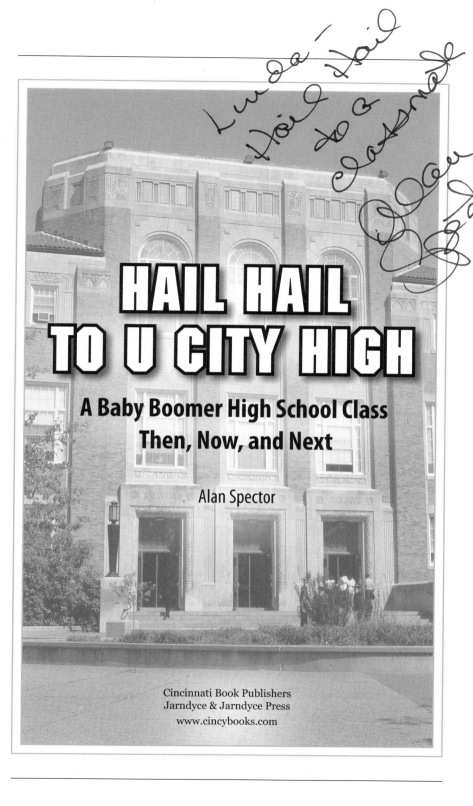

HAIL HAIL
TO U CITY HIGH

A Baby Boomer High School Class
Then, Now, and Next

Alan Spector

Cincinnati Book Publishers
Jarndyce & Jarndyce Press
www.cincybooks.com

Hail Hail to U City High
A Baby Boomer High School Class
Then, Now, and Next

by Alan Spector

Cover and text design: Brent Beck, www.brentbeck.com
Published by Cincinnati Book Publishers
Anthony W. Brunsman, President
Cincinnati Book Publishers World Wide Web address is http://www.cincybooks.com

ISBN-13 978-0-9817269-1-5
ISBN-10 0-9817269-1-7

Printed by John S. Swift Co., Inc.
Printed in the United States of America
First Edition, 2009

DEDICATIONS

This book is dedicated to two very special people in my life.

Dana Michele Spector
Sycamore High School Class 1988

To daughter, Dana Spector DeBlasi, who, with her husband, Vince, and their sons, Jordan and Aaron, chose to build their family in my home community and live across the street from University City High School.

Kevin Robert Spector
Sycamore High School Class 1991

To son, Kevin Spector, who, with his wife, Lisa, gave us the gift of another grandson, Jacob, while I was writing this book.

This book is additionally dedicated to those from the University City Class of 1964 who have passed away, yet will always be our classmates.

Terry Mitze

"A man he seems of cheerful yesterdays and confident tomorrows."

ACKNOWLEDGMENTS

This book is a self-assigned class project—an "A-plus" for the nearly 150 of you who allowed me to use your life experiences and memories to help tell our class story.

Thank you especially to classmates Tim Arnold, Joanna Slotkin Baymiller, Jill Friedman Chapin, Laya Firestone Seghi, David Pactor, Stephen Kowarsky, Adrienne Nadler Hirschfeld, Don Pearline, Elaine Levin Unell, Zara Haimo, Andrea Kolker Muchnick, Shellie Klevens Ritterman, Judy Fortus Growe, Ed Friedman, Kay Rudolph, and Jerry Weiner, who applied their creativity, capability, time, and energy, to each create a meaningful segment of the book.

Thank you to my *Tom-Tom* (school newspaper) research team, classmates Leslie Berger, Carol Enger Canis, Ellen Polinsky Cohen, Marla Schukar Levinson, Mickey Leon Sandmel, Gary Singer, Elaine Levin Unell, and Ron Unell.

Thank you to Mr. Wallace Klein, a 70-year denizen of the halls of University City High School as student, teacher, and school historian. Mr. Klein contributed his historical documents, time, knowledge, and passion for the school.

Thank you to Peter Schiff, who once again generously applied his thorough and insightful editing expertise to keep me on track.

Thank you to others who helped with the manuscript, especially classmates Arleen White Bly and Elaine Levin Unell, both career teachers. Special editing thanks to Dunieka Benjamin, Thomas Kenyon, Stephanie Perry, Ted Moses, Michael Pope, Tiffany Belger, and Calvin Johnson, all students in Mr. Rick Wilson's 2008 Creative Writing Class at University City High School.

Thank you to Tony Brunsman and Sue Ann Painter at Cincinnati Book Publishers and graphic designer, Brent Beck, for making the publishing process feel like a family project as well as a class project.

The biggest thank you goes to Ann, my wife, who has been adopted by my high school class as one of their own. She encouraged and supported me, contributed her editing skills, and, as always, provided insight just when I needed it most.

TABLE OF CONTENTS

PREFACE

I'll Be There

Alan R. Spector

"A good student, a good athlete, a good friend."

To an insecure high school student in the early 1960s, the future looked like: Who will I sit with at lunch today? Will I have a date on Friday night? How will I do in the football game on Saturday? How will I ever finish my term paper for next week? Will the green baggers accept me? Will I get the role in next month's school play? How will I tell my parents about that "D" I got on my math test?

Even for a "mature" senior, the future was only a little more expansive. Who will I ask to the prom? Will I be asked to the prom? Who wants to go to that silly old prom anyway? Where will I apply to college? What summer job can I get that will help me pay for college? How will I ever finish my term paper that is due tomorrow?

Few, if any of us were perceptive enough to be asking long-term questions. Who, what, and where will I be in 45 to 50 years? What will my relationship be with my high school classmates when we are in our 60s? Will I go to my 40-year reunion? If a classmate needs my help in the future, how will I know it and what support will I provide?

As graduating seniors, we signed each others' yearbooks with deep, insightful phrases.

"We have everything to base a marriage on—we disagree on everything. But alas, it cannot be. Jane" (Horzmann)

"We really caught some grins in US History! It's been great knowing you. Best of luck. Love, Joie" (Mary Jo Gottlieb)

"You'll do in a pinch; in fact, you'll do in a squeeze. Luck always, Elaine" (Levin)

"Keep up with baseball. You'll never make it as a football player. Bob Cooper"

"Specks—It has been your pleasure being with me all of these years. Seriously, Al, you are one of..." (Marc Tenzer—thought never finished)

"May your future wife be fruitful and bear you many offspring. W. J. F." (Bill Fuchs)

"Best of luck. I know whatever you strive for will be yours. Love, Barb" (Glick)

"It sure was different. Have a good time. Tom Norman"

While we would have liked to believe we would all remain friends, we knew we were heading off to different colleges and lives. Based on what we knew at the time, the yearbook messages could have simply been translated as, "Bye." As it turned out, that would have been shortsighted.

Although a substantial nucleus remains in St. Louis, the University City High School Class of 1964 is widely dispersed geographically. We are also separated by time and by our individual post-high school educational experiences, families, careers, and lives.

We could have easily left high school and our class far behind, perhaps only to be brought back together by an occasional reunion. That is what happened to many of the people I have talked to from other high school classes, both from different schools and from different years. It also happened to some members of our class. Yet, now in our 60s, a meaningful number of classmates from U City's class of '64 are in many ways as close now as, if not closer than, when we were in school together.

Perhaps we should have written in our high school yearbooks, "I look forward to still caring about you when we're in our 60s. If you need someone to talk to, I'll be there. If you want to visit, come see me, I'll be there. If you need support, I'll be there. I look forward to staying connected and seeing you as often as I can. I'll be there."

Who were we during our high school years in the early 60s? Who are we now that we are in our 60s? Why are many of us as close as we are? Why is it important that we are close? What have we learned and what can others learn from our common experience? Searching for answers to these questions is what inspired me to write this book.

There are other reasons as well. I had a fulfilling experience creating, publishing, and promoting my first book, *Baseball: Never Too Old to Play "The" Game*. It was just plain fun. Thus, writing another book was inevitable, and my high school class was an obvious choice for the subject matter.

If you read the first book, you may be surprised that this one is not about baseball. But in many ways neither was the first. It was fundamentally about life lessons derived from the game, playing it as a youth, and now playing it as I grow older. *Hail Hail to U City High* is similar, in that it explores life lessons learned from the journey of my high school class and, hopefully, of other early baby boomer classes.

My classmates often attempt to express how fortunate we are to continue to be so close. We stay with the discussion for awhile then give up and settle into the comfortable knowledge that it is just so.

Friends and family outside my class find our relationships hard to comprehend. Upon hearing how our class is still close, they frequently say something like, "You're kidding, aren't you? My class has reunions, but they are nothing like yours, and only a few keep in touch between reunions. How did your class get that way?"

While we could live with never being able to fully articulate the answer, my hope was that writing *Hail Hail to U City High* would help.

I also wrote this book because I envisioned the process bringing our class even closer together. As you will see throughout the book, I chose to write it interactively with my classmates, thinking about it as a class project. The book is filled with the perspectives of those who had positive high school experiences, those whose experience was negative, those who have stayed closely connected, and some who have not. The book also includes a number of significant contributions from classmates who eagerly jumped at the chance to write with me and from those who had created meaningful musical lyrics, poems, and prose over the years.

There are a number of other points about this book to share before getting on with it. First, to be clear, it is not about "my class is better than your class." Rather it is simply our story told in the absolute. Sure, we are generally proud of who we were and what we have become. But many deservedly feel the same way about their own high school class. I hope that our story is one everyone can relate to.

So, while this book is about my specific high school and class, it is also about yours. You can substitute the timeframe, the characters, the stories, and the perspectives with your own and those of your classmates. If you are an early baby boomer, this should be easy for you to do, because we have a shared culture and have experienced the same historic events.

If you are older, you should also be able to relate. You shared the same history along with some of your own. You also lived through our era and understand how it was so different than the times and culture of earlier and later generations.

If you are younger and, perhaps, even still in high school, you should still be able to relate. In fact, you may be the one(s) who would benefit most from the story of my class. If I knew in 1964 what I know today about my classmates and myself, I would have acted differently in high school. Perhaps you can learn from who we were, what we experienced, and who we have become.

If you are a child or grandchild of one of my classmates or another early baby boomer, this is a chance for you to understand better why your parents or grandparents are the way they are, and, perhaps a little about who you are and why.

A second point about the book; similar to *Baseball: Never Too Old to Play "The" Game,* my story runs throughout, but is presented as only one of many examples of the broader themes. You will read others' stories here as well. While you may or may not be mentioned in the book, may or may not be from University City, and may or may not have graduated high school in the early-to-mid 1960s, I hope you can also find your story here.

Thirdly, I am not, nor am I trying to be an historian, sociologist, psychologist, or member of any other discipline that can provide expert analysis of our class, our times, or each of us as individuals. Rather I am just one member of a high school class with one perspective and the desire to reflect on the perspectives of others.

Finally, I recognize I was not then, nor am I now the most culturally aware person around. I am relatively insensitive to things like fashion, the latest movie, the hottest song, or which celebrity is not speaking to which other celebrity. I remember a lot, but I have also relied heavily on classmates, research, and Ann, my wife, to shore me up.

Three housekeeping notes—first, for simplicity throughout the book, I have used each female classmate's maiden name as her middle name—that is, except when I am referring to her in her girlhood.

Secondly, each senior picture in the book is accompanied by a current picture and my classmate's full name as shown in the *Dial*, our high school yearbook. Below each name is a quotation that we called a "quip." The *Dial* publication staff included a committee that was charged with selecting or creating an appropriate quip for each senior. As you learn more about my classmates, you will find, as I did when I went back to the yearbook, that the quip committee did a consistently wonderful job.

Finally, you will find a continuing dialogue that runs throughout the book. It is in italics and is at the beginning of each period. The conversation is fictitious, but the characters having it are not. Each actually attended the 40-year class reunion event in the gym, and they could have very well had this conversation, which introduces the essence of each period.

The U City Class of 1964 was exceptional by any measure. We valued education, and the vast majority of students went on to college, most earning a degree, many earning advanced degrees. We had more than our fair share of athletic success during our high school years. Our school music and arts programs were acclaimed and well-attended. And there were a myriad of activities, both organized and not, to engage anyone who wanted to participate—and most did. Perhaps everyone feels this way about his or her high school class. Well, so do we. We appreciate where we have come from and where we are now, and we look forward to where we are going—together. Hopefully, you can also appreciate our story.

Allow me to tell you about the University City High School Class of 1964—a class that is still close four-plus decades after graduation. We will go through the six periods of our school day together and then "I'll meet you under the clock." Perhaps our high school alma mater means even more today than when we sang it at our graduation. Its first line is "Hail, hail to U City High."

Alan Spector
University City High School Class of 1964

UNIVERSITY CITY HIGH SCHOOL ALMA MATER

Hail, hail to U. City High,
All hail to our old gold and black . . .
Hail, hail to U. City High,
Our friendship may she never lack . . .
Ever faithful, ever true
As we raise our song anew . . .
Of the days we've spent with you,
All hail U. City High.

FOREWORD

Then and Now

Thomas E. Arnold, Jr.

"With fleet foot and happy heart he goes through life."

There are certain metaphoric truths about high school. It is a cauldron of dreams and unfulfilled opportunities and what ifs – to be marinated and exaggerated over the years. And it is a womb of permanently-intertwined connections with classmates, fellow travelers, seemingly buried in the long ago—connections that will not and should not go away.

Dreams will grow, and diminish, come and go; some will be realized, others discarded, replaced by new ones. With the passing of time, we come to realize that those lost opportunities were really youthful improbabilities anyway - if they indeed really were opportunities —something to get over, after all. Or not. But the rest of it is an enduring, unavoidable pull on our life-strings, a continuous stream of outtakes on the horizon of our mind's eye that hover back there, and then come rushing up at a given moment, uninvited but persistently welcomed, to remind us of our roots, our youth. Our imperfections, warmed over by the years—the improbable distance — all of it becomes a benchmark for our lives as they have evolved these many years later.

The 1964 graduating class of University City High School, first suburb west of the St. Louis city limits, bloomed, together, in the same fertile garden, from gangly teenage angst into hopeful young adults during perhaps the most remarkable four years of our country's history. From September 1960 to June 1964, our nation saw the birth of civil rights, the launch of the women's movement with the publication of Betty Friedan's *The Feminine Mystique,* and the seeds of the environmental cause sown by Rachel Carson's *Silent Spring.* We launched our first man into outer space and heard our president state the improbable goal of landing a man on the moon before the end of the decade. Our nation's presence in Vietnam grew from fewer than 1000 troops to an incendiary conflict, interrupted momentarily by the assassination of our president, whose death would prevent him from seeing his dream realized.

And these firsts: Ford Mustangs, The Beatles, The Beach Boys, zip codes, seat belts, IUD's, panty hose, The Berlin Wall, birth control pills, "Smoking can be hazardous to your health" on cigarette packs – that cost 25 cents, *The Tonight Show* with Johnny Carson, the first man in space and the St. Louis Arch.

With more than four decades gone by since we graduated U City High School, we've all had numerous reminders of the vast chasm between then and now, between youthful hopes and dreams and reluctant, semi-adult acceptance of our shortcomings, between opportunities both realized and not.

More telling realizations have come of late, given the opportunity to reconnect with old classmates we shared some of those dreams with so long ago. Or, even more remarkable, connections with others we had nothing in common with back then, or so we thought, only to discover that what we do have are our roots, our memories, and our awakening perspective of all of it - the most important things of all.

Forty-five years, as of this writing - seems like a long time ago, doesn't it? Or, does it? Forty odd years is long enough to discover who we really are, or can be; long enough to become something different than we thought we would be or could be.

Four decades is long enough to have children and grandchildren, cave in to male-pattern baldness, take on new partners in life, gain and lose countless pounds, and, finally, begrudgingly, lose a half step on the dance floor. Perhaps time enough to see our parents in a different light. Time plenty enough to savor great victories, suffer enormous losses, and, blessedly, put them all into some kind of tolerable context.

A lifetime, literally, for some of us - the classmates we've lost along the way. Time enough to realize that whether or not they were close friends or simply classmates, and whether or not they had the same interests we did, or dressed the way we did, they shared every one of these remarkable experiences with us and held to some of the same dreams we did.

Time enough to know that all of them have contributed to the pull on each one of us to have come back to past reunions and attend future ones—to reach out to each other through the gift that is our internet connection, to evoke more memories, discover new friendships, and weigh in on another impassioned debate.

These things can cause all of it to feel like a mere heartbeat ago, the memories of those times within an itch of yesterday, yearning to be scratched.

The memories will come, too. Sometimes they'll ascend along with a song on the radio. Or a rerun on television. Some old *American Bandstand* footage. A whiff of English Leather. An email evoking the past. The moments will sit there on the horizon of our mind's eye, waiting to be observed, and savored, and be as fresh as when they happened.

And then, with the luxury of the years and the miles, we're left to decide that we all had much more in common back then than we ever could have or would have acknowledged. Certainly what matters now is to know that we all faced life's first real steps together, and drew from each other and from the same collective well for inspiration and direction and affirmation. It is, all of it, a testament to the power of our shared experiences at University City High School. We are blessed with that, and with each other. Then, and now.

We've come back to this touchstone of a class journal to gather it all back in and share it with each other, and with the ones who have left us behind, and with you.

A special thanks to one of us, Alan Spector, who decided that there is something about our collective memories and hindsight and emerging lives that might connect with others who grew up when we did—or with those who have wondered about the "children of the 60s," who may have been their parents—or found our music, or are facing life now themselves, and wondering if their ancestors worried about the same things, or shared the same hopes and dreams, or faced the same temptations. Well, we did, and we do. Then and now.

Tim Arnold
University City High School Class of 1964

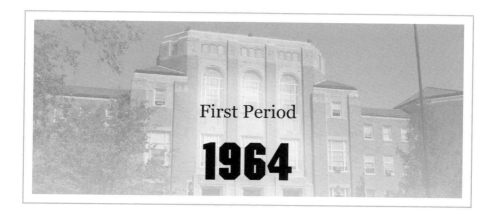

First Period

1964

"A child miseducated is a child lost."
John Fitzgerald Kennedy

"The real truths in our lives don't make the
six o'clock news or the morning paper."
Bob Greene

Marla   *Mark*   *Judy*   *Anne*   *Steve*

In the dark recesses of an imposing high school building opened in 1930 is a small gym with most of its limited seating in a balcony that overhangs both ends and one side of the gym floor. The balcony seats are empty this Friday evening, October 8, 2004, but the floor is packed with people. There are about 300 men and women in their late 50s. They are classmates, more than 200 strong, from the high school's graduating class of 1964, many joined by significant others. It is the Friday night opening event of their 40-year reunion weekend.

The gym evokes memories of the sounds and energy of

cheerleaders, the blast of a pep band, the odor of two-a-day indoor practices, the grunting of "running the steps," the loss of a 5-3 basketball game before the era of shot clocks, the excitement of senior carnivals, and the music, now referred to as "oldies," of proms and sock-hops.

Five alumni are clustered in one corner of the gym. Since the class celebrated its 50th birthday party together eight years earlier, they have, like other classmates, e-mailed and phoned often. While they live thousands of miles apart, like other classmates, some have found a way to visit each other. For this weekend, they, along with more than a third of their graduating class of about 600, have made the individual and collective effort to come together.

After extended hugs and wonderful-to-see-you kisses, they begin to catch up with each other and to revisit the memories, some of which were among the best of their lives. This is not idle small talk filling the time—their conversation, insulated from the din that surrounds them by their attention to one another, is filled with the sincerity and familiarity that comes from deep and growing relationships and from a common and valued history.

They could have been together in this same gym corner or some other corner of the building 40 years earlier, but it feels as if it were only yesterday, allowing them to quickly get into a rhythm of give and take that can only be derived from a special connectedness. What else could explain how they feel when surrounded by people that they have seen so infrequently since high school, yet with whom they are so comfortable?

Steve Novack lives in Glencoe, Illinois, a Chicago suburb, with childhood sweetheart, classmate, and wife, Ilene Weinstein Novack. The class knows Steve as the mild-mannered, sharp-shooting varsity basketball player and the starting second baseman on their state championship baseball team. Chicago knows Steve as the mild-mannered founding partner of the law firm of Novack and Macey, which the Chicago Tribune called, "A high-powered litigation boutique." Steve thinks of himself as Ilene's husband, a father, and a grandfather.

Anne O'Brien was a cheerleader—she is a cheerleader. She was prom-queen beautiful—she is beautiful. She was fun and caring and a great friend—she still is. Anne lives in Sebastopol, California, where she owns a private teaching and counseling business. A free spirit, Anne has followed the loves of her life to Scotland, Spain, Greece, Chicago, Las Vegas, California, St. Louis, and now back to California, where she is with her children, the forever loves of her life.

Marla Schukar Levinson was and is a feisty redhead and a friend to all. Her journey from high school in suburban University City has taken her, and husband Bruce, to an expansive ranch in rural Missouri. Her stories, once of high school activities and dates, are now of riding horses, birthing calves, and nurturing grandchildren. Marla's brother, Steve, was also a classmate, one of too many who have already passed away. Marla, Steve, and Elsie, as Marla calls her mom, created a classmate gathering place during their high school years, a home alive with laughter and energy. Marla still brings that to the class—she is a gathering place, alive with laughter and energy.

Mark Glickman lives in Davie, Florida with wife Jean. He is warm, sincere, and uplifting. Even when he is communicating via e-mail, the smile on Mark's face and the twinkle in his eye shine through. His marketing degree serves him well in his role as a textile sales representative. Florida is a great location for Mark as his business has taken him to Columbia, Barbados, and the Dominican Republic. Mark played on the school's state championship baseball team. He still loves the game and remains a devoted St. Louis Cardinals fan.

Judy Inger Shanfeld lives in St. Louis and is one of the foundation stones of the reunion-planning committee, adroitly handling the job of treasurer. Judy, married to Jerry, U City Class of '63, is a legal secretary, grandmother, and class stalwart. An inspiration to all, Judy carries herself with grace and brightens up any room she is in. She is a breast cancer survivor, but the disease does not define her—Judy defines herself.

Judy: *"I can't believe we graduated so long ago.*

Mark: *"Yeah—I can remember it like it was only 40 years ago yesterday."*

Anne: *"This gym brings back memories. We didn't have a very good basketball team—no offense, Steve— but we sure had a lot of fun."*

Steve: *"You're right about our team, but we enjoyed playing anyway. I think the problem we had is that you don't find a lot of really tall Jews."*

Mark: *"Basketball was certainly not the only thing going on in the world in the early 60s."*

Marla: *"Right—we grew up in pretty exciting times. When we were born, television had barely been invented and before we graduated, JFK told us we'd put a man on the moon. Pretty heady stuff."*

Anne: *"The cold war, Vietnam, civil rights. We also had to deal with how we were going to get a date for Saturday night. No wonder we were insecure."*

Judy: *"You were insecure? I thought I was the only one."*

Mark: *"We each thought we were the only one."*

Marla: *"Maybe that's why we never figured out the sex thing. I'm not sure if that was the good news or the bad news."*

Anne: *"Well, the people in this gym have a lot of children and grandchildren—so we eventually figured it out."*

Steve: *"Speaking of all these people, I wish I could get them all out of the way, find a basketball, and see if I still have a jump shot."*

Parkview 7-0682

Arleen White threw the ID bracelet at me—it bounced off my chest and fell into a puddle formed by the cool steady evening rain in which we stood. I was bright enough to get the hint that we would no longer be going steady. In 1961, during our sophomore year at University City High School, the symbol of eternal love or, at least, assurance of a date for next Saturday, was the linked chain of an identification bracelet.

Arleen Sue White

"Not very short, not very tall,
but loved respected,
and honored by all."

Adam Langer captures the limited horizons of high school romance in his coming-of-age novel, *Crossing California*. Langer writes of his teenage characters, "...could Jill imagine that she was not supposed to be with Muley Scott Wills forever and always. Or at least until they graduated from high school. Or at least for a little while."

Arleen and I went steady for months, a high school eternity, and to this day, I remember her old telephone number, Parkview (PA) 7-0682.

Little did we know that more than 40 years later she would be wearing my ID bracelet again.

As is true with so many of our classmates, Arleen and I have connected and reconnected many times over our post-high school years. She went to the University of Missouri-Columbia (Mizzou), and I went to the Rolla School of Mines and Metallurgy (name changed during my tenure to the University of Missouri-Rolla).

Ann, my wife-to-be, graduated from neighboring Clayton High School, class of '66. She also went to Mizzou, where Arleen became Ann's convenient excuse not to be back to her dorm by curfew when I visited her for the weekend. Yes, in the mid-1960s, there were curfews at college dorms, and the dorm buildings were even segregated by gender. Ann merely signed out of the dorm, indicating that she was going home to St. Louis, but stayed at Arleen's apartment for the weekend.

Arleen went on to live in Maryland, the Philippines, and New York before returning to St. Louis, and I lived in Northeastern Pennsylvania before settling in Cincinnati. We both married and built families and careers. And we both now have grandchildren to visit, play with, pass along wisdom to, show pictures of, and brag about.

We have had our separate life experiences, yet every chance we get, Arleen and her husband, Howard, and Ann and I get together.

Prior to our 40-year high school reunion, I came across my old ID bracelet. In the gym at the Friday event, I asked Arleen, with Ann's blessing of course, to go steady with me for the evening.

Arleen wearing "our" ID bracelet at our 40-year high school reunion

At the end of the evening, she returned the ID bracelet as planned. This time, however, I did not have to retrieve it from a puddle.

My current friendship with Arleen is not based solely upon going steady in 1961. We have not stayed connected over these years because of our sophomore "romance." How do I know that? Because I have similar longstanding relationships with many other high school classmates, at least half of whom (the guys) I have never even kissed. Well, actually—oh, never mind—that is another story.

Long-term friendships like these are by no means unique in our class. Friendships and connections, while not universal, are common. They are sought, nourished, valued, and sustained. Why are so many classmates still so closely connected? What was it about the shared high school experience that became the basis of lifelong and growing relationships? Why are so many now close with those who they were not as close with in high school? Who was the University City High School Class of 1964? Who are these people?

Walking to School

Prior to moving to University City in the middle of third grade, my family lived in an apartment on Clara Avenue in the city of St. Louis. From Clara, beginning in kindergarten, I walked to Hamilton Elementary School through the Food Center grocery store, past the Winter Garden ice skating rink, across DeBaliviere (a major thoroughfare) just up the street from the Goodie Train restaurant, through several neighborhoods, and past Phil Hertzman's house. In the summer, I made the same trek to PlaySkool, the playground program at the school, or to play at Phil's house.

Playground mates (I have the ball) at the Hamilton School Summer PlaySkool in 1954. Seven eventually moved to University City and the high school class of 1964

Phil Hertzman (second from the teacher in the front row) had a great house across from the schoolyard. The house had an in-ground concrete "swimming pool," albeit only the size and depth of an oversized bathtub, and featured a breezy wraparound front porch on which to play board games out of the relentless heat of the St. Louis summer sun. Perhaps most importantly, the house had a great wiffle ball backyard.

At least we thought it was great for wiffle ball until one day I hit the ball up on Phil's flat garage roof. I got the ladder from the garage and was ready to climb when Phil said he would get the ball. He scaled the ladder and craned his neck to see where the ball had settled. Wasps! Swarming! Stinging!

Somehow he got down the ladder without falling. It took hours for him to stop shaking from the stings. Phil "took one for the team" that day—it could have been me. More than 50 years later, when I visited Phil in Santa Fe, New Mexico, where he is a physician, I reminded him of the incident. He recalled it vividly and responded, "I guess if I had a better curve ball, you would have never gotten the ball up on the roof."

Why tell this story? It is not to remind Phil of the wasp incident. Rather, it is to acknowledge the times in which we grew up. Not only did I take the 15 minute urban walk to Phil's house as an eight-year-old, but I played at his house and in his neighborhood all day before taking the walk back home. It was safe and accepted then—it is what we did.

Moving to University City

University City, Missouri was incorporated just two years after the 1904 Louisiana Purchase Expedition, better known as the 1904 World's Fair. Until the turn of the 20th century, the land on which the city would eventually be developed was rolling countryside and farms, with public infrastructure limited to a few businesses that serviced travelers on the wagon road that linked St. Louis and the Missouri River.

E. G. Lewis, a Connecticut native, was a visionary who made his money building a local St. Louis magazine into a nationally-distributed periodical with circulation over 1.5 million readers. It was the first major publication specifically targeted to women and, fortunately for Lewis and for University City, available just as women were becoming interested in suffrage and other issues.

In 1903, Lewis built the magazine's publishing office building just outside the St. Louis city limits. He later bought and developed what he called a "model community," University Heights, in which the streets were named for prominent American universities. The office building and the development were near the site of the World's Fair and the growing Washington University.

Lewis's community of a hundred-plus acres eventually grew to become University City; six square miles that now house 35,000-plus residents. The original five-story octagon-shaped publishing office building eventually became City Hall.

In the late 40s and early 50s, University City's proximity to St. Louis and its modestly-priced housing made it relatively easy for city apartment dwellers to find and afford homes. Another factor also helped establish the demographics of University City and its high school class of 1964.

A number of the community's prominent Jewish temples and synagogues were either located very near University City or had relocated to the developing community. This made University City one of the suburbs and school districts in which there was a significant Jewish population.

In 1955, my family moved from our urban apartment into our first house at 8340 Fullerton in University City. I entered Daniel Boone Elementary School where I would earn the nickname "Monkey," because I was going through a phase of eating bananas without peeling them. The nickname did not bother me until one day my mother came to school for a parent-teacher conference. She was walking down the hall toward the meeting when she heard, "Hey, there's monkey's mother."

I heard about it at dinner that night, and we had a good family laugh. The nickname eventually wore off as did my banana eating habits.

Our house was a small three-bedroom, one-bathroom ranch that really stretched the family finances when we bought it for $15,500, in the range of the national average.

Families in U City were generally middle class, which, according to the US Census Bureau, meant an annual 1955 household income of just under $5000. In my case, both Mom and Dad worked. My dad drove a delivery truck, and my mom was a nurse at a time when it was not yet the norm for women to be in the workforce.

My family's migration to University City was being repeated hundreds of times as St. Louis city apartment dwellers moved to suburban homes and enrolled their children in new schools. Some families had found University City before their children were born. And some families moved in from outside the St. Louis area.

Regardless of the path of our respective family journeys, we were all to become part of the nearly 600 members of the senior class who would participate in graduation on Wednesday, June 10, 1964, at 6:30pm in the football stadium at University City High School, its largest graduating class to that point.

Karen Paulsen moved south only two miles to the very northwestern edge of the school district to 1723 Gulf Drive, where she entered Daniel Boone Elementary School in 1954. Karen Paulsen Bauch now lives over 1000 miles from Gulf Drive in Winnipeg, Manitoba, where she is a violinist with the Winnipeg Symphony Orchestra.

In 1958, Laya Firestone moved into the University City school district at 725 Old Bonhomme Road, but attended the Epstein Hebrew Academy before entering the public school system for high school. Laya Firestone Seghi now lives over 1200 miles from Old Bonhomme in Miami, Florida, where she is a psychotherapist.

Richard Gimpelson moved four miles from 857 Clara Avenue to 7444 Anrose Drive, where he entered Jackson Park Elementary School in 1956. Richard and I lived in the same apartment building and attended Hamilton School together in the city of St. Louis. The Gimpelsons and Spectors found University City a year apart. Richard Gimpelson still lives in St. Louis where he is a doctor of obstetrics and gynecology.

Judy Becker was born in University City. When she was two, her family moved from an apartment in an area referred to as "The Loop," near University Heights and City Hall. From her house at

7265 Creveling Drive she attended Flynn Park Elementary School. Judy Becker Plocker still lives in St. Louis, where she is a real estate agent.

These stories are typical. One that is not is of classmate James Morris Bright, who was born Moishe Breitberg of Polish parents in the displaced persons camp in Bergen Belsen. Moishe's parents were Holocaust survivors. His family lived in Europe after they were liberated and eventually moved to the United States and to University City.

Jim's history of survival ended when he passed away in January, 2005. Before he did, he was able to travel back to Poland to see the camp where he was born. Also before his passing, Jim established himself as an articulate conservative spokesman in our class.

Upon news of Jim's death, classmate Judy Elbom Cameron summed up feelings when she wrote to the class, "He will be missed... I am very saddened to lose a great friend way too soon. I hope he is riding his Harley in Heaven, wearing his red thong, and continuing to brag about his President. And may he rest in peace with our other classmates. Hugs, Judy."

Whether through a short hop across town or from horrors halfway around the world, we were converging on University City in the 1950s and establishing a base from which we would launch our individual lives, each of which would pass through University City High School.

Party Line

While most of University City was reasonably well established by 1955, our end of town, the furthest from the original development, had a way to go. When we moved to our home on Fullerton, there was a farm across the street, and it was not uncommon for the horse to get loose and roam the neighborhood.

Parts of our infrastructure were underdeveloped, yet on the verge of improvement. Our street was not paved, and there were no sidewalks. We shared our phone service with several other homes on a party line—we only knew a phone call was for us by the number of short rings. When we picked up the receiver to make a call, it was not uncommon to hear someone from another household already having a conversation on the line.

No, I did not listen in, but I could have. Apparently, some did. Arleen White recalls a girlhood phone call with Marsha Klibansky in which they were gossiping about Doug Taylor. Well into their deep personal discussion, they heard a voice, "OK, girls, this is Doug. I'm listening, so you better not say anything more about me!"

Arleen and Marsha were mortified and hung up without saying goodbye. The worst part of the incident was facing Doug the next day at school.

Eventually private lines replaced party lines, our street was paved, and sidewalks were installed. The farm acreage was acquired by the school district, and in 1959, Greensfelder Park Elementary School opened. My sisters attended Greensfelder; Carol transferring from Daniel Boone in the fourth grade and my youngest sister, Marti, being in the school's first kindergarten class. Their walk to school was literally across the street.

Both Carol and Marti also went on to graduate from U City High, in 1968 and 1971, respectively. Marti, along with several of her Greensfelder schoolmates skipped third grade and graduated high school at age 16.

I graduated from Daniel Boone Elementary School in 1958. Even then, my elementary school classmates had sown the seeds of lifelong relationships. We vividly remember those years. We can still easily name the 60-plus students in the sixth-grade photograph of Mr. Walker's and Mr. Warren's classes, despite not having seen a number of them for five decades.

Among these Daniel Boone graduates is the core of the planning committee for our high school reunions. It is little surprise that we also planned and held a sixth-grade reunion nearly four decades after leaving elementary school.

Others who would become my high school classmates were graduating from Blackberry Lane, Nathaniel Hawthorne, Pershing, Delmar-Harvard, and other elementary schools. Each would be attending one of two junior high schools in the district, Hanley and Brittany, for grades 7, 8, and 9. Because building capacity was strained at the high school, we would spend our freshman high school year at one of the junior highs.

Television Generation

Do you remember what you did right after school was over each day in the sixth grade? Many of us would hurry home so we would not miss *The Three Stooges*. I was captain of the Patrol Boys; a group of sixth graders who each wore a white bandolier belt with an official-looking metal badge firmly affixed. It was our job to help fellow students get across the busiest intersections safely as they walked home. On my rounds as captain, I needed to make sure that the other patrol boys were at their corners and that everything was going well. But as soon as our shift was over, it was *Three Stooges* time.

While some of us rushed home for the Stooges, many were doing so to catch *American Bandstand*. They recall many years of dancing with invisible partners while watching the show; joining fan clubs for regulars Pat Moliteri, Justine Carelli, Bob Clayton, Arlene Sullivan, Carmen Jimenez, and Kenny Rossi; and collecting pins and pictures and autographs.

While our addiction to the Stooges was short-lived, we continued to tune into Dick Clark and *American Bandstand* throughout Junior and Senior High School.

Sitting in front of the television was something that we had grown up with—we were the first true television generation. 1946, the year most classmates were born, was the first in which there were more than 10,000 working televisions in the country—only nine local stations were on the air nationwide. When we were five, there were only 25 working color television sets in the country. Brandon Tartikoff, an early baby boomer and the youngest-ever president of NBC's entertainment division said, "Television itself is a baby boomer, it's a baby boomer instrument."

Today, there are, on average, more than two TV sets per household and two-thirds of homes have three or more. When was the last time you watched a black-and-white set?

In his book, *Boomer Nation, The Largest and Richest Generation Ever and How It Changed America*, Steve Gillon wrote, "...the average Baby Boomer had viewed between 12,000 and 15,000 hours of television by age 16."

By the middle of our high school years, therefore, we had spent about 1.5 years of 24-hour days staring at a television set, an average of more than two hours every day for 16 years.

Gillon also wrote, "...children raised on shows like *The Mickey Mouse Club* and *Howdy Doody* saw more than 500 hours of ads by the age of 6. By the time they were age 21, most Boomers had seen more than 300,000 commercials."

These are frightening statistics, but they have an upside. Given there were only three national networks and a couple of local stations, we had limited viewing choices compared to today's seemingly hundreds of channels—we shared a common experience every day from birth through high school. We watched the same shows, heard the same jokes, saw the same news, and, yes, were influenced by the same commercials.

The programs we watched generally avoided controversy, showcased family values and togetherness, and celebrated rugged individualism. Television was a primary building block of our shared culture.

If you are an early baby boomer or older, you will likely remember the following television genres and shows. It is by no means a complete list, but should be enough to whet your nostalgia whistle.

Saturday morning cartoons, like *Deputy Dawg, Heckle and Jeckle, Rocky and Bullwinkle,* and *Mighty Mouse* ("Mr. Trouble never hangs around when he hears that mighty sound. Here I come to save the day—that means that Mighty Mouse is on the way.")

Westerns, like *Wild Bill Hickock, The Cisco Kid, Bonanza, Gunsmoke, Have Gun Will Travel, Annie Oakley, The Roy Rogers Show, Maverick, Rawhide, Fury,* and *The Lone Ranger* ("A fiery horse with the speed of light, a cloud of dust and a hearty 'Hi Ho Silver.' The Lone Ranger. 'Hi Ho Silver, away.' With his faithful Indian companion, Tonto, the daring and resourceful masked rider of the plains led the fight for law and order in the early west. Return with us now to those thrilling days of yesteryear. The Lone Ranger rides again.")

Situation comedies, like *Father Knows Best, Make Room for Daddy, The Donna Reed Show, I Love Lucy, Ozzie and Harriet, The Honeymooners, Leave It to Beaver,* and *The Many Loves of Dobie Gillis* ("Hey, Dobe, let's go downtown and watch them knock down the old Endicott Building.")

Variety shows, like *The Ed Sullivan Show, Milton Berle's Texaco Star Theater, The Show of Shows,* and *The Perry Como Show* ("Letters. We get letters. We get stacks and stacks of letters. Dear Perry, would you be so kind, to fill a request and sing the song I like best?")

Quiz shows, like *The $64,000 Question* (Teddy Nadler, the $252,000 winner on the spinoff show, *The $64,000 Challenge,* lived in University City less than a mile from my house and was classmate Adrienne Nadler's uncle*), Beat the Clock, What's My Line?, The Price is Right, I've Got a Secret, To Tell the Truth, Truth or Consequences* ("That's Beulah the Buzzer.")

News commentators, like Edward R. Murrow, Chet Huntley, David Brinkley, John Cameron Swayze, and Walter Cronkite ("And that's the way it is.")

Children's programs, like *Kukla, Fran, and Ollie; Captain Kangaroo; Rocky and His Friends; Watch Mr. Wizard;* and *Howdy Doody* ("Kawabonga.")

Walt Disney shows, like *Disneyland, The Wonderful World of Color,* and *The Mickey Mouse Club* ("Now it's time to say goodbye to all our company; M-I-C, See you real soon; K-E-Y, Why? Because we like you; M-O-U-S-E.")

Detective and Police Dramas, like *Dragnet, The Untouchables, Highway Patrol, 77 Sunset Strip, Naked City,* and *Sergeant Preston of the Yukon* ("Well, King, this case is closed.")

Other popular shows, like *American Bandstand, This is Your Life, Omnibus, Hallmark Theater, Candid Camera, The Twilight Zone, Your Hit Parade,* and on and on and on

On Wednesday, June 10, 1964, the day of our high school graduation, the TV schedule from the weekly insert in the Sunday

St. Louis Post-Dispatch revealed some interesting things about television from our era.

- There was nothing "on the air" from about 1:50am, when the local NBC affiliate (KSDK-TV, channel 5) finished its last weather report until 5:15am when the CBS affiliate (KMOX-TV, channel 4) began the morning with *Devotional News*. NBC did not start its daily broadcasting until 7:00am with *The Today Show*, ABC (KTVI-TV, channel 2) at 7:15am with something called *Credo*, and the local independent station (KPLR-TV, channel 11) began at noon with *Yesterday's Newsreel*. The public broadcasting station (KETC-TV, channel 9) only had an evening schedule, running from 6:30pm to about 10:00pm.

- Programming was dominated by game shows, westerns, family dramas, and comedies, like those mentioned above, and by soap operas like *Love of Life, Guiding Light*, and *Search for Tomorrow*.

- Those shows being broadcast in color were specially noted. On June 10, 1964, there were five; a number exceeded by the eight shows that were designated as "repeats."

- The ABC evening national news was only 15 minutes long as was ABC's local news. ABC was competing with NBC's *Huntley-Brinkley* and CBS's *Walter Cronkite*, both half-hour newscasts, and with *Zane Grey Theater*.

- Very few of the shows from that day still exist—*The Today Show* (originally hosted by University City High School graduate Dave Garroway), *Price is Right, Jeopardy*, the soap operas, the nightly national news shows, and the *Tonight Show*.

- Remember this?

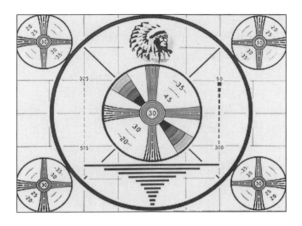

"...to the moon..."

We loved our television as we grew up in the 1940s, 50s, and 60s. It was a large part of our lives and, importantly, a part of the shared culture that brought us together in a simpler time and became part of the foundation for remaining close four-plus decades later.

Television helped us reflect on the hope and promise of the time in which we lived. In January 2008, Ann and I visited the Kennedy Space Center in Cape Canaveral, Florida on the way to baseball tournaments in Sarasota and Fort Myers. We spent two full days at the Center, and it brought back the memories of the space race and what it meant to us.

It is ultimately appropriate for the complex to have been named for President Kennedy. We remembered the televised news report of his speech at Rice University in Houston, Texas in September 1962. If you want to be inspired, review the entire speech, but here are two excerpts that capture the essence of John Kennedy and of that time in our history.

> "Those who came before us made certain that this country rode the first waves of the industrial revolution, the first waves of modern invention, and the first wave of nuclear power, and this generation

does not intend to founder in the backwash of the coming age of space. We mean to be a part of it—we mean to lead it. For the eyes of the world now look into space, to the moon and to the planets beyond, and we have vowed that we shall not see it governed by a hostile flag of conquest, but by a banner of freedom and peace. We have vowed that we shall not see space filled with weapons of mass destruction, but with instruments of knowledge and understanding."

"We choose to go to the moon. We choose to go to the moon in this decade...not because (it is) easy, but because (it is) hard, because that goal will serve to organize and measure the best of our energies and skills, because that challenge is one that we are willing to accept, one we are unwilling to postpone, and one which we intend to win..."

Today, unlike when we heard this from President Kennedy, we are barraged by extended local newscasts, national network news, 24-hour cable news channels, and web-based news every time we logon. But the visual media was relatively young in 1962 and having the president in our living rooms was still a novelty. We watched him together, were inspired by him together, and were energized to follow him into space—together.

Pluralistic Ignorance

We were fortunate that our families moved us into the University City School District. Our elementary school experience and our tenure in junior high prepared us well for the senior high school, where we were afforded an outstanding and balanced menu of academics, sports, and extracurricular and social activities. Despite being surrounded by excellence, we felt the insecurities of our teenage years. In fact, we were typical in that each of us also likely thought we were the only ones who felt insecure.

I met Professor David Kennedy of The City University of New York's John Jay College of Criminal Justice through a violence reduction program we are working on together in Cincinnati. Professor Kennedy taught me a concept that he applies to how chronic violent street groups think that also seems to apply to our teenage feelings of insecurity.

The concept is "pluralistic ignorance"—when "everybody in a group thinks that everybody else in the group thinks something that nobody else in the group really thinks."

It is likely that in high school we all thought that everyone else thought they were confident and secure, yet very few really were. It took many of us 40-plus years to be able to share those insecurities with classmates, only to find out that we were not alone.

Grandma Never Looked Like That

Debbie Brownstein was elected "Prettiest Girl" of our senior class. Five daughters, 12 grandchildren, and four-plus decades later, Debbie Brownstein Pulley is still beautiful. At our 30-year class reunion, I was reminiscing with friend and class-clown Howard Danzig when Debbie, who had just become a grandmother for the first time, walked into the room in a sleek white lace dress. Howard sighed, put his hand on my shoulder, leaned toward me, and whispered, "Al, I don't remember my grandmother ever looking like that."

Our generation's grandparents had lived hard lives. Many of them had emigrated from the "old country"—in my case from Brusilov, Ukraine (a town near Kiev) and from Lithuania. Many grandparents of Jewish descent had lived through persecution in their home communities and taken the drastic step to travel across the world to the United States.

They set out to build new lives, but having barely reestablished themselves, they were hit by the Great Depression. Through all of this, they reared solid families that converged on University City in the early 1960s, bringing us to the time and place in our lives when we had the freedom to be insecure teenagers.

The opportunities to feel insecure were unlimited. For example,

I might muster the courage to ask Debbie to slow-dance to a Johnny Mathis song at WigWam, our weekly school-sponsored Friday-night party venue. Yet I would find myself wondering throughout the entire dance whether she was really thinking about dancing with me or, in her heart-of-hearts, wishing she were dancing with Terry Mitze, the high school love of her life.

Arleen White Bly recalls similar feelings when dancing with Terry. They were close friends and enjoyed dancing together, but Arleen could always tell when Terry was thinking about Debbie and would tell him to go find and dance with her.

Debbie's relationship with Terry was an interesting one. Like a significant percentage of the class, Debbie is Jewish. Terry, who very sadly passed away in 2006, was not. With an apparently sufficient choice of "nice Jewish boys," Debbie's mother expected her to be dating within their faith, and Mom made sure Debbie was fully aware of that expectation.

So, what did we do? We joined the conspiracy and one of us "nice Jewish boys," Steve Schukar, would pick Debbie up for a date and take her home at the end of the evening. Debbie's mom always believed Debbie was dating Steve. Thirty years later, her mom asked Debbie, "Whatever happened to that nice blond boy you knew in high school?"

Debbie could still not tell her it was Terry Mitze and admit he had been her steady boyfriend. Some insecurities never die.

Walk the Walk

In 1964, University City was a relatively homogeneous community and high school. Not only did we have a large Jewish population (we were occasionally and crudely referred to as "Jew City"), our class was all white, as were neighboring school districts, including Clayton. When a black student enrolled at Clayton High School during our era, it was such big news that I remember his name to this day—Decatur Agnew.

Although we had no blacks in our school, fellow students were teaching us the importance of racial awareness. Classmate Lisa

Rosen now lives in Seal Beach, California. When in high school, Lisa was at the center of an effort to urge the Board of Education to allow "Negro" students to enter University City schools. Her group believed that even if blacks were to be living in U City and wanting to attend the schools, they would likely have been discouraged from doing so.

Lisa had attended a speech by Dr. Martin Luther King at a local synagogue. She was moved by Dr. King and by the fact that *Brown v. Board of Education* had been handed down nine years earlier with apparently no effect on her local schools or most others for that matter. She rallied more than 30 students to her cause, held a number of meetings in the fall of our senior year, got an audience with the Board of Education, but saw no action before we graduated. Although she was disappointed, there is no doubt that she had moved both students and Board members to a higher level of racial awareness. Integration of University City schools began in earnest shortly thereafter.

Classmate Stephen Kowarsky also helped us think about race when he wrote a piece that was published in the school newspaper, "Several Impressions of a Young Man on the Pure Innocence of Childhood."

Stephen wrote, "I was riding home from work on my bicycle, passing by Flynn Park, and I stopped to watch three little boys playing there—two of them were white and one was a Negro. They were playing catch with an immense cardboard box. Now and then one of the boys would be knocked over trying to catch the box and the other two would help him get to his feet and they would go on with their game.

"I pondered over the innocence of these children. Did they notice that one of them had a different color of skin and did they care? In the honest and simple words of children I thought those were merely 'friends.' They do not need the artificial distinctions posed by our world.

"I was about to ride away refreshed by the afternoon and by this moving scene when one of the white boys tossed the box off to the side. He said something to the other white boy and they seized the

Negro by his hands and feet and began swinging him back and forth. The Negro boy squealed. Higher and higher they swung him as if to throw him into the air when suddenly they stopped and let him down.

"I moved closer to hear as the Negro boy struggled to catch his breath and speak, dizzy from his experience. One of the white boys yelled, 'Now swing me.'"

While Lisa Rosen and Stephen Kowarsky were raising our awareness on an intellectual level, we had a classmate who had to deal with racial prejudice or, at least, gross insensitivity on more personal level. As did Lisa and Stephen, this classmate helped us take a giant step in racial awareness and social justice.

David Pactor grew up in two worlds. When he was very young, he began working in his father's grocery store, "Po Boy's," which was located in a predominately black section of North St. Louis.

He learned, as he puts it, to "walk the walk" and "talk the talk" of the black community. In fact, when customers came into the grocery and spoke to his father using various street dialects, David's dad would ask him to "translate."

Many of David's boyhood friends were the North St. Louis neighbors who hung out at and near the store. While his skin was dark by white standards, David had light skin relative to most of his black friends. Accepting his skin tone and what his friends referred to as "good hair" (wavy rather than tightly curled), the neighborhood accepted David and thought of him as "colored." He was comfortable living in both worlds.

In the mid-50s, the Pactor family moved to an apartment in "The Loop." Being more racially aware than most U City 12-year-olds, David noticed that blacks were rarely seen in nearby University City shops or on the streets with a notable exception. He observed waves of African-American women arriving by bus daily only to then be dispatched to their work as maids throughout the suburbs. "The Loop" was a transfer area for the St. Louis public transportation system. As David says, "None of them were coming in to teach, to prosper, to stay."

It was not until he moved to University City that David had

his first personal experience with racial prejudice. His darker skin prompted some of his new elementary school classmates to call him racially-charged names, and he was not immune to an occasional fight. These incidents further raised David's racial awareness, and he became more accustomed to the insensitivity of others. It was not uncommon for him to be asked questions like, "What are you?" "Why are your brother and sister so white and you so dark?" "Did your mother sleep with the mailman?"

David was still occasionally confronted by racial insensitivity at the senior high school. But instead of lashing out or crawling inside a shell, he stepped up to help his classmates understand the hurt of racial injustice. As an officer of our Senior Cabinet organization, David was asked to contact Hodges Skating Rink to make arrangements for Hodges to be the venue for a party. The management of the rink made it clear during the planning that they would be happy to have us come, but it would be unacceptable for blacks to attend—it was their policy not to admit African-Americans. At the time, of course, the terms "Negroes" or "Coloreds" were used. I suspect that Hodges Rink people used different terms.

Despite the fact that there would have been no blacks coming anyway, David made it clear that if the Hodges venue were accepted despite its exclusionary policies, he wanted no part of the party, the Senior Cabinet, or the class for that matter. The party was cancelled. David views it as his first, but not last, human rights victory.

David went on to become the first in our class to join VISTA, America's domestic Peace Corps, and the first from University City to attend predominately-black Howard University in Washington, D.C. It was so unusual for a classmate to be attending Howard that someone on the ten-year class reunion committee thought David's biographical information was a mistake. The reunion book reported that he attended Harvard University.

David now lives in San Francisco, where he is an art dealer, bartender, and community activist; from where he is still connected to the class; and where he is still occasionally asked insensitive questions.

Prisoner in the Back

As well as having a large Jewish population and being all white, the vast majority of us were from middle-class families in which the father worked, the mother stayed home, the house was on the small side, and there was a single family car. A few had his or her own car in high school, but most needed to borrow the family car. I was really cool picking up dates in my family's '57 Chevy station wagon and later in our Plymouth Valiant. Yeah—right.

Steve Schukar was among the first to have a car of his own. His sister, Marla, recalls Steve buying a '56 Ford stick shift. She also remembers that she and her sister, Judy, later paid off the car and used it while Steve was in the service.

We would cruise U City, stop at Hamburger Heaven with their unique "H" sauce (a recipe that was lost when the drive-in restaurant closed, although attempts are being made to recreate it), head for Tropicana Bowling Lanes to play pool, meet friends on "the strip," and just enjoy the freedom that was Schuk's car. I can now reveal that Steve would let me drive, even before I was old enough to have my license—pretty rebellious stuff at the time.

Classmates who did have cars fondly remember them as well as the stories associated with them. Gary Singer had a '56 silver and white Chevy convertible, which was stolen in '63. After graduation, Gary went on to own a '67 Shelby Mustang 428 with two four-barrels and a '68 Corvette. He now sarcastically refers to his Honda Civic as his newest "muscle car."

Arleen Inger drove a Chevrolet Corvair convertible and recalled it being one of her favorite cars. Her Corvair gave Arleen 110,000 miles before she sold it in 1970—surprising, in that Ralph Nader, in his book, *Unsafe at Any Speed*, referred to the Corvair as "the one-car accident" and panned its overall safety performance.

Before getting her Corvair, Arleen drove her mom's 1956 Pontiac. On the day she got her driver's license, she was driving the Pontiac to pick up her friend Anne O'Brien. The plan was for the two to then pick up other friends to go do dinner, a ritual they followed as each earned her license.

Arleen recalled, "I had to ease out onto Midland before making the right turn as there was a blind curve from my left. I kept turning my steering wheel to the right, then pressed the accelerator and took down the solid concrete lamp post on the corner...not a scratch on the car, yet we faced a bill from U City for $389.89. I was also placed in the back seat of the police car and when he radioed hq, he said, 'I have my prisoner in the back.' Scared me beyond explanation. Mom had to bail me out, not literally, but it felt that way. No dinner out that night!"

The incident definitely made an impression on Arleen as she remembered the exact amount of the bill from the city after more than 45 years.

Tim Arnold copied the class on a note to Arleen as he reminded her of another car story that involved her. "Dear ex-cheerleader Arleen, you were the cause of my first car wreck, as a 16-year old wannabe, cool enough to date a cheerleader. I'm driving toward the school one Saturday afternoon and damn(!), here comes Inger walking down the other side of the street. We were semi-buds but that's it. And I'm driving my parents '64 Chevy Biscayne, the cheapest model available, no radio, no whitewalls, no nothing. But, what the hell? I whip this hot rod thru an open space in the parking medium that separated the lanes and jammed the best teenaged U-Turn I could manage and roar up beside you. I slam on my brakes, screeching to what I thought was a totally cool hoodlum stop right next to you, thinking somehow that this would be really, really impressive. Not. Somebody's right behind me and rear ends me in the worst possible way; as a naïve teenager. Bam! Wrecked! And for the first and maybe only time in the history of Missouri traffic law, for getting rear-ended, it's my fault, not his. And worse, it made absolutely no impression on you. Or my parents either. That is what I remember, about you and my first one. Car wreck, that is. And I still think you're cool."

Signal 30

While it is hard to picture now, before we had our licenses, our parents would drive us on dates. It seemed very natural at the time; like an early teenage carpool. But we could not wait to get our driver's license; doing so was one of our teenage rites of passage, as evidenced by Arleen Inger's and Anne O'Brien's dinner ritual with their friends.

The written license test was pretty straightforward, little different from studying for a school exam. But the driving test was fraught with uncertainty—insecurity rears its ugly head once again.

Will I make a critical mistake? Will I get that one inspector who I hear flunks everybody? How will I ever parallel park the '57 Chevy station wagon? How will I tell my friends if I fail the test and have to take it again?

Driver's education at the high school was designed to help us survive the licensing process. We sat in a classroom full of car simulators, drove a route dictated by a movie projected on the large pull-down screen in front of us, and were scored based on our faux driving proficiency. This may have been the first video game.

Remembering the driving simulators, classmate Adrienne Nadler Hirschfeld says, "For years I went around telling people that I learned to drive on stationary cars watching a movie, and nobody knew what I was talking about, even the driving teacher at my children's school."

In the simulators, we learned how to shift gears (remember manual transmissions?), hit the brakes in an emergency, stop for school buses, and generally drive defensively. One day we settled into our simulators and were told we would not be practicing driving. I do not remember our instructor's exact words, but I recall they came across something like, "We're going to watch a film called *Signal 30* that is intended to scare the hell out of you and to make sure you drive safely. We'll be showing you terrible car crashes and actual injuries and fatalities. So pay attention."

Apparently, at the time "signal 30" was the code used by the state police when there was an accident with a fatality.

You can watch *Signal 30*, produced in 1959, on *YouTube*. The film's opening ominously reads, "This is not a Hollywood production as can readily be seen. The quality is below their standards. However, most of these scenes were taken under adverse conditions, nothing has been staged. These are actual scenes taken immediately after the accidents occurred. Also unlike Hollywood our actors were paid nothing. Most of the actors in these movies are bad actors and received top billing only on a tombstone. They paid a terrific price in these movies, they paid with their lives."

And, yes, the film did scare the hell out of me, and I remember it to this day.

The driver's education room also housed a device intended to test our reflexes. We would sit in a driver's seat with a gas pedal and brake pedal below us in their proper positions. On a panel in front of us was a red light, a green light, and a timer capable of measuring in hundredths of a second.

Step on the gas and the green light would come on. The red light would then come on at random times. Our task was to see the red light and as quickly as possible move our foot from the gas pedal to the brake and jam it to the floor.

The timer told us how quick we were. I was proud that I was always among the fastest, but was never able to beat Sandy Cytron. She was too quick for me.

Wholesome Recreational Program

With license in hand and mobility assured, our activity horizons expanded. Whether single or double dating or just meeting a group somewhere, the choices seemed endless.

Movies at the Varsity, Tivoli, or Beverly—*Beckett, My Fair Lady, Dr. Strangelove*

Movies at the Drive-ins—*Tom Jones; Promises! Promises!* with Jayne Mansfield (both billed as "Adult Entertainment")

Cinerama movies-*How The West Was Won; Circus World; It's a Mad, Mad, Mad, Mad World*

Dinner or late-night snacks at Hamburger Heaven, Via's, Nino's, Rinaldi's, Parkmoor, HoJo's, Frank & Helen's

Stopping at Jack & Jill, the family-owned and operated hole-in-the-wall restaurant. Sid Ladin, the owner, seemed to know everyone in town. We can still picture him behind the counter with messy white shirt and cap and can still hear him talking with customers as though they were family. His wife and daughter worked there and so did his mom, who made the best chili. Jack & Jill had no printed menu—all of the offerings were on signs of various shapes and colors plastered all over the walls. And every item had a name related to something or someone local or to the gestalt of the offering.

There was a four-scoop (all different flavors), four-topping delight called "The Four Sisters," named after classmate Leslie Berger's mom and her three sisters. There was the "Darktown Strutter's Ball," all chocolate—ice cream, fudge, and even the whipped cream (the only place I have ever seen where even the whipped cream flavor was a choice). The "Griper's" sundae had four scoops (your choice of flavors) and three toppings (your choice).

There are different memories of the name and size of Jack & Jill's largest concoction. It was either "Physician's Delight" or "Idiot's Delight" or "Kitchen Sink" and had either 25 or 50 scoops of various flavors of ice cream with all the toppings—all for $5.00. Whatever the name or size, if you ate it yourself without any help, it was free. The concoction and the eat-it-all-for-free offer lasted only until someone dropped and broke the huge platter on which it was served.

It may sound like we only went there for the ice cream, but the restaurant had lunch and dinner short-order fare, as well. Oh, there was one item that was not on a sign on the wall. It was a sign on the ceiling—some pineapple upside-down treat.

Pickup basketball games in front of Gary Oxenhandler's garage (played shirts and skins one December when we had a abnormal heat wave), on Marc Tenzer's patio (watch out after a layup; the drop-off was about a foot), in Steve Novack's driveway (the whole side of his house could be used as a backboard making a game of H-O-R-S-E more interesting)

Concerts like the one in which Dick Clark sang the male part for an ailing Paul of Paul (Ken Hildebrand) and Paula (Jill Jackson)—"Hey, Hey Paula, I wanna marry you"

Seeing Peter, Paul, and Mary in concert at Kiel Auditorium for $2.00 a person

Taking dates home, then meeting at the lighted tennis courts at the large city park to play touch football at midnight

Going to Gaslight Square to listen to Dixieland or, on more adventuresome nights, to the Blue Note Club in East St. Louis to listen to live jazz

Dancing for hours on Friday evenings at WigWam with live local bands like Patty McCoy and the Renegades, Little Walter and his Band, Winston and the Afftones, and Deacon and the Preachers

There were as many as 1000 people at WigWam on any given Friday evening. But dances were not the only WigWam activities. There was a Board of students, who planned well-attended events throughout the year. There were Cardinal games; cruises on the Admiral, a riverboat on the Mississippi; trips to the Municipal Opera, an outdoor venue for locally-produced Broadway musicals—our senior year, 200 students went to see *Calamity Jane*.

Classmate Eddie Friedman came across an old WigWam pass that reminded us of that special time. The back of the card read, "The purpose of WigWam is to provide a wholesome recreational program and the facilities for such an activity. General Rule: Enjoy one's self in the group and with the group. Specific Rules: 1) No smoking except where designated. 2) No alcoholic beverages may be brought into the WigWam and no person who has been partaking of such can be admitted. 3) A guest who enters by paying fifty cents must be accompanied by a member who will be responsible for this guest's behavior. The WigWam board will have the power to deal with violators of the above rules and may, if they feel it necessary, expel them for any period of time they deem wise."

When was the last time you saw an event referred to as a "wholesome recreational program?"

Going to St. Louis Hawks games at Kiel Auditorium and Cardinals games at Busch Stadium (the old Busch Stadium, previously called Sportsmans' Park) or listening to the games on KMOX on the car radio

Going to the Highlands amusement park and riding the Bobsled and the Comet, the longest and highest roller coaster in the country at the time, or, sadly, watching the spectacular fire that burned the Highlands to the ground in the summer of 1963

Attending midnight mass on Christmas Eve at the St. Louis Cathedral because, despite being Jewish, we found the experience inspirational

Playing pool at Tropicana Bowling Lanes and eating one of their flame-broiled burgers—in my judgment, the best in town

Meeting on "the strip," the gathering place near the high school just to see who would show up and what might be going on that evening

Just driving around and listening to our music, Motown, the British Invasion, and a little Dean Martin, Andy Williams, Beach Boys, Peter, Paul, and Mary, and Johnny Mathis sprinkled in on WIL, KXOK, KATZ, and other stations

And listen to music we did. For many classmates, recalling their favorite song or singer or group brings back a flood of memories of their entire high school experience. Judy Inger Shanfeld recalls two songs that were important to her and, apparently, still are.

"One of my favorite songs from before high school was 'To Know Him Is to Love Him' by Phil Spector and the Teddy Bears. It was the time of the first crush, when you thought the guy did not know you were alive... 'Why can't he see? How blind can he be?'

"In high school, the song with meaning for me was 'You Belong to Me' by The Duprees. The summer between our junior and senior year, my parents took us on a three-week vacation to the New England area and through Canada. I'm sure I made them miserable as I did not want to go when I had a boyfriend in St. Louis. The song talks about 'Fly the ocean in a silver plane'...'just remember 'til you're home again, you belong to me.'"

Carol Enger Canis says, "I associate the song by Johnny Mathis, 'Misty,' with Les Zuke and me. If I saw Les now, I'd like to give him a big hug. Hmmmmmmm."

Adrienne Nadler Hirschfeld, "My favorite song in high school was 'Gee Whiz' by Carla Thomas. We girls were so into drama with the boyfriend relationships. And the songs had so much feeling in those days."

Alan Spetner, "My favorite song and most memorable was 'The Bird is the Word' by the Trashmen. On New Year's Eve our senior year, we had a party at my house and for two hours straight we played 'well, uh, everybody's heard about the Bird...Bird Bird Bird...Bird is the word...' until Charlie Wiener threw up on my mom's living room floor, and we had to take him home and dump him in his front yard."

Mark Glickman, "...one that sticks out the most is 'Runaround Sue.' When we all would take showers after practice and Mitze would hold the soap in his hand like a mike and sing like he was Dion and we would all sing along. That was a super time and tons of memories with it."

Alan Resnick, "...my gut tells me to pick, 'She Loves You,' because the Beatles really hit me with that one. I wasn't a big fan at first, but a Beatles fan I am today."

Paula Glovinsky Sigel, "My favorite was Bobby Darin's 'Splish Splash'...I love the song and the singer...I was fortunate to see him in person when he was in St. Louis...and I still have the souvenir book."

David Nemon, "50s and 60s music is what I know best. I still listen to it like they were still on the charts. My favorite song on the 50s was 'At the Hop' by Danny and the Juniors. It got it all started. Then in the 60s it was 'Fun Fun Fun' by the Beach Boys."

Joanna Slotkin Baymiller's favorite song from our high school era is "Will You Love Me Tomorrow" by The Shirelles. For her, it had a kind of yearning—it expressed her vulnerability as a 15 year old. "What if I fell in love?" "What if he didn't love me back?" "What if he was there for a day and then gone?" "What would I do?" Whenever she hears the song, Joanna sings along. She knows every word, and the lyrics take her back to when she was 15.

Elaine Levin Unell remembers "Shake a Tail Feather" by The Five Du-Tones because when she hears it, she can still see Alan Spetner on the dance floor, bent over waving his hands where tail feathers would be.

Marla Schukar Levinson recalls loving anything by The Temptations. She loved to watch them dance and practiced doing their moves for hours.

Debbie Brownstein Pulley fondly remembers "Traveling Man" by

Ricky Nelson. It still reminds her of Terry Mitze, who was one of the few of us who traveled extensively with our families. Terry returned from a trip to Europe one summer when "Traveling Man" was gaining popularity and would sing it to Debbie.

Ellen Polinsky Cohen loved anything by Martha and the Vandellas—the beat, the feel of the music.

Harold Sanger remembers "Good Night My Love." He recalls, "A favorite for me and a special young lady. One of the stations...used to play it every night at midnight. So, one great summer we usually found a place to drop the convertible top, soak in the moon & enjoy..."

There was music to listen to in the car and always something going on—our driver's license made it all accessible.

We Did Not Get It

While we were very active, frequently out late, and, by the standards of the day, challenging the norms of acceptable behavior, we were, compared to today's high school students, in a very safe and comfortable environment. Although many classmates smoked, the majority did not. There was also relatively little drinking, although there were definitely exceptions. While a few were experimenting with marijuana, in general, drugs were not yet part of the conversation; that is, if you do not count the use of physician prescribed "diet pills." And only a few were sexually active.

Those who smoked at school were restricted to a small courtyard hidden between wings of the building. Even in the early 60s we were relatively well aware of the risks of smoking. Our student-edited school newspaper ran editorials about the risks and even suggested a full smoking ban on school property, a point of view well ahead of its time.

In the fall of our senior year, the school held a debate. Classmate Stephen Kowarsky took the side of pro-smoking arguing that there was no solid evidence that smoking caused cancer. Classmate Lynne Marschak argued anti-smoking, citing the number of lung cancer deaths in the country. It was in January of our senior year that Dr. Luther Terry issued the *First Surgeon General Report: Smoking and Health.* At the time more than 40% of US adults smoked. The percentage has been in decline since the report and is about half the 1964 level.

Both of my parents smoked, and lung cancer eventually overtook my father. I was exposed to secondhand smoke at home and will likely never really know the effects of that. When I was about eight years old, my dad, who, while he smoked, knew it was not a good idea, put a lighted cigarette in my mouth and told me to inhale. Two hours later I finally stopped coughing, and I have never had another cigarette in my mouth.

Drinking was also not an issue for me or for most classmates. I did not drink in high school until my senior year when I went on a trip to the Lake of the Ozarks with Steve Schukar and older friends Pat Morris and Larry Appel. They introduced me to gin and Fresca, which tasted OK but did not impress me much. Other than on that trip, I cannot recall ever going out on a date or hanging out with the guys when alcohol was involved.

There were some classmates for whom drinking was an integral part of their social scene. They recall stories of attending collegiate purple passion parties while still in high school, of figuring out how to buy beer for the evening, of trying to explain hangovers and smelly clothing to parents, and of risky driving incidents. But these stories were not reflective of the majority of students.

So, some smoking, some alcohol, and less drugs—and not a lot of sex. We often kid each other today that we regret not figuring out sex earlier. But I do not think we really mean it. There was little pressure to be sexually active. I felt lucky, no pun intended, to have gotten "to second base" a couple of times. Making out mostly meant endless kissing.

Most of us did not know much about sex. We knew something was going on occasionally, but there was not much discussion about it. We were so naïve that even when there were clear signals, we missed them. A couple left the stands at a football game and returned an hour later looking somewhat disheveled and wearing different clothes. We did not get it. Some friends showed us the condoms in their wallets, typically ones that had been there for a very long time with no opportunity to use them. We did not get it. We may hold the local, perhaps national, high school record for the most consecutive years of having a junior cheerleader named Sharon get pregnant. But there was relatively little attention given to that at the time. We did not get it.

I was telling Jill Friedman Chapin that I was going to address our general sexual naiveté in the book. She put it in perspective when she said, "My sex life was nonexistent. But if you're going to share this with anyone, feel free to say I was a slut. At my age, it can only enhance my reputation."

As I was writing this section of the book, a *Bloomberg News* article appeared in the *Cincinnati Enquirer* with a headline reading, "More teen sex, less caution, CDC says." In part the article reported, "The percentage of teens who said they had sex rose to 47.8 percent last year...Condom use fell...to 61.5 percent..."

We would not have been able to relate to this report in the early 60s at University City High School. We did not get it.

Sex, drugs, and rock and roll? No, no, and yes. Our relative naiveté was not the bad news—it was the good news. High school students have enough pressure without dealing with these issues.

They're Full of ...

To be clear, the high school experience at University City was not something that everyone from the class of '64 remembers fondly or wants to remember at all.

One of my favorite adventure writers is Randy Wayne White. I enjoy his continuing characters, his style, and his love of baseball. His protagonist is Marion "Doc" Ford, a marine biologist and ex-government black ops agent who cannot quite separate himself from his past.

In White's novel, *Dead of Night*, Doc Ford is talking with his teenage son, Lake, as they wait outside the emergency room while their friend Tomlinson is being treated. Ford had just returned to the waiting room and learned that his son had been talking to the attractive female doctor.

"'Any word on Tomlinson?'

'Naw, Doctor said it'd be about an hour. She's funny. I like her. We had a pretty good talk. Know what she told me? She said, 'When adults tell you that adolescence is the best time of your life, they're full of shit.' Said she didn't really start feeling comfortable, having fun, until she was in her late twenties. Hated her teens.'

'A smart woman; she's right. I was a little older. Early thirties.'

'No shit?' Lake had been experimenting with profanity. I had to force myself not to smile.

'I shit you not. Early thirties.'"

A number of classmates recall their time at U City with something less than fondness. Some of them have reconnected over the years and are glad to have done so. Yet some understandably continue to distance themselves from their high school experience.

Whether we had an excellent high school experience, a bad one, or, like most of us, somewhere in between, the members of the University City Class of 1964 are a collection of personal and shared stories. We entered high school having been formed by our families' journeys, our cultural heritage, and our middle-class values.

By the time we graduated, the school itself and our experience there had greatly influenced each of us. Our lives would be forever affected by our time at University City Senior High School.

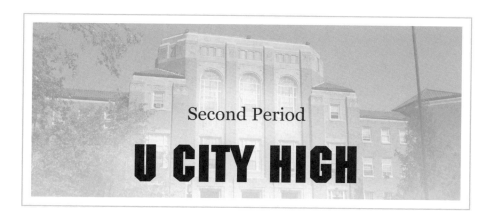

Second Period

U CITY HIGH

*"Education is what survives when what
has been learned has been forgotten."*
B. F. Skinner

"I am still learning."
Michelangelo

Anne O'Brien

*"She creates beauty with her eyes,
And enthusiasm with a cheer.
Confidence with a smile."*

Marla: *"Sometime before the end of the evening I'm going to find
someone to meet me under the clock—it's been a long time."*

Mark: *"I would have met you there anytime—all you had to do
was ask."*

Judy: *"The old traditions die hard. I feel really comfortable in this
building."*

Steve: *"We spent a lot of time here. Classes, sports, clubs, concerts,
dances, hanging out—what did we call 'hanging out'
back then?"*

Anne: *"Don't remember, but we did a bunch of it. I think I was doing something after school almost every day, or at least it felt like it."*

Judy: *"I've heard our principal, Dr. Boyer, and some coaches and teachers will be at the dinner tomorrow night. I appreciate them even more now looking back."*

Mark: *"We had a lot of things going for us. We won some state championships."*

Judy: *"Our arts program was first class."*

Steve: *"We had so much going for us that sometimes it seemed like we had too much going for us. We started each day early, went through challenging classes, played sports or did something else after school, got home late, ate supper, did homework, wore out, and went to bed. Then it started again the next day."*

Marla: *"Are you complaining?"*

Steve: *"No, I wouldn't have had it any other way."*

Marla: *"I definitely need to get someone to meet me under the clock."*

Truth Courage Wisdom

The building is imposing. Classmate and architect David Nemon describes it as "majestic." Classmate Ron Brown, also an architect, describes the façade as "neoclassical." Regardless of the word used, the University City Senior High School is impressive.

Entrance to University City High School

No less impressive is the entranceway itself and these sets of words, each set carved on a granite lintel over one of the three sets of double doors:

TRUTH COURAGE WISDOM
LETTERS ARTS SCIENCES
IDEALS SERVICE CHARACTER

Although the words are profound, they tended to disappear into the routine coming and going through the doors. Yet, what better charge could we have received every day at school and for the lives that were ahead of us?

When it was opened in 1930, University City High School stood alone amidst nothing but open land textured with the streets that would become the residential community that would soon surround the school. The feeder roads converged on a large rotary in front of the school. While designed to facilitate traffic patterns, the rotary also served us well when we earned our driver's license and were dared to drive around as often as we could in a set amount of time.

Between the traffic circle and the school is a large landscaped plaza—named in 1988 for long-time art teacher Tom Lawless. The plaza transitions to a short but broad flight of steps leading up to the landing in front of the entrance doors. The plaza was the location of the senior prank of a class ahead of us—they somehow lifted the Principal's car from its parking space and placed it on the steps in front of the school.

Another senior class used the last couple of weeks of their tenure to check virtually every book out of the library and then return them all in one day. Our class slowly rid the cafeteria of silverware as our final semester wound down. I do not recall whether or not we returned the silverware—so much for truth, wisdom, and character.

It Feels So Right

The school building is the dominant feature on the grounds that are also shared by the football field, track, natatorium, and significant landscaped green space. Note that I am using present tense to describe the school I attended more than four decades ago.

The reason is that, as I approach the school today, it looks the same and feels as though I never left.

As I am writing this section of the book, I am visiting family and friends in St. Louis from my home in Cincinnati. I am sitting in a school desk in a classroom at University City High School, the kind with the desk surface attached to the chair, perfectly designed for right-handers. The last time I sat in one was to take final exams in 1964.

I am honored to have been asked to speak to Mr. Wilson's third period creative writing class—asked to do so after my first book, *Baseball: Never Too Old to Play "The" Game*, was published.

The desk should feel the same, because I am about the same size as I was then—five-foot-ten and a little under 200 pounds. The classroom, however, has some noticeable differences. The writing boards on the walls are white, not black; my hair is gray, not black; the students are black, not white; and there is a computer on Mr. Wilson's desk.

The school and its classrooms seem old, but have aged well, which feels no different than when we were here more than four decades ago.

Our school nickname was the Indians but is now the Lions. By making the change, U City joined other high schools and colleges around the country exhibiting increased sensitivity toward Native Americans. Perhaps the Lions would have been best all along. Large regal statues of lions stand on 30-foot pedestals on either side of the street greeting those who enter University City near City Hall.

Engraving on a granite slab that now sits in a corner of the school as a memory of the previous nickname

In general, the feeling of sameness outweighs the differences and is confirmed when I notice the writing on the whiteboard in the front of the classroom, "Next time: Quiz on *For Esme, with Love and Squalor.*"

The students enter the room from the energy and din of the hallway. They are engaging as they politely greet and welcome me while struggling to work out from under their heavily-laden backpacks. We did not have backpacks. Instead we made more frequent stops at our lockers, and the boys carried our books and notebooks under one arm, while the girls carried theirs pressed against their chest.

The class has yet to begin; the students are settling in. There are differences, but it feels so right.

Under the Clock

I am looking forward to roaming the hallways after class and know, based on some earlier visits, that the remainder of the school will feel comfortable as well. Every time I go through the entrance doors, it feels like home—that is, with the exception of a security desk now stationed just inside.

After class, I return to the cavernous front hall, the centerpiece of the school and of our high school experience. The hall looks the same and sounds the same as students meet and greet and hustle to their next classes.

The front hall is huge and serves well as a meeting place. The area is about 2500 square feet, has a high ceiling, and features a small but very helpful clock just above the eight-foot-high, three-glass-door trophy case that faces the school's entranceway. For us, the benefit of the clock went well beyond keeping the school running on its regimented schedule.

"I'll meet you under the clock."

Hall of Fame

While walking the halls, I made sure to visit a relatively new feature in the school, one that was established in 1999. Lining the walls on both sides of one long hallway are plaques celebrating members of the University City High School Hall of Fame. The alumni in the Hall are highly accomplished, including those prominent in entertainment and the arts, world renowned scientists, noted athletes, educators, business leaders, and community activists. It would be worthwhile to profile each of the members of the Hall, but that may be the subject of a separate work. Here is a sampling.

Among writers and performers of note are Carl Dennis (class of '57), winner of the 2002 Pulitzer Prize for poetry (one of three University City High School graduates to have been awarded this prize); Cornell Haynes, Jr. (class of '93) , better known to his hip-hop and rap fans as "Nellie;" Dave Garroway (class of '31), the first host of NBC's *The Today Show*; and Thomas "Tennessee" Williams (class of '29), the great playwright and two-time Pulitzer Prize winner (*A Streetcar Named Desire* and *Cat on a Hot Tin Roof*; also authored *The Glass Menagerie*, *The Night of the Iguana*, and *The Rose Tattoo*).

On April 6, 1929, *The U. City Pep*, the school newspaper of its time, published "The First Day Out," a story written by Tom Williams. He had already won awards for his writing and had been published outside of school. This reflection of a sea cruise taken during summer vacation before his senior year, however, was among his earliest works. If you are a fan, you may enjoy seeing the last paragraph of his high school story.

"You congratulate yourself that you are such an excellent sailor. However, just at that moment, something very peculiar happens to your head. It seems to come loose and to bob up and down, just like a kite on a windy day. Your legs wobble and the sea and sky whirl dazzlingly around you. You sink into a chair and close your eyes. Only one thought consoles you in your misery. And that is that in five more days you will be once more upon firm land."

University City also contributed to the world of sports. High School Hall of Fame members include Vaughan "Bing" Devine (class of '33), prominent baseball executive with the St. Louis Cardinals, San Francisco Giants, and Montreal Expos. We had the honor of having Mr. Devine as the keynote speaker at our spring sports banquet in 1963, the year we won the Missouri high school baseball championship.

I had the privilege of playing with and occasionally catching University City Hall-of-Famer Ken Holtzman (class of '63), the number-one pitcher on our state championship team. He went on to play with the Cubs, Athletics, Orioles, and Yankees, pitching two major league no-hitters. I am convinced, however, that his most important no-hitter came in the semi-final game of our drive for the state championship, but there is no mention of that one in Cooperstown. Ken was part of the great pitching staff that led Oakland to consecutive World Series championships from 1972 to 1974. He boasted an ERA of 2.55 and a batting average of .333 in World Series play. Most recently, Ken was a manager of a team in the fledgling Israeli major league.

University City Hall-of-Famer Robert Person (class of '87) played with a number of major league clubs but was most successful with the Phillies. He was voted "Phillie of the Year" in 2000, had a career-high 15 wins as a pitcher in 2001, and set a Phillies record in 2002 by batting in seven runs in one game with a three-run home run and a grand slam.

Bernard Gilkey (class of '84) played with his hometown St. Louis Cardinals and with the Mets and Diamondbacks. Gilkey had a solid major league career, hitting over .300 three times. Perhaps some know him better for his brief role in the movie *Men in Black*. Recall the scene at Shea Stadium in New York when a Mets outfielder is distracted by a massive spaceship over the stadium. He watches the ship instead of the fly ball that hits him in the head. That was Bernard Gilkey.

Rounding out this sampling of U City Hall of Famers are those who were from my era at the high school. Classmate Allen Brockman and his wife, Ronnie Goldberg Brockman (class of '66) founded and are the Directors of Camp Rainbow, a program for seriously ill children, ages six to 13. It provides the children with the opportunity, at no charge, to attend a week-long sleepover camp. Allen and Ronnie have a long list of other accomplishments, most focused on the needs of children.

Classmate Ronald Gould is a circuit judge of the United States Court of Appeals for the Ninth Circuit and former Clerk for Supreme Court Justice Potter Stewart. Judge Gould (it is hard not to just call him Ronnie—so I will) was nominated by President Clinton and confirmed by the Senate in late 1999. Ronnie has also been deeply involved in the Chief Seattle Council of the Boy Scouts of America, following his scouting passion that led him to his Eagle Scout award while still living in University City.

Perhaps the kind of person Ronnie is was best stated by fellow classmate Tom Norman, when he responded to a message from his friend, Ronnie, to the class. Tom wrote, "But I have to say you are much too modest. For those of us who don't know, you are not 'only' a judge, which already is a great honor for our class to share in—that one of us rascals has gotten to be a judge (me, I got to be an edible nut broker). You are one of the appellate judges on the Western Appellate Court of the United States, covering Washington State, Oregon, and California.

"I wanted to put that in and acknowledge the incredible disposition and indefatigable sense of humor you continue to have, as you wrestle with grace and art your life with MS and as a U. S. Appellate Judge. As I understand it, your day begins with a workout routine of some hours, sandwiches in your work responsibilities, and then ends with a routine of some duration.

"I hope I am not embarrassing you, but know that you are an example for any of us who are physically challenged and in my book, a hero. I say that as I count my blessings and acknowledge your gift."

What he wrote says a lot about Tom as well.

Dr. Ira Herskowitz (class of '63), his PhD from MIT, was a prominent research geneticist, who was posthumously inducted into the Hall of Fame in 2003. His work in the early 1980s helped develop a patented process for producing insulin for diabetics. He was also a pioneer in the effort to learn how genes can influence a person's response to drugs. He cared about the high school so much that his family established a yearly award to recognize and reward outstanding teachers.

Rabbi Myron Kinberg (class of '63) was a friend and teammate. Myron was the catcher on our state championship baseball team, a fierce football player, and a state championship wrestler. He converted his athletic focus to that of his rabbinate and his passion for human rights. He was awarded honors from the Eugene (Oregon) Human Rights Commission, the NAACP, the Inter-religious Commission for Peace in the Middle East, and Peaceworks, from which he earned a lifetime achievement award. His lifetime of helping was cut short when Myron passed away in 1994.

There are 88 University City High School Hall-of-Fame graduates who represent all who have contributed to society in special ways.

New deserving members will be inducted every two years. It is good to see the plaques on the walls of the school building as they remind students and other passersby what is possible. The Hall of Fame serves to make stronger the heritage and culture of the institution that is University City High School.

Herr Klein, Professor Bobbitt

University City High School was an exceptional academic institution. Our parents demanded, the faculty and administration provided, and we received a quality education.

Mr. Wallace Klein attended University City schools beginning in the sixth grade at Delmar-Harvard Elementary School and graduated from the high school in 1940.

He attended Washington University, where his undergraduate degree path was interrupted by World War II and a stint in the military. The Army sent him to a German language school at UCLA, an opportunity that became a building block for the remainder of Herr Klein's academic career. He returned to and graduated from Washington University with High Honors and was inducted into Phi Beta Kappa, Pi Sigma Alpha, and Delta Phi Alpha, national Liberal Arts, Political Science, and German honoraries, respectively.

He went on to earn his Master's Degree in Political Science and History, began teaching at the high school level, and was eventually offered a job at University City High School, his alma mater.

Upon his retirement in 1983, Herr Klein wrote, "I took the job at University City because my own memories of the school were very positive, because the reputation of the school had been and still was excellent, because almost all of the teachers were still there, and because I wanted to teach German. The school is what it is because the tradition of excellence is still strong...and because the community has been, in the main, appreciative of and supportive of the fine educational opportunities students enjoy here."

Since retiring, he has taken on the role of University City High School historian. Herr Klein is a frequent visitor to the school and is amused by the reaction of today's students when he tells them he has been roaming the halls for more than 70 years. Appropriately, he was inducted into the school's Hall of Fame in 2001.

Herr Klein says of the early 60s at U City, "In your era, the students knew that the faculty cared about their education—the faculty knew the students cared—and, importantly, both knew that the parents cared deeply."

His perspective is borne out by other data. In 1964, the Council for Basic Education (CBE) conducted a statistical study to assess the relative quality of the thousands of secondary schools throughout the country. Founded in 1956, CBE is a nonprofit educational organization whose primary purpose is to strengthen the teaching and learning of the basic liberal arts subjects in American undergraduate schools. The statistical population for the national study was all applicants for, including the 3207 students who had been awarded, the Woodrow Wilson Foundation Fellowship between 1958 and 1963. U City was tied for 19th in the entire nation and one of only five high schools in the entire Midwest in the top 25.

This was only one indicator of the quality of our education. During our school years, as measured by the Iowa Test of Basic Skills, which include vocabulary, language, reading, work-study, and arithmetic, the students in University City schools consistently performed one to two grade levels above the national norms on average. Teachers at the high school were chosen by the US government for the Fulbright exchange program with other countries. University City was selected as one of the two top schools in Missouri for teaching mathematics by the Society of Actuaries and the Mathematics Association of America. In 1964, 45% of the nation's high school graduates went on to attend college. Our class sent about 80%.

Despite the school's qualities, the administration was always looking for ways to improve. The Board of Education accepted a proposal from Washington University to participate in an Asian Area Studies Program and introduced the teaching of Chinese into the high school curriculum. Classmate Kay Kruvand Watts recalls enjoying an experimental two-year Humanities class, which combined art, history, and literature and was taught by a team of three teachers from their respective disciplines. A committee was formed to improve the library and its use by students. Principal Dr. Mark Boyer visited other schools around the country with a special interest in such innovations as independent study programs and flexible scheduling.

It was not uncommon for representatives from other schools to visit us as well. For example, in early 1962, nearly 100 principals toured University City during their annual convention of the National

Secondary School Principals Association to learn how the school was achieving such good results.

I was to get another indicator of U City's status from an unexpected source. In my first freshman semester at the Missouri School of Mines and Metallurgy, I had a dynamic English professor, Jack Bobbitt. It was not easy to be dynamic and an English professor at a predominately engineering school of 5000 college men.

Professor Bobbitt asked me to stay after class one day saying he wanted to talk about an assigned paper I had submitted earlier in the week. He quickly eased my obvious concern when he said that he had enjoyed my paper and my writing structure and style. Then he said that he wanted to add a data point to an informal experiment he had been conducting. He explained that he had been teaching at the college level in Missouri for a long time and had found that he could identify students from one of two high schools in the state by their grammar usage and writing capability. One was a small Catholic school in mid-Missouri. The other was University City. He then asked if I had gone to either.

Joe Hale—a Great Teacher

At U City in the early 60s, we were fortunate to have more than our fair share of excellent teachers. One of our favorites was Chemistry teacher, Joe "The Toe" Hale. We called him "The Toe" because he told us at the beginning of our junior year that he had cut off his big toe in a lawn mower accident over the summer. Perhaps we were not as sensitive as we should have been.

Mr. Hale made class exciting and memorable, helping us learn by using mnemonics that many of us remember to this day.

While learning about the concepts of oxidation and reduction, he shared with us, "LEO the lion says GER." LEO: Loss of Electrons—Oxidation and GER: Gain of Electrons—Reduction.

The rings of electron orbits are each identified by a letter. How could we possibly remember the order of rings from the nucleus outward? "Sober physicists don't find giraffes hiding in kitchens."

s, p, d, f, g, h, i, k

During a lab experiment, Mr. Hale taught us the correct order by which to add materials when mixing an acid with water. "Do what you ought to—pour acid into water. Don't be a gas-head by pouring water into acid."

Classmate Don Pearline, who works in pharmaceuticals development, recalls Mr. Hale's "Dance of the Prairie Chicken" that he performed to teach us about the differences between rotational and translational energy. Don describes Mr. Hale's dance, "...he starts by raising both hands over his head, like the Hokey Pokey, and both shakes his hands and waves them...revival tent type of shaking them. Then he starts turning around and around in place...a bit frenzied with a bit of a hop from one foot to the other—rotational energy. Then, while all of this is going on, he starts moving from the front of the room to the back—that's the translational energy... together is total kinetic energy. Joe Hale—a great teacher."

My favorite Hale mnemonic helped us remember the positive valence of many of the elements. He used the rhythm of a sports cheer.

HAgLiNaK, HAgLiNak

CuBaCaFe

PbZnMg, PbZnMg

AlFeBiNiCr, AlFeBiNiCr

SiC, SiC, SiC

The first line elements have a valence of +1. The second two lines of elements are +2. The fourth and fifth lines have +3 and +4, respectively. I learned this cheer in 1963 and remember it today.

When I reminded classmates of the cheer, Mike Fleischmann, who is a graphics designer for NBC, wrote back, "I remember it well, even shared it with my daughters when they took chemistry in high school."

Mike's daughters, Hannah and Laura, who went to high school in Mamaroneck, New York, were touched by Joe Hale from University City High School across decades and distance.

As Don Pearline said, "Joe Hale—a great teacher."

Classically Educated

Mr. Hale was not the only great teacher. According to Herr Klein, "The faculty was excellent across the board. A Master's Degree was required—the faculty was highly and classically educated."

He attributes the quality of the faculty to a number of reasons. The school attracted extraordinary teachers because the community strongly supported education, the School Board was trusted and respected, and the pay was better than in most other districts.

Despite the pay being better at U City, many teachers still needed to supplement their income with other jobs. Mr. Klein taught English as a Second Language in the evenings and was a bookkeeper at a local shoe company in the summers.

Another positive trait of our faculty was continuity. My aunt, Ethel "Tappy" Spector Harris, graduated from University City High School in 1934. Greater than 25% of the faculty/administration listed and pictured in her 1932 sophomore yearbook were still on staff in my senior year 32 years later.

The 1932 yearbook was dedicated to Miss Leliaetta Bruns, that year's senior class sponsor and Head of the Mathematics Department. While I could not determine whether she held the position throughout the years, Miss Bruns was also the Chair of the Mathematics Department in 1964.

As Senior Sponsor, Miss Bruns figured and recorded all senior credits by hand; everything a Registrar does today by computer. She generated the entire school's schedule by hand. She even personally tied the ribbon around each of the senior's diplomas. When she retired, she had been teaching and the Senior Sponsor for 44 years.

A highly trained and regarded faculty was the norm. Miss Wanda Bowers was no exception. Unlike Miss Bruns, she was not at University City in 1932. Rather, she was teaching in Southern Missouri and came to U City about 1940 after receiving her Masters Degree. Classmate Joanna Slotkin Baymiller was profoundly influenced by and remembers Miss Bowers.

By Chance

Joanna's home is in Guilford, Connecticut, but she lives several days each week in Manhattan, where she is a writer and Vice-President of Strategic Planning for a theater design and planning firm. She describes her life as that of a "bohemian/urban/progressive/Volvo-driving/artsy-fartsy/intellectual/activist."

Joanna and I have a special connection, one that we only accidentally discovered. When my aunt Tappy moved from her home to Crown Center, a senior living apartment complex, she told me of and, eventually, introduced me to a new friend she had made. Sylvia is an independent, insightful, and witty nonagenarian. She is also blind.

Months after I had met Sylvia at Crown Center, classmate Leslie Berger sent an e-mail saying that Joanna would be in St. Louis and inviting others to join Joanna and him for lunch.

By chance I was also in St. Louis the day of the lunch with Joanna. By chance I was able to join the 15 or so classmates who could make it. By chance I sat next to Joanna. By chance we talked about relatives who still live in St. Louis. By chance she mentioned her mother lives at Crown Center. By chance she told me that her mother is blind. I said, "By chance is her name Sylvia?"

Since then, Joanna and I have become very close, unlike in high school, where we barely knew the other existed.

Joanna's life has been and is a creative one, deeply influenced by, among others, Miss Wanda Bowers of University City High School. Following our 40-year reunion, Joanna was inspired to write "Our Miss Bowers."

Joanna Slotkin

"If I had a dream—
past the wit of man to say what
dream it was."

Our Miss Bowers
By Joanna Slotkin Baymiller

At 96, the lady takes no prisoners. And she still dazzles.

The lady is our Miss Bowers. Our fierce, mysterious, magical English literature teacher. And we're in her home.

During the weekend of our 40th class reunion, classmate Shellie Klevens has pre-arranged for us to visit—on Saturday, October 9,

2004, with great anticipation, we visit our high school influence in her sunlit and spotless apartment on a high floor.

She is ageless and positively waltzes us through with a graceful wave of her arm. She could be a dancer. She's also lucid, focused, and stunning, with a handsome, hawk-like beauty that has deepened over the four decades since I began staring at her.

She's tall and slender, and wears a fashionable black top and long skirt. She wears high heels too, until, when she sits down, she drops her shoes on the carpet and sits with her legs crossed in her stocking feet. She wears a single piece of jewelry, a large flat stone wrapped in a slim piece of silver on a long cord. Her hair is exactly as I remember it, pure white with braids neatly wrapped on top of her head. The high school yearbook photo of her shows the same face; the same open, curious, and slightly amused expression.

"Come meet my family," she says, and takes us through the apartment introducing us to photographs and paintings that she cherishes. There are photos of her brother, Charlie; of her parents, who came from Cape Girardeau, Missouri; and one arresting portrait that someone took of her on the street ("you don't mind if I take your picture, Madam, do you?" she recalls being asked.) The pose is of a woman in a wide brimmed ribboned hat and cream colored suit, looking at the camera with a steady gaze that seems to say, "yes, I know I'm photogenic, take the picture already..." You could put it on the cover of *Vogue*.

This powerful, yet delicate, woman commands our attention as she did standing in front of us in high school when she shared with us her high standards and expectations of us. We have felt obliged to live up to those expectations throughout our lives.

We continue on our guided tour of her apartment. There is a painting by Miss Bowers that was done when she was an adolescent, which would mean some time in the mid-1920s. Possibly a self-portrait—it depicts a young girl and shows that a talent for visual art as well as literature was developing at an early age.

There are two books in sight; one a book of poems by the poet laureate Billie Collins, a gift from our classmates Judy Fortus and Sue Fischlowitz, who visited her a few days previously, and another, *Dancing with Cats*, a gift from her brother.

I look at Miss Bowers. She strikes me as feline: lovely, lithe, watchful, delicate, a touch mischievous, and saucily independent.

Half woman, half cat. The poetry book is tender and insightful. I think together they embody her spirit.

She's accessible – up to a point. Ask a personal question, and the wall comes up, ever so gently and politely, but ever so firmly as well. She answers our questions ("who are you really" is what they're all about) carefully. I respect anew the value of NOT revealing all. I learn something yet again from this woman who has taught me so much in the past, who selected my stories for the high school literary magazine; who made me work harder on them to make them better, and who let me know that yes, I was a writer.

My mother has some of her qualities. Katharine Hepburn had them, too. It's a sense of self-awareness coupled with a sense of self-worth that allows a person to give, to share, but does not require them to give themselves away in order to be loved. Miss Bowers and Hepburn were born only two years apart. They both embody that spirit. I aspire to that as well.

Shellie wants to read what she's been writing, and Miss Bowers curls up to listen. She sits—she tilts her head slightly and cups her cheek and chin, exactly as she did in class when she sat on her desk and read to us.

Later, of course, we are full of questions. We are curious about her background: how did she get to U City? What was it like for her? A farm girl, from the southern part of the State, she brought a very different background to the classroom. She recalled that when she first came to U City to teach, she felt that she was viewed as an oddball by the rest of the faculty. No wonder I loved her so: I was an oddball. Being an oddball, it was necessary for me to find other oddballs: for me, it was the group of green baggers -- we'd call ourselves Bohemians now, but who knew then what we were. We were just kids looking for an accepting peer group. She too, wanted to belong.

How did she become a teacher? She had a great teacher herself—one who loved to read aloud. Anyone who had Miss Bowers in English Literature class will recall that she read to us – particularly from Charles Dickens. Today, I read things I love, and some things I have written, to my mother and my friends.

We kept asking questions.

Why didn't she marry? One class sent an emissary to ask her. She told him, and repeated to us that the men who she thought were interesting were, she soon realized, not "suitable" as long term relationships. "They would not have worked out," she says. I'm thinking "bad boys." Like me, she loved the wild ones, the ones who break your heart. And she was wise enough not to choose them.

How many of us, looking back, could have benefited from that piece of wisdom in our 20s, 30s, and 40s?

But she doesn't speak about these men. She makes it clear that these particular memories are private. She doesn't write about them either – not yet. But she tells us that she is working on her memoirs, and those will undoubtedly be something to read.

We leave, dazzled. In a few weeks, I tentatively mail her some of my stories, the successful ones that have been published as well as a few others that are still undergoing changes. She replies, with graceful and positive and interesting comments. But it's her stories I now want to read. Her memories, adventures, and dreams. Who is she? We still don't know. And I wonder how much she will reveal.

(On June 22, 2008, Elaine Levin Unell forwarded a note to the class from Miss Bower's family. The note began, "Miss Wanda Bowers will be 100 years old on August 14, 2008...she is quite well, still lives independently, and has a mind that is very sharp and quick...As you might guess, Miss Bowers is still 'in control.'")

Mr. Wallace Klein

Mr. Joseph Hale

Miss Wanda Bowers

Divine Intervention

The quality of the academic faculty was matched by the quality of the school's athletic department—enhancing our high school experience, whether we participated as an athlete, a member of the school band, a cheerleader, or a fan.

During the sports seasons, many of the social events revolved around the game schedule. For example, the weekend football game ritual began on Friday evening when everyone met at WigWam, anticipating our Saturday afternoon game.

As football players, we had a curfew, which, of course, we followed religiously. Yeah—right.

An exception to the football weekend ritual occurred on Friday, September 27, 1963. When the year's league schedule was issued, it showed us playing the McCluer Comets on Saturday, the 28th. Insensitive to the fact that U City had a large Jewish population, the league had scheduled the game on Yom Kippur, the holiest of Jewish holidays. When confronted with the problem, the league's compromise was to play the game right after school on Friday, such that it would be over in time for us to get home before sundown, the official start of the holiday.

Going into the McCluer game we were 0-2, having lost our two non-conference games prior to the start of our league season by a cumulative score of 56 to 6. To make matters worse, McCluer was coming into the game with a city-high ten-game winning streak and was ranked fourth in the polls among large St. Louis schools.

The odds were not good. What are a bunch of undersized Jewish guys supposed to do in a game just before the eve of Yom Kippur? Play the game. Play it we did—I can remember the game vividly to this day.

Later in our senior year, Mr. Fendelman gave us an assignment to write a paper describing a time when we had a personal encounter with an "out-of-body experience." There was no doubt what I would write about, because on that eve of Yom Kippur in the Hebrew calendar year of 5724, there was a two-minute period during which everything was perfect, and I was watching myself quarterback my team from outside my body.

We were, to the surprise of many, perhaps mostly ourselves, behind only 17-13 with less than two minutes left to play. We forced a McCluer punt and had the ball on our own 35-yard line. I was fortunate to have already had a good game, having scored one touchdown running and thrown a 65-yard touchdown pass to Steve "Mouse" Moran.

As I sit writing this account, it is approaching the 45th anniversary of the game, yet I still vividly remember the three plays that led to our victory.

- 800 left end down-and-out pass to Jim Cohen
- 900 short-side-option pass to Phil Shanker
- 800 left end z-in pass to Jim Cohen

Each pass was complete, the last for a 45-yard touchdown. The Jewish guys won an unlikely game and were home in time for sundown on the eve of Yom Kippur.

We won only one other game that season and tied another, finishing at 2-7-1. Was the McCluer game divine intervention? What else could it have been?

Jim Cohen (wide receiver) and Alan Spector (quarterback)
40 years after the McCluer game

Champs

Despite our general lack of football prowess as seniors, we had more than our fair share of athletic success while we were at U City. I had the opportunity to be the first baseman on the 1963 Missouri state championship baseball team.

University City also boasted Missouri state championships in swimming and in both indoor and outdoor track and field. We also had two state champion wrestlers (Myron Kinberg and Bernie Steinberg, both class of '63), a water polo conference championship with two third-team All-American water polo players (twins Dan and Don Casey, class of '65), a third-place finish in the state cross-country championships, and a conference runner-up golf team. Not bad for one high school over a couple of years.

Despite all of these reasons to be boastful about our athletic achievements, there was more of a quiet pride at U City. While other schools filled their letter jackets with stripes and stars and pins and graduation years and school mascots, at University City there was an unwritten rule. We wore only the letter. The U said it all.

Are there regrets looking back on our athletic program? Yes. We grew up in a time before Title IX opened up interscholastic athletics for women as preparation for collegiate sports. Our female classmates participated primarily in intramurals; field hockey, basketball, volleyball, and other sports.

Surprisingly, my aunt's yearbooks from her U City high school years, 1932 through 1934, show the school had girls' varsity basketball, volleyball, and field hockey, each with a substantial schedule, league play, and varsity letters awarded. In 1933, there was even a girls' varsity "baseball" team, although based on the size of the ball in the yearbook picture, the game seemed to be softball. In 1933, University City also boasted a varsity archery team that competed against other schools.

What happened to girls' varsity teams between the 1930s and the 1960s is not clear. We had active girls' intramural sports programs, but varsity sports were limited to a two-game field hockey schedule and a three-game volleyball schedule. I would have loved to have seen classmates Alice Schneider, Sandy Klayman, Vicki Aubuchon, and others compete for the high school in an extensive varsity sports program. And I would have loved to see Lois Rosenberg run track— she could fly.

Denuttem

Our athletic achievements would not have been possible without an exemplary coaching staff. While we did not have a successful football season our senior year, it was clearly not the result of a weak coach. Clarence "Stub" Muhl began coaching at University City in 1928 and when he retired in 1966, he had amassed 225 victories and 20 championships.

Coach Muhl was a five-foot-five, 130-pound end (both offensive and defensive) for the University of Illinois, having played with Red Grange. In 1924, Coach Muhl was an honorable mention All-American. Even then, when players were of a more modest size, he had to be tough to play end. He was still tough when he coached us 40 years later.

When Coach Muhl was dissatisfied with our practice execution, he would insert himself into the drill to show us how to do it right. We were bigger than he was, 45 years younger, and had full pads on, but that did not stop him from showing us how to block at full speed. He taught us toughness.

One particular play was not working well in practice because the blockers, especially the pulling guards, were not opening a running lane. Coach Muhl started screaming in his high-pitched voice, "Denuttem, Denuttem."

We all looked at each other, then at him—we had no idea what he was saying. So Coach dropped his clip board and whistle, pushed our right guard aside, stepped into the slot on the line, and told us to run the play. As he pulled around the left end to block, he lowered his shoulder and hit the defensive end right in the crotch. The end went down, the running lane was open, and the play was successful. We all, especially the defensive end, then knew exactly what Coach Muhl was telling us. "Denuttem, Denuttem."

Nice Guys Finish First

The other coaches at the school were not as colorful as Coach Muhl, but still made long-lasting impressions on us. Coach Ron Bergmeier was the entire assistant coaching staff for football. It takes a multitude of coaches to do that job today. He coached us with respect—his for us and ours for him. He also taught us to respect the game; something all of our coaches emphasized.

Thinking about our football coaches brings back memories of our team physician, Dr. Guy Magnus. Although he had a successful private practice that included families of classmates, Dr. Magnus' gruff approach did not instill confidence in his high school athletes. During one game, Bobby Blitz (a great name for a football player) suffered a dislocated shoulder just before the end of the first half.

When we went into the locker room for halftime, there was Bobby moaning on the trainer's table. I walked over to see how he was doing. Just after I entered the trainer's room, Dr. Magnus showed up to "help." Bobby looked up, his moaning stopped, his eyes got wide in horror, and he jerked away from the doctor's touch. He jerked so hard, he reset his own shoulder and was fine. Nice job, doc.

Coach Henry Buffa was our varsity baseball coach. He was able to attend our 40-year reunion in 2004, but passed away in August 2007, at age 84. Condolences from former players and students poured in from around the country and around the world. Ken Holtzman summed up Coach Buffa beautifully when he wrote from Israel, where Ken was managing a team in the inaugural season of the Israeli major leagues.

Ken wrote, "I am sorry that I had to learn the sad news while in Israel, but I feel it's necessary to put Coach Buffa's contribution to U City baseball and my career in proper perspective. More than anyone I know, he disproved the logic of another of my old managers (Cubs manager Leo Durocher) who said, 'nice guys finish last.' He was a tough ex-marine who would give you the shirt off his back and in the next instant pounce on you if he felt you were not giving it your best. His greatest achievement is not the '63 State Championship but the hundreds of former pupils and players who turned out to be good citizens and caring people. So rest easy coach, now we know for sure that nice guys finish first."

Coach Buffa taught us that excellent performance, high standards, and being a nice guy are not incompatible.

Coach Dick Greenblatt was the school's head basketball coach and our assistant varsity baseball coach. Coach Greenblatt believed that attention to the game's details made winners; a viable philosophy of sport and of life. On the bus on the way to our away baseball games, Coach Greenblatt would tell us toward which field the wind would be blowing and how strongly. He paid attention to details and believed in preparation—he taught us to do the same.

Coach Ed Mickelson was our sophomore baseball coach and a guidance counselor at the school after having a brilliant minor league and all-too-brief major league playing career. In 1953, Coach Mickelson got the last hit and drove in the last run ever scored by the St. Louis Browns before they became the Baltimore Orioles. In 2007, he authored *Out of the Park: Memoir of a Minor League Baseball All-Star.*

Coach Mickelson would tell us, "You have million-dollar arms and ten-cent heads."

He did so to teach us that physical errors were an expected part of the game, but mental errors were unacceptable—true both on and off the field.

U City's swimmers report that Coach Ron Goldenberg taught them hard work and discipline. His approach motivated and trained the swim team to the school's first state championship and our water polo team to the conference championship.

Although I never had the honor of being coached by Coach Henry Schemmer, the high school's track coach, his mere presence at the school was meaningful to every athlete and student. He retired at the end of our senior year after coaching track for 43 years, the last 37 of them at U City. In those 37 years, Coach Schemmer led the school to 19 indoor and 15 outdoor state championships and was inducted into the St. Louis Athletic Association Hall of Fame.

One of Coach Schemmer's championships was in our senior year; a team led by classmates Jim Cohen (hurdles), Greg Tsevis (mile run), Neil Davis (shot and discus), and Steve Moran (sprints). In a newspaper interview, "Mouse" Moran said of Coach Schemmer, "We did it all for him."

The track/football field has since been dedicated to and named for Coach Muhl and Coach Schemmer.

Coach Clarence Muhl

Coach Henry Buffa

Coach Ed Mickelson

5-3

You will notice little mention of our basketball team. While some years before, the University City Indians had an honorable mention All-American, Sandy Pomerantz, and while we had a number of excellent players, we lacked height. Our school newspaper, the *Tom-Tom*, referred to the team as the "Ten Little Indians."

Perhaps the highlight of our basketball adventures during our tenure at U City was a game that we lost. Our arch-rival in every sport was Ladue. In fact, it is still hard for me to write the name that we referred to as the "L Word," well before that took on a different meaning.

In our senior year, Ladue had an excellent basketball team. Yet in a tournament only one month before the fated game, we had squeaked out a one-point upset. Coach Greenblatt concluded that there was little chance that lightning would strike twice. Not to be one to yield to inevitability, Coach devised a strategy that almost worked.

This was the era before shot clocks. As Jerry Stack reported in the *Tom-Tom*, "It's not whether you win or loose, but *how* you play the game. Even though UC's Cagers almost shut themselves out in a heartbreaking 5-3 loss at Ladue, the Indians stalled admirably.

"The stall, believed by Coach Dick Greenblatt to be UC's 'best chance' because of the Indians' height disadvantage and the Rams' man-to-man defense, nearly backfired. But the Indians, stealing the ball four times in the last 1:10 seconds, came close to pulling this rather pointless affair out of the fire."

What Stack did not report was that, in the absence of action on the floor, the two sides of fans spent the game chanting cheers and jeers at each other. Tensions were high and there was chanting of another sort as the game wore on. There was no brawl because that was just not what we did at the time. But it was as close to there being one as we could imagine.

In March that year, the *Tom-Tom* reported, "Because of the furor caused by the 5-3 game against Ladue, Coach Richard Greenblatt has decided to cancel basketball games with Ladue for the next two years. Mr. Greenblatt said that this decision was entirely his own and that no one influenced him."

Assistant Principal Lloyd Brewen, who had been the varsity

basketball coach before Mr. Greenblatt, announced shortly before we graduated that the Ladue ban was being rescinded.

Yes—that was our basketball highlight.

Whew

Playing sports in high school was a learning experience, exciting, and fun. But it could also be draining. Going to school early; being in classes all day; practicing your sport after school and playing weekend games; getting home late for supper; and finishing homework late was grueling. In my sophomore year, I played football, basketball, and baseball—there was no break in the year. For my last two years I decided not to play varsity basketball. I opted rather to play in a recreational league on the weekends with classmates Mark Tucker, Russell Tims, Dickie Jacobs, Ricky Golubock, and Ron Blumoff. Marc Tenzer, who was on the school's varsity team, could not play with us in the recreation league—he coached us instead. We had a great time, and it gave me a mid-year break—oh, and we won the championship game 60-51 in April 1964.

"The Beats"
Top Row: Dickie Jacobs, Coach Marc Tenzer, I am the sweaty one, Ronnie Blumoff
Bottom Row: Russell Tims, Ricky Golubock, Mark Tucker

There was another downside to being involved in athletics at U City in the early 60s, especially football and wrestling—it was the smell. Just off of the locker room was what was called "the drying room." It was a small cave of a room in which we hung our football practice gear after the morning session of late summer two-a-days (two practices each day, one in the morning and one in the afternoon). The intent was that the large exhaust fans in the room would dry our sweaty uniforms before the afternoon session. Humid St. Louis, non-air conditioned school—no way. Not only did the place stink, but it was not at all pleasant to don a damp practice uniform. And there are few things worse than putting on a moist athletic supporter.

Despite the shortcomings of the football uniform drying room, the conditions paled to the odor and oppressive environment in the cramped confines of the wrestling room during their season—whew.

Hallelujah

Academics and sports were not the only prominent features making up the landscape that was University City High School in the early 60s. The arts and other school activities were not only plentiful—they were highly valued and participation levels were high. Envision a Chem-Physics Club that numbered nearly 100 members. There was a club for virtually anyone with a special interest—Russian, German, Latin, Bridge, Debate-Current Events, Pen-In-Hand (literary), Radio, Stamps, Audio-Visual, Mathematics, Future Nurses of America, Coins, and more. Although it would likely be controversial today, there was even a Bible Club with a faculty sponsor.

The organization for those of us who had earned varsity sports letters was called "The Tribe." I had the honor our senior year to be its president and, as such, to act as the master of ceremonies at the Fall Sports Recognition Banquet. It was at that banquet that Coach Muhl captured the essence of our 2-7-1 varsity football season by declaring, "Well, we built a lot of character this year."

The arts, like academics, sports, and activities, had a long and strong tradition at U City. Although I was unaware of it, a current student, Calvin Johnson, told me about a labyrinth of rooms under the stage of the performance auditorium referred to as "the catacombs." Included is one room the "green room," where performers wait to come on stage. Calvin told me that it has been a longstanding tradition for students to autograph the walls of the room as they waited.

I asked classmates if they knew about this stage substructure, but few did. Curiosity overtook Adrienne Nadler Hirschfeld. She visited the school and was guided to the locked green room. Adrienne reported she had found the autographs. Calvin says he has seen them from as far back as the 1930s.

Creative Writing teacher Mr. Rick Wilson reports that some years ago a new School Superintendent wanted to get the green room cleaned up and ordered the walls sandblasted. There was an uproar among students, faculty, and parents; tradition was upheld—the autographs were untouched.

The arts were prominent in our era. Mr. Lang's Concert Orchestra numbered 68. Mr. Warner's Symphonic Band and Dance Band numbered 98 and 15, respectively. Dr. Procasky's A Cappella and Concert Choirs numbered 77 and 29, respectively. But the numbers involved tell only part of the story. Attendance at orchestra and choir concerts and at school plays and musicals rivaled that of sporting events. The quality of performances attracted not only students, faculty, and parents to the school's large performance auditorium, but the community-at-large as well.

I was a percussionist in the band in elementary and junior high school, but was regrettably faced with a conflict at the senior high school. Band was scheduled during sixth period, our last of the day. This was the same period those of us playing football were scheduled for our "physical education class," so that we could start our practices an hour early versus waiting until after school. I was also reminded by both football coach and band director that I could not play in a game and the halftime show on the same day. While I am glad that I played high school sports, I regret not having had the band experience.

U City's musicians were doing much more than just going through the motions. In the fall of 1963, 25 members of our school orchestra were named to the local "63-64 All-Suburban Orchestra," by far the highest representation of any of the 12 schools participating. Four Indians occupied first chairs—Sam Goldstein (French horn) and classmates Judy Biegelson (cello), Donna Heicher (flute), and Richard Patterson (trumpet). Judy also played in the St. Louis Philharmonic Orchestra during her high school years, following in the footsteps of her brother, who was three years ahead of us at U City.

Phillip Grossman, (class of '65), was a brilliant violinist and appeared on *Ted Mack's Amateur Hour*.

Orchestra members were recognized for their abilities. So was the school Symphonic Band. In the spring of 1964, it was selected as one of only five nationwide to play in the Chicago National Band Clinic.

During our senior year, the high school chorus sang selections from *South Pacific* and *Porgy and Bess* with the University City Community Symphony Orchestra in a fund raising concert for a college scholarship fund for those graduating from U City and going to Missouri state schools. I appreciated that, as I was able to take advantage of the scholarship.

Perhaps the highlight of each musical year was Dr. Procasky's winter choir concert. The choir would conclude the annual program by performing Handel's *Hallelujah Chorus*. What made the performance even more memorable was that choir alumni were invited to the concert and welcomed to the stage to join the finale. The power and beauty of the sound coming from a choir of nearly 200 voices was an emotional experience for singers and audience alike.

Dr. Procasky was also the producer of the annual school musical, referred to lovingly as the "Pro Show."

Classmate Kay Rudolph, who lives in Chicago, recently wrote, "I remember Dr. Pro was an exceptional, creative, supremely talented man. Because of him I earned a degree in Music Ed and had my own high school choir for two years. After I returned to St. Louis, I taught music for three years in the early 70s. Our music department got together occasionally, once at Pro's home. A glorious experience to spend time with him as a colleague. Do you detect a certain hero worship?"

The Pro Show our senior year was the musical *The Boyfriend*. The choice of the show was perfect as we could easily relate to the story and to the lyrics of the title song, which, in part, were:

A girl who'd reached the age
Of seventeen or thereabouts
Has but one desire in view.

She knows she has reached the stage
Of needing one to care about.
Nothing else will really do.

Childhood games are left behind
And her heart takes wing.
Hoping that it soon will find
Just one thing.

We've got to have,
We plot to have,
For it's dreary not to have
That certain thing called "The Boy Friend."
We scheme about
And dream about
And we've been known to scream about
That certain thing called "The Boy Friend."

Dear Flabby and Sonic Booms

Activities were not limited to clubs and the arts. We were busy writing and publishing the school newspaper, going to school-sponsored parties, participating in student government, creating and editing our yearbook, acting as counselors for sixth-grade camp, going on class trips, writing and publishing the school literary magazine that was creatively called "The Magazine," and getting involved in sundry other pursuits.

The wide range of school-related activities was well-reported in the school newspaper, the *Tom-Tom*, co-edited our senior year by classmates Elliot Atlas, Kim Cohn, and Leslie Zuke. Archived *Tom-Toms* are a treasure-trove of memories. Because this book is a class project, I recruited classmates to help me research the old papers. The result was a *Tom-Tom* party in the school library, where the old newspapers are stored.

I was joined by Leslie Berger, Mickey Leon Sandmel, Carol Enger Canis, Ellen Polinsky Cohen, Ron and Elaine Levin Unell, Marla

Schukar Levinson, and Gary Singer and by school historian and former teacher, Mr. Wally Klein.

In a back room of the school library, we pored over the old newspapers that brought back memories as well as informing us of some things we did not remember.

Classmate Carol Eisenberg had written an advice column titled "Dear Flabby."

We had a student exchange with Shawnee Mission High School. The cost of traveling by bus to Shawnee Mission, Kansas and attending other weekend events was $20 per person. The senior trip to Washington, DC cost only $160 for all expenses, including the plane ride.

The girls played football in the Lipstick Bowl, raising $200 for UNICEF.

The game of "Bullwinkle" became a favorite student pastime. You have never played Bullwinkle? Take a penny, nickel, and dime. Sit across from your opponent at a smooth table, like one you might find in a school cafeteria. Your opponent forms a goal by placing a fist (palm down) against his side of the table, then extending his pointer and little fingers over and resting on the table. These fingers become the goal posts.

Drop the three coins in the middle of the table from about six inches high. Advance your coins by flicking any coin between the other two. You do this until you have a clear shot on the goal, or until a coin falls off the table (lose your turn), or does not travel fully through the other two coins without touching one (lose your turn). If you have a shot on goal, flick that coin through the other two and toward the goal. If the coin hits the middle two fingers of the fist between the goalpost fingers, you have scored—one point for the penny, two for the nickel, and three for the dime. If you score, you stay on offense and drop your coins again. Play the game up to any prearranged number of points. You are ready to play Bullwinkle.

President Kennedy's Council on Youth Fitness recommendations prompted the school's physical education program to include more running.

When asked by the "Inquiring Reporter" about what she would do if she were President of the United States, Phyllis Lieberman, after a moment of thought, answered, "I'd play touch football on the front lawn of the White House."

We drew 5000 people to our Senior Carnival, held in the gym from noon to midnight. Proceeds went to the Edgewood Children's Home, a center for treatment for emotionally disturbed young children.

Schneidhorst's, a local restaurant placed an ad featuring U City students. "Seen at Schneidhorst's: Phyllis Lieberman with Steve Kamenetsky, Alice Schneider with Jon Pollack splitting a Big Bevo, and Larry Abrams sipping a cup of tea." (Schneidhorst's must have been a special place—Phyllis and Steve went on to become Dr. and Mrs. Steve Kamenetsky.)

The Velva-Tones, a band formed by classmate Howard Danzig, in which classmates Lloyd Palens, Ron Unell, and Mark Feldman played, would say anything to get a gig. Their *Tom-Tom* advertisements contained such catchy tag lines as:

"Separate the men from the boys but not from the girls."

"We provide the best music to resurface floors by."

"Roses are Red; Violets are Blue; We Want Jobs!"

We enjoyed a costumed sock-hop at which many of the boys dressed as girls and vice versa. No, the Velva-Tones did not play.

Ken Brown, Steve Novak, and Marc Tenzer in drag at a sock hop

Fifty U City boys collaborated during a winter break to set a world record, playing a continuous Monopoly game for 161 hours. In preparation for the game, they wrote Milton-Bradley describing what they intended to do. Milton-Bradley sent them one-million dollars of Monopoly money.

The Earl Newman Band played at the Beer Garden Spring Dance—all the dancing, root beer, and pretzels you could handle for one dollar per couple.

The Pep Club kick-off mixer was a real bargain—15-cents for members; non-members "slightly higher."

Seventy-six students "took over" City Hall as we shadowed University City officials for a day to learn more about local government during High School Day. I remember being sworn in as Councilman-for-a-Day.

School Administrator Mr. Kettlekamp led a group of citizens to protest against jets flying over metropolitan areas. He said, "I attribute directly to sonic booms the jamming of the door on room 211, causing students to be constantly late to their fourth period classes." (This was one of many such articles reported in the *Tom-Tom's* annual April Fools issue.)

Our research party felt as though we were still in school during lunch period, when *Tom-Toms* were distributed, and we would quickly scan the paper to learn what was going on, trying to keep up with everything.

We finished our library research, but our *Tom-Tom* party was not over. We headed to lunch at Frank and Helen's, one of the restaurants in our old stomping grounds. Classmates Debbie Brownstein Pulley and Sue Corman Slater and my wife, Ann, and Leslie Berger's wife, Judy, joined us for lunch. What is a party without food?

1964 Was a Unique Time

In 1987, Bob Greene, reconstructed his high school diary and wrote, *Be True to Your School: A Diary of 1964*, a year in his life and that of his friends in Bexley, Ohio. One of the first things I did after deciding to write this book about my class of 1964 was to read Greene's book. The Preface of his book stuck with me. He wrote, "All of us, no matter when we are born, have years that touch us in a similar way to how 1964 touched me. But 1964 was a unique time. America still had one foot in the Fifties, while tentatively stepping into the Sixties. When most people hear about the Sixties today, they think about the decade in terms of stereotypes: the radical change in musical styles, the revolution in sexual attitudes, the urban race riots, the student activism on campuses, the pain of Vietnam.

"It is easy to forget that at the beginning of 1964, all of that had yet to happen. The year was part of the Sixties, yes, but it was very much the ending of one era and the beginning of the next. Like most other things that happen in our society, it took place so gradually that we hardly noticed it at the time.

"There were important events happening in the outside world that year—events that journalists were chronicling every day...my friends and I paid little attention to those things. Probably most of us, teenagers or not, are like that. The real truths of our lives don't make the six o'clock news or the morning papers."

Although we paid attention to TV news and the *Post-Dispatch* and *Globe-Democrat* newspapers, and we discussed current events with parents, teachers, and each other; Bob Greene was largely correct. Our high school lives were primarily driven by personal events and the people with whom we were close. These were the "truths of our lives"—classes, tests, papers, games, plays, concerts, driver's licenses, jobs, dates, college applications, cars, music, parties, families, friends, teachers. The days and nights were full but manageable and, looking back, seemed carefree.

We were generally insulated from the outside world by the protection of our parents, our community, and our school and by immaturity, a relatively narrow range of interests, Midwestern values, and the serene times in which we lived. But things were about to change dramatically.

Goodman, Schwerner, and Chaney

When we graduated in 1964, more than 40% of the country's population was under 20 years old. The Beatles had been on the *Ed Sullivan Show* only four months earlier. The Ford Mustang had recently been introduced. The last electric street car had run its route in University City.

President Lyndon Johnson was running for his first full term and was on his way to a November landslide victory over Senator Barry Goldwater. Nelson Mandela had just been sentenced to life imprisonment in South Africa.

Civil rights workers Andrew Goodman, Michael Schwerner, and James Chaney would soon be murdered in Philadelphia, Mississippi. Shortly thereafter, the Civil Rights Act of 1964 would be signed into law, outlawing segregation in schools and public places.

The first computer program written in BASIC (Beginner's All-purpose Symbolic Instruction Code) had just been run. Forty hidden microphones had been discovered by the State Department in the newly constructed US Embassy in Moscow.

The "Gulf of Tonkin Incident" was about to occur (or not, depending on which story is to be believed) leading to our open involvement in the Vietnam War.

Seemingly crucial high school happenings, like picking up my ID bracelet from the puddle and realizing that Arleen White and I were breaking up, paled when compared to what we as individuals and as a society were about to experience.

We had grown up in the relative calm of a post-war economic and emotional high. We had lived in a protected environment. And we were leaving 1964, University City High School, and our secure past behind.

Senior Song-1964

Stephen Kowarsky, who now lives in Melville, New York, wrote the lyrics for our senior song (Kay Rudolph wrote the music) and insightfully foreshadowed how many of us would feel looking back on 1964. Note Stephen's reference to "Three years"—we were at the high school building as sophomores, juniors, and seniors while being housed for our freshman year at one of two local junior high buildings. He wrote:

Three years have we learned together, our hearts and our
*   minds to know*
We always knew time would come when we would have to go
Soon we will all be gone and never meet again
But the years were good to us and we'll always remember them

Our tears and our laughter have echoed thru the halls as we
walked along
To class and clubs and sports and everywhere that we belong
We may not all be here but the echoes will remain
And the spirit of U. City High our lives will all contain

The only thing Stephen did not get quite right was "we will all be gone and never meet again." While that is true for some classmates, it is far from what has come to be for so many others. Thankfully, Stephen's foresight was just a little blurry.

The time did "come when we would have to go." But as we ventured out on our individual life journeys, we remained bonded because, "the spirit of U. City High our lives will all contain."

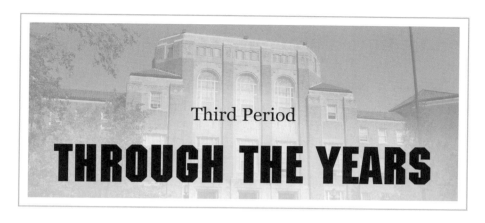

Third Period
THROUGH THE YEARS

""*I am not young enough to know everything.*"
Oscar Wilde

"*It takes a long time to grow young.*"
Pablo Picasso

Judy E. Inger

"*A loving heart is the truest wisdom.*"

Steve: "*We went to high school in the 60s, and we're almost in our 60s. A lot has happened over those 40 years.*"

Mark: "*A lot of history—Vietnam, the moon landing, losing King and the Kennedys, Nixon and Watergate, the Berlin Wall coming down. It's hard to keep track.*"

Judy: "*Those events affected us, but we've had our individual stories as well.*"

Marla: "*Kinda like high school. We were each our own person, but we had a lot in common.*"

Judy: "*Here's what I find amazing. The people in this gym went to different colleges, moved to different towns, and lived their own lives. Yet every ten years and sometimes in between we come back here like homing pigeons."*

Marla: *"There was a special comfort in our high school years despite all of our insecurities. It's not surprising we would want to recapture that feeling. And I think we do that pretty well."*

Steve: *"It looks like more than 200 classmates feel the same way."*

Mark: *"Hey, how 'bout them Cardinals."*

Anne: *"Glick, you still love those Birds, don't you. I can call you Glick, can't I? Or is that nickname reserved for your old baseball buddies like Steve here?*

Judy: *"Speaking of baseball buddies, I've heard that Spector is looking for both of you guys. He says he brought two gloves and a baseball and is looking to play catch in the gym just like you did 40 years ago. I can't wait to see that."*

Anne: *"I hear that Terry Mitze is going to be here this weekend, but I haven't seen him yet. It's been way too long. We've all lost touch with him."*

Marla: *"OK—who wants to meet me under the clock? Or do I have to wait another ten years?"*

Mr. Fendelman Wept First

Since high school graduation in June 1964, we have witnessed four-plus decades of human history in the making, from the elation of remarkable progress to the sadness of overwhelming tragedy. In parallel, we have lived the history of our own lives in which we have experienced the full range of personal emotions. During those intervening years, we have also each been an integral part of the history of the University City High School Class of 1964. We have partied and remembered together at every-ten-year reunions and class birthday parties, kept in daily contact electronically, traveled to see each other at regional mini-reunions, gone on class cruises, met at monthly happy hours, and mourned together the loss of classmates at funerals and from afar.

While human history, personal history, and class history have each run their separate course, there is also an integrated rhythm among the three. Our personal lives have been affected by human history and by the collective experience of our class.

On November 22, 1963, we became deeply aware that historical events could and would affect us individually and become an integral part of our shared experience. It was the first semester of our senior year. I was sitting in Mr. Fendelman's English class, which had begun only moments before. We had settled into his comfortable teaching style.

An electronic click drew our attention to the public address speaker high on the wall in front of the room. Although the click was familiar, it was unusual for the PA system to interrupt class at any time during the day other than for early morning and late afternoon announcements.

Yet, here we were, just after one o'clock, drawn to the voice emanating from the box on the wall. Dr. Boyer, our principal, cleared his throat and hesitantly announced that he was sorry to have to inform us that President John Fitzgerald Kennedy had been shot only a half hour earlier in Dallas, Texas. The president was dead.

The class, the school, the nation, the world fell silent—then wept. Mr. Fendelman wept first. Class dismissed. School dismissed. We would reconvene after the funeral, which everyone watched—in our own homes; yet together.

Lying in state—the procession—the coffin on the caisson—the riderless horse—the constant drum beat—"Hail to the Chief" played at dirge speed—Arlington Cemetery—the eternal flame below the Custis-Lee mansion—Mrs. Kennedy in shrouded black—John Junior's salute—President Johnson being sworn in on Air Force One—Lee Harvey Oswald—Jack Ruby.

Perhaps Elaine Levin said it best and simplest in her diary entry. "Friday, Nov. 22, 1963 KENNEDY ASSASINATED by Lee Harvey Oswald. At about 1:00 pm ...Dallas, Texas ...broadcasting during school. Kids sobbed in classes ...walked around the halls in a daze. I never heard U City's halls so quiet. Unbelievable!"

Our yearbook, the *Dial*, would be dedicated to President Kennedy, as I suppose were most 1964 class yearbooks around the country. The dedication page carried his presidential photograph. The inscription below the picture read:

JOHN FITZGERALD KENNEDY (1917-1963)

"Grant to us Life that though the man be gone,
The promise of his spirit be fulfilled."

John Masefield

The assassination would be the first but only one of many historical events that would affect us through the years. We would all and always be burdened by knowing the answer to the question, "Where were you when President Kennedy was shot?"

Deferments-Where Did They Go?

Soon after our high school graduation, the Vietnam War became an increasingly prominent feature on our national landscape and in our individual lives. American society was conflicted about the war as was each of us individually.

Vietnam was and is a very emotional subject for those who supported the war and those who did not, for those who were drafted and those who were not, for those who served in Vietnam and those who did not, and for those whose families were directly affected and those whose were not. It is neither my intention to open old wounds nor to relive the classic debates about the war, the veracity of its rationale, how it was conducted, or how individuals dealt with the prospect of serving. It is my intent, however, to reflect on the war from the perspective of the time and its effect on classmates and others in the mid-to-late 1960s.

While America had been active in Vietnam for decades by the time we were in high school, the involvement was primarily limited to political activities and intelligence gathering. However, there had been American casualties as early as the late 1950s. Soon after we graduated, President Johnson, responding to the events following the Gulf of Tonkin incident in August 1964, ordered the first combat troops to Vietnam. They arrived in early 1965.

By the end of 1965, more than 184,000 US troops had been deployed. The military draft was in full swing. Eventually, about ten percent of the 22,000,000 who would come of draft age during the war would actually be drafted.

There was constant personal and societal pressure to decide whether or not to support the war, whether or not to express our points of view publicly in protests or rallies of support, whether or not to fulfill a military obligation regardless of our stance on the war, and, if for whatever reason we chose not to serve, how to proceed.

The law required that each male register with the Selective Service within 30 days of his 18th birthday. Most classmates and I were assigned to Draft Board 101 in Clayton, Missouri. I was not immediately concerned, because when we graduated high school, those going to college were exempted from the draft. This would later become a problem, however, because the percentage of those registered for the draft at 101 who went to college was very high. Our draft board was desperate to meet its quotas for draftees.

Perhaps only classmate David Pactor got a break from 101. He left the University of Missouri after a lackluster and unhappy experience, but quickly enrolled in classes at Washington University and Meramec Community College in St. Louis in an attempt to sustain his college deferment.

Being fearful that he was not meeting the draft board requirements, David crafted what he calls the "most significant and meaningful piece I have ever written." In it, he promised that if the draft board allowed him to retain his deferment, he would commit to repaying the country with public service many times over. Incredibly, the board relented and, not incredibly, David has been dutifully fulfilling his promise all of his life.

For those of us not wanting to volunteer or be drafted, our choices seemed to be to join the National Guard or Public Health Service, leave the country, attain conscientious objector status, or find a way to maintain a deferment. After college, our deferment hopes rested on marriage, fatherhood, or a job in a vital industry. But, as the war intensified and the deployment of troops significantly increased, these deferment options were either terminated by Presidential Order or were made much harder to earn.

When deferments were in doubt, young men took action. Classmate Steve Novack's objective was to "do anything I could do to not get into that damn war." Steve joined the reserves, committing himself to basic training, summer camps, and reserve meetings. He spent 119 days (but who was counting) training in Fort Jackson, South Carolina, in 1967. He feels it was worth it, because he avoided going to "Nam."

After unsuccessfully trying to get into a reserve unit, classmate, friend, and now stepbrother, Marc Tenzer, looked for ways to avoid going to Vietnam or, at least, to minimize his combat risk. He took two steps. He entered ROTC with classmate and friend Mark Tucker, and spent parts of college summers at Fort Knox (after sophomore year) and Fort Sill (after junior year) to be commissioned as a Second Lieutenant. We would later learn that this rank not only increased the likelihood of being deployed, but also meant a greater probability of seeing combat.

Secondly, a relative of Marc's arranged a personal meeting with Senator Stuart Symington of Missouri. When the senator asked Marc how he could help, Marc replied simply that he did not want to go to Vietnam.

Marc Wayne Tenzer

*"I would rather make my name
than inherit it."*

Despite the meeting and the senator's encouraging words, Marc was deployed to Vietnam. He found himself, however, in a non-combat outfit that was responsible for helping local civilians rebuild their infrastructure. Marc's first assignment was to be in charge of a supply motor pool, which he found interesting, because he barely knew where the engine of a vehicle was. He then had an assignment that he refers to as "scrounger."

While most of his job responsibilities and acquisition talents were focused on providing building materials, school books, and other needed supplies to help Vietnamese locals, he did have some requests that were reminiscent of James Garner's role as Charlie Madison in the 1964 movie *The Americanization of Emily*. Marc "acquired" a fender for a '69 Chevy for a General, air conditioners for officers' hooches, and an 8-milimeter projector for "stag flicks" that had been smuggled into camp.

Marc had a plane and helicopter at his disposal. He recalls the plane having "Air America" markings. Recently, Marc ran into a guy he refers to as having been the Radar O'Reilly of his unit—the guy knew everything that was going on and had access to personnel files. "Radar" told Marc that their unit had had a CIA affiliation, which was news to Marc.

Although he had been deployed to Vietnam, Marc saw no combat and was back in the States in less than a year. Perhaps the meeting with Senator Symington did help, but Marc will never know.

Fat Boys' Platoon

I graduated from college in January 1969, by which time there were well over 500,000 American troops in Vietnam with casualty rates at their peak. I did not believe in our role in the war and, despite inner turmoil about my obligation to serve, I decided I did not want to go. By then, the marriage deferment had been terminated. In April 1970, the fatherhood deferment was also ended for any child born after that date—our daughter, Dana, was born in July 1970.

While job deferments were still being granted for those working in "critical" industries, my opportunity to take advantage of this option was short-lived. Just days after graduation, I began working for the Charmin Paper Products Company in Mehoopany, Pennsylvania. Charmin was a wholly-owned subsidiary of The Procter & Gamble Company.

P&G wrote a three-page letter to my draft board making it sound as if I were running the entire corporation—a company that had been so vital to provisioning the troops in all of the country's great wars. My role was critical to the capability of the company, and the company was critical to the country and the war effort. The letter did not point out that, at the time, I was working as a production supervisor in an operation making Pampers Disposable Diapers.

The draft board saw through the message, and shortly thereafter I received my draft notice.

I had moved my young wife to Mehoopany, Pennsylvania away from her home and family in St. Louis, Missouri. We had begun to build our future. Dana had been born, and I had been drafted.

In anticipation of the draft problem, I had already begun to search for options. My leading candidate was to join the National Guard and hope that I would not be deployed to Southeast Asia. At the time, because the draft was designed to supply the right number of troops for deployment to the war zone, it was unlikely that National Guard troops would need to go. I was lining up the National Guard option when my draft letter came, rendering the Guard decision moot.

The letter was not totally unexpected. On December 1, 1969, the Selective Service held the first draft lottery since 1942. The good news was that the lottery brought more certainty to the 850,000 young men trying to figure out where they stood in the draft process. A blind drawing determined the birth date to be drafted first, second, and so on until the draft requirements were met for each draft board.

The other good news was that my number was 183, relatively high. The bad news was that my draft board still had a large number of men with college deferments causing the board to go beyond 183 to meet its quota.

The letter ordered me to report to the induction center in Clayton, Missouri. I formally requested a change of venue to one closer to where we lived. The change process took two months to complete. OK, so what do you do if you have been drafted, you do not support the war, you have a family, and you have two months to figure it out?

Some were avoiding the draft by moving to Canada, hoping, yet not knowing, that years later, they would be pardoned and able to return to the United States legally. While the Canada option was never a serious consideration, it was also made moot when I learned about an approach that could work for me.

The military has certain mental and physical requirements that an inductee must meet in order to be accepted into service. One of these requirements assures that the inductee is neither too frail nor too heavy to be an effective soldier.

At the time I learned about this requirement, I was five-foot-ten, weighed about 210, and was reasonably fit. I had played baseball and football in high school and four years of varsity baseball in college. In Pennsylvania, I had stayed in shape playing softball, basketball, and flag football four to seven days a week.

There was a chart in the Selective Service manual that gave the minimum and maximum allowable weights by height. The chart told me that at five-foot-ten, I could neither weigh less that 119 pounds nor more than 219 pounds to be acceptable to the military. 219 pounds was in sight.

I began to eat. Ann recalls me eating a cake and a half-gallon of ice cream every day along with oversized meals and anything that was not tied down. We were confident this plan was going to work, but we also put a contingency plan in place. Ann's mother would come to Pennsylvania to be with Ann and Dana just in case something went wrong during the induction physical and Ann had to manage without me.

One evening, several weeks before my physical, the phone rang. I probably had to stop eating for a few minutes to answer the call. A gentleman introduced himself and told me he was a draft attorney. My family in St. Louis had contacted him, and he was ready to help. He and I talked through how I was to act at my draft physical and what I should do if it looked like the personnel at the induction center were not paying attention to the height/weight requirement.

It was finally my day to report. Ann, her mom, and Dana drove me to the Wilkes-Barre induction center. We semi-confidently reviewed our plan for me to call Ann to pick me up after I was released. While we knew that I was now physically unfit for the draft, we hugged as though I was going away for a long time.

The process went as expected with the requisite and less-than-congenial "strip and line up," "open and say aah," "turn your head and cough," and "bend over and spread 'em," all of which immediately endeared me to the military. Only a couple of times during the morning did I think I might have to do the things my attorney and I had reviewed. When I stepped onto the scale to be weighed, the guy logging in weights said, "That can't be right. Step off and get back on the scale."

The scale had registered 263 pounds.

When I did get back on the scale, he said, "You don't look that heavy, but I guess it's right."

Later in the process, a few of us, apparently those with some kind of detected physical or mental problem, were herded into a separate room. A soldier came into the room with our files and went from man to man addressing each of us with regard to our individual malady. To me he said, "You know, son, you can sign a waiver that will allow you to join the Army at your weight. We'll put you in the fat boys' platoon and get those pounds off of you quick. You'll be in the best shape you've ever been."

I politely said, "No thank you, sir (I may have been older than he, but thought I should play his game while I was on his field). What happens next?"

He scowled, had me sign the right paperwork, told me I would be getting notification of my 1-Y draft status, and dismissed me. I excitedly called Ann from a pay phone in the hall—she came to pick me up—we hugged again knowing how close the call had been—we got on with the rest of our lives.

I soon received my 1-Y notification. The 1-Y classification signifies a mental or physical deficiency that the Army would like to check about every six months to see if you have been cured. My followup strategy was to reduce weight down to 225 to 230, beef up a little before each six-month weigh-in, and keep doing so until I was out of the woods. I did not know how long that would be, but did not care.

I returned twice for six-month checks. After the second, I received my permanent draft status in the mail. I was 4-F, physically unfit for service.

Our life decisions were being influenced by the folk music of the day and vice versa. Among these songs was *The Draft Dodger Rag*, introduced by Phil Ochs at the Newport Folk Festival in late July 1964. The song's protagonist, "a typical American boy from a typical American town" is conflicted. He is fully aware of his responsibilities and that "when it came my time to serve I knew 'better dead than red.'"

However, "when I got to my old draft board," for his draft physical, he meets the Sergeant in charge and his innermost feelings take over. He's afraid, and he admits it to himself, "buddy, this is what I said,"

...one thing you gotta see
That someone's gotta go over there, and that someone isn't me
So I wish you well, Sarge, give 'em Hell, Yeah, Kill me a thousand or so
And if you ever get a war without blood and gore, Well I'll be the first to go

It becomes his mission to find a way to convince the Sergeant that he should not be going to war.

Sarge, I'm only eighteen, I got a ruptured spleen
And I always carry a purse
I got eyes like a bat, and my feet are flat, and my asthma's
getting worse
Yes, think of my career, my sweetheart dear, and my poor old
invalid aunt
Besides, I ain't no fool, I'm a-goin' to school
And I'm working in a DEE-fense plant

I've got a dislocated disc and a wracked up back
I'm allergic to flowers and bugs
And when the bombshell hits, I get epileptic fits
And I'm addicted to a thousand drugs
I got the weakness woes, I can't touch my toes
I can hardly reach my knees
And if the enemy came close to me
I'd probably start to sneeze

Ochs did a great job of capturing our inner conflict, but he missed one of the possibilities his young man might have shared with the Sergeant.

Sarge, I stayed up late and as crazy as it sounds
I ate and ate and gained 50 pounds
It took me only two months which was none too soon
And I'm not signing up for your fat boys' platoon

Forty years ahead of my time, I followed what I called the "high protein/low carbohydrate" diet—later be known as the "Atkins Diet." I returned to my playing weight of 210 and subsequently went down to 190. Today I range from 190 to 200, about 75% of my draft physical weight.

While my experience was different than most, what was not different was the enormous strain on our generation individually and collectively. Every male between the ages of 18 and 26 was going through the uncertainty of balancing personal beliefs, personal priorities, available options, and difficult decisions.

Some classmates went to Vietnam, some seeing combat. Some had sufficiently high lottery numbers to avoid the draft. Some found ways to stay out of the service. Classmate M. J. Savoy died in Vietnam.

The relative stability of high school was shattered as we dealt with college, new careers, and new families—and with Vietnam—all at the same time.

By 1974

By 1974, the tenth anniversary of our high school graduation, the war in Vietnam was officially over. For many, regardless of whether they or their relatives served or chose not to, the wounds would slowly or, perhaps, never heal.

By November 1974, the Warren Commission had concluded that Oswald acted alone. Khrushchev had been deposed, quarks had been discovered, PBS had been created, the DNA code had been deciphered, Martin Luther King and Bobby Kennedy had been assassinated, the Beatles had broken up, and 11 Israeli athletes had been killed at the Munich Olympic Games. Nixon and Agnew—elected, inaugurated, resigned.

We were in the middle of the Cold War, the pace of scientific innovation had accelerated, Israel was fighting for its life, the Civil Rights Movement had won some hard-fought battles, and citizens, especially the younger generation, had begun to distrust many of the institutions that we had previously believed in without question.

UCLA was dominating college basketball, Green Bay had won the first two Super Bowls, Joe Namath had led the American Football League New York Jets to the upset of the National Football League Baltimore Colts, and University City pitcher Kenny Holtzman was well on his way to winning 60 games for the Oakland A's over the three years in which they won consecutive World Series.

Neal Armstrong had walked on the moon as President Kennedy had promised we would, and the Space Race was well underway. It had also been the decade of Kent State, the Pentagon Papers, Roe v. Wade, the Tet Offensive, My Lai, Patty Hearst and the SLA, *American Graffiti*, *In Cold Blood*, *A Clockwork Orange*, *All in the Family*, and DDT.

By 1974, most of our class had completed our education, begun families, and begun careers.

Events, both of national and personal significance, were fodder for discussion when 223 classmates and 181 significant others converged on St. Louis the weekend of June 28-30, 1974 for the first high school reunion of the University City Class of 1964.

Two Key Decisions

We were easily recognizable to each other at the ten-year reunion, and we still tended to cling to those with whom we hung out in high school. Phyllis Lieberman Kamentesky was kind enough to invite our old crowd to her home prior to the start of official reunion events. Ann and I were among the first to arrive and joined a few others in Phyllis's basement recreation room. I knew the evening and weekend were going to be comfortable when I heard someone coming down the stairs and, without seeing her, knew it was Marla Schukar Levinson—ten years gone by, and I could still recognize her voice.

By 1974, most of us were in a similar life stage, having made what can be considered the two most crucial decisions of our lives.

Peter Graham, a Procter & Gamble colleague explained this best when, at his retirement party, he said, "There are only two decisions in your life that are of any real consequence—all others pale by comparison. One is who you choose to marry; the other is who you choose to work for. And I was fortunate to have made the right decision is both cases."

In the late 60s and early 70s, we were significantly less likely to change careers and jobs as often as would our children's generation. And we were more likely to marry young and have children early in our marriages. As a result, by the time of our ten-year reunion, most of us had made the two consequential life choices.

Many of us had already had children—others would soon. Three female classmates recall the ten-year reunion in relation to where they were in their stage of childbearing.

"Many people then were married and had begun their families. It was a year before I had my first child."

"At the reunion, many of the girls were pregnant. I was less than two months from the birth of our second child."

"I was six months pregnant and feeling slightly fragile and very vulnerable."

Thinking of the ten-year reunion brought back a different memory for classmate David Nemon. He recalls driving to the Saturday night gala at the Sheraton Westport Plaza and hearing Paul Simon's "Kodachrome" on the radio.

When I think back to all the crap I learned in high school
It's a wonder I can think at all
And though my lack of education hasn't hurt me none
I can read the writing on the wall

While these were neither desired nor accurate sentiments about our high school experience and our pending reunion, the timing of the song on the radio makes David's recent recollection understandable.

One of my key decisions, who to work for, began to unfold in the second semester of my junior year in college when I was contacted by a pre-recruiter from Procter & Gamble's Charmin Paper Products Company. He told me he had gotten my name by looking at lists of officers of campus organizations and had noted that I was the Vice-President of the Student Government and Master of AEPi, my fraternity, among other campus activities. He asked me to interview with the company while they were visiting the school.

I reminded him that I was only a junior and had yet to make any plans to interview, but I would be glad to do so if he still wanted me. I was interviewed and offered a trip to the company's manufacturing plant in Mehoopany, Pennsylvania. At the end of the plant day visit, P&G made me a job offer.

I told them I would still be going through the interview process with other companies during my senior year and would get back to them. Despite many interviews, a number of company trips, and lots of job offers, nothing ever matched what P&G had to offer in the kind of work I wanted to do, career opportunities, and pay. I made the choice and began working for them immediately after graduation in January 1969. Playing college baseball had caused me to lighten my class load, requiring a ninth college semester.

Ann and I were married on August 25, 1968, just before that final college semester. We knew the marriage would last for a lot of reasons, not the least of which was surviving four months in our very old, rundown, cramped, poorly heated, sometimes buggy, pink trailer located in rural Rolla, Missouri.

Ann Sachar

"Exuberance is charm."

We subsequently moved from small-town Rolla to small-town Tunkhannock, Pennsylvania, located only a short drive from the manufacturing plant where I would be working. We were young and naïve—Ann was 20 when we were married, and I was 22. However, having moved far from home, we learned quickly and began to build our lifelong relationship.

We were also building our family. Dana got a little brother when Kevin was born in January 1973.

As my P&G colleague said, the two key decisions are who you choose to marry and who you choose to work for. By 1974, I had made each of those decisions, and I was fortunate on both accounts—marrying Ann and working for P&G.

By 1984

By 1984, Watergate sentences had been served, President Ford had pardoned Richard Nixon, and President Carter had pardoned the Vietnam draft evaders.

The country had celebrated its bicentennial. Our family celebrated July 4, 1976 by unpacking boxes to complete our move from rural Tunkhannock, Pennsylvania to suburban Cincinnati, Ohio.

By 1984, the first space shuttle had been flown. Jim Jones' Peoples Temple sect committed suicide in Jonestown, Guyana. Anwar Sadat and Menachem Begin agreed to a "framework of peace" at Camp David. The first test tube baby was born. Ayatollah Khomeini replaced the Shah of Iran.

Three Mile Island nearly melted down. Ted Turner launched CNN. Unsuccessful assassination attempts were made on President Ford, Pope John Paul II, and President Reagan. The assassinations of Anwar Sadat, Indira Ghandi, John Lennon, and Benigno Aquino were successful. AIDS was first identified. Toxic gas leaked from a Union Carbide facility in Bhopol, India killing 2000 and injuring 150,000.

Michael Jackson released *Thriller* to eventually sell 25 million copies. MTV was born. The Cardinals won another World Series. Cats opened on Broadway to close almost 7500 performances later.

By 1984, MRI (magnetic resonance imaging) technology was introduced. Barney Clark received the first artificial heart and died 112 days later. IBM introduced the first personal computer running MS-DOS. Compact disks became available. The FCC authorized Motorola to begin testing cellular phone services. Apple introduced the MacIntosh computer.

Terrorists killed 237 US Marines in Beirut. The Soviet Union shot down a South Korean commercial 747. Crack cocaine was developed in the Bahamas. University City High School graduate Tennessee Williams died.

Satchel Paige also died. Satch is the source of my favorite quotation and what is more becoming my philosophy of life, "How old would you be if you didn't know how old you was?"

Lost Indians

During the Thanksgiving weekend, 1984, at our 20-year reunion, we could look back on nearly 75% of us having earned a degree, almost 30% advanced degrees, based on those who had answered the reunion questionnaire. We were averaging about one and a half children per classmate. Almost half of us had stayed in Missouri; the others spread over 38 states. And six classmates had died.

Out of our class of about 600, there were 69 listed in the reunion booklet as "Lost Indians," those the reunion committee had not been able to locate. Among these were Anne O'Brien and Jeff Rifkind.

Anne O'Brien was "lost" to the reunion committee, but they apparently did not check with her close friend and fellow cheerleader, Arleen Inger, who had already reached Anne and convinced her to come to the reunion. The committee could not be faulted however. By 1984, Anne had been, as they say, "around."

In 1970, Anne traveled to Europe, met a Scotsman, got married and stayed in Scotland, where she became a teacher and took advantage of the opportunity to travel throughout Europe. The marriage ended, and Anne returned to the US, settling in Chicago and teaching in Winnetka; but not for long.

Anne reconnected with a former boyfriend from a neighboring St. Louis high school. They moved first to Las Vegas and were on their way to live in Oregon when they traveled through Bodega Bay, California, the town in which Alfred Hitchcock's *The Birds* was set. They loved it so much, they stopped and stayed.

That relationship ended, and Anne met Tim, a fisherman, who was to become the father of her first child. Anne then met and married Steve, a musician and computer programmer, just before our 20-year reunion. Steve and Anne would later have a daughter together. By this time, Anne owned and operated a Montessori Pre-School and Kindergarten and had moved to Sebastopol, California to be closer to work.

Anne was not lost—she knew who she was and where she was in her life. She had merely been "around" enough to make it difficult for the committee to find her. Thankfully, she never lost her connection with Arleen Inger.

Arleen Inger and Anne O'Brien

In 1984, classmate Jeff Rifkind lived across the bay from San Francisco—we just did not know it. Jeff recalls 1984 as one of his very best years. In that year, he married his second wife, Stephanie, and his son from his first marriage was living with them. The year before, partnering with the Clark Oil family, Jeff founded CrossCheck, Inc., which became one of the nation's largest check approval and guarantee companies. He was President and Chairman of the Board.

Before 1984, Jeff's life was far from being settled. He was expelled from Southeast Missouri State for a woman's dorm drinking episode. He enlisted in the Navy where, through a series of IQ tests, the first of which he scored 86, it was discovered that he was dyslexic. Once that was identified and his real IQ, which is high, could be ascertained, the Navy sent him to Maryland to study math, advanced electronics, and code. They put him to work in Naval Intelligence.

Although he enjoyed the challenge, Jeff says, "The first rule of Naval Intelligence is to get out of the Navy." He was honorably discharged in 1968, moved to Cleveland, where his father was living, got a sales job with Hertz, climbed the corporate ladder, moved to Philadelphia, became a Vice-President at PepsiCo Truck Rental, and moved to San Francisco. Jeff immediately fell in love with the Bay Area, especially the music scene, and has lived there ever since.

Jeff had what he called "two trains running." He was a corporate VP by day and an "art buying, pot smoking, hippie rocker" the rest of the time. He was hanging out with Crosby, Stills, and Nash; Santana; The Grateful Dead; Jefferson Airplane; and others.

The music scene and the drug scene went hand-in-hand. Jeff recalls, "By 1984, the rocker days were over, and the coke madness that everyone I knew had gone through had ended, and we were all trying to beat Bill Gates."

Since then, Jeff's son earned his business degree, married, and has given Jeff three grandchildren. Sadly, Jeff lost Stephanie to breast cancer in 2001 and spent "several years sitting in a dark room." He has now been able to move on, buy a beautiful home on the Russian River on several acres of redwoods, and has moved from CEO to DDN, which he says stands for "Don't Do Nothing."

Actually, Jeff does more than nothing. He owns a medical marijuana delivery company, still jams on the harmonica with friends, paints and draws, and is working with a publisher on a book he has written entitled, *Roll-Up*. The book was inspired by some time Jeff spent in California's San Quentin State Prison before being released when the charges brought against him were disproved—but that is another story, and Jeff is telling it.

The committee that chose quips for our senior yearbook in 1964 did a great job when they selected Jeff's. It reads, "I count no time lost I gave to pleasure."

Jeff and Anne both enjoy life and we are glad they are no longer Lost Indians.

Building Families and Careers

The vast majority of classmates were leading pretty traditional lives. We were well settled into families and careers. Not everything was necessarily going well, but most of us could be considered in the mainstream.

By 1984, Anna Yaffe Sauer had earned her BA from Brooklyn College, was living and working in her husband's business in Baltimore, Maryland, and was staying busy with their six children, the most in our class. Anna's children have since blessed her with 31 grandchildren.

By 1984, Leslie Zuke had been a newspaper reporter and had hosted a radio public affairs program. He had been the Public Relations Director for the Arts & Education Council, the Repertory Theatre, and the Museum of Science & Natural History—all in St. Louis. After holding the position of Director of Corporate Affairs for the Canadian branch of the Seven-Up Company in Toronto, he had been appointed Vice-President of Public Affairs for the entire corporation.

By 1984, Gary Oxenhandler and Marvin Tofle had each earned his law degree from the University of Missouri, had chosen to continue to live in Columbia, Missouri, and had founded the law firm of Tofle and Oxenhandler.

By 1984, Janice Goldberg White and her husband Kenneth had lived in Israel for two years, one year volunteering and one year in Jerusalem while Kenneth was in Rabbinic School, before returning to the States. Janice was working as a secretary for the State of Nebraska Retirement Services.

By 1984, Marsha Weltman had earned her BA and MA in Education from Washington University and her MA in Dance/ Movement Therapy from UCLA, where she stayed to become a therapist in UCLA's Neuropsychiatric Institute.

By 1984, Robin Segal Lent had been divorced and remarried, had two daughters from her first marriage, had received a Masters Degree in Library Science from Columbia University, and had worked at the Teachers College Library in New York and the University of New Hampshire Library. She had also begun work toward a Masters in English, which eventually led to a second career teaching in the English Department at the University of New Hampshire.

By 1984, Debbie Brownstein Zetcher and her husband Ron had five daughters. In response to a reunion questionnaire inquiry as to what was the most interesting and adventuresome thing you have done, Debbie responded, "Raising 5 daughters...an experience that I am truly grateful that I have had."

Don Serot—Orthopedic Surgeon in St. Louis and father of four sons.

Jim Resnick—Architect in St. Louis and father of three.

Arleen Inger—Accounting Manager for Cincinnati's Spring Grove Cemetery, the second largest not-for-profit cemetery in the country, and mother of a daughter.

Joyce Arky Lewin—Running a gift business called "Perfect Presents" from her home and mother of three with husband, classmate Tom Lewin, an attorney.

The list goes on and on, but these classmates well represent what most of us were focused on in our late 30s—building families and careers.

I'm OK Now

Two hundred thirty-eight classmates and 174 guests convened in St. Louis for the 20-year reunion of the University City Class of 1964. Andrea Kolker Muchnick captured the essence of that reunion when she wrote a welcoming letter on behalf of the planning committee. In part, Andy's letter read, "We all shared that certain time and culture with its own rules and rituals. We had one common bond—the transformation from adolescence to early adulthood. For some, it may have been the most painful time of our lives, or one of the happiest. We were all on the threshold of something. We wanted to be adults. Old roles didn't seem to fit. Many of us moved in expected directions—college, jobs, marriage, kids. Others did not. Some of us took on the old roles and struggled to make them fit, to make them our own. Some of us changed directions in midstream; an amazing number in fact. There were career changes, divorces, and cross-country moves. Some of us achieved fame, others experienced loss and grief. But for whatever reason, none of us have forgotten those years of our lives."

Andy concluded the letter, "We hope that tonight will be a

very special form of time travel to recall old memories, renew old friendships, and share whatever wisdom we've accumulated over the years. The reunion committee wishes you an evening of nostalgia that will stay with you till we meet again."

By halfway through the Saturday evening party at the Holiday Inn Clayton Plaza, I had learned a couple of things. One was that, despite being out of touch with most of them since the last reunion, I was still remarkably close to these people, both as a group and as individuals. Reconnecting was quick and easy and comfortable, as though we had been together all those years.

The other thing I learned was that the seemingly innocuous question, "How are you?" was anything but. It was not uncommon to hear a response like, "I'm OK now."

This might be followed by a story of drug addiction and rehab or by a story of a difficult divorce or the loss of a parent or the loss of a classmate. What was also remarkable was that listening to these stories did not feel like a burden, at least most of the time, but rather a bonding, as if to say, "I'm here to support you, and I'm glad you're OK now."

We had each lived long enough to have experienced personal setbacks. I had lost my mom to cancer in 1976. Classmates who knew my parents asked about them. The look in their eyes was sad and sincere when I told them about Mom. In the same way our parents bonded together to rear us, so too had we bonded together to share feelings about each other's parents. In so many ways, we were like an extended family.

A highlight of the evening was a gift to the class by Tim Arnold. At the time, Tim was living in St. Louis and was a Senior Vice-President and Management Supervisor for D'Arcy Advertising, where he was running the Budweiser advertising campaign.

Tim used his creativity and resources to produce a 20-minute video tape of memories, including live-action footage of when we were in school. The tape also included historic images of world, national, and local events, as well as movie and TV clips from the era. It was all accompanied by our music—the soundtrack alone brought back all of the memories. Tim's tape was shown and thoroughly enjoyed at both the 20-year and 30-year reunions, and I have watched it frequently over the years.

Ann and I were able to share with my classmates that we had

moved to Cincinnati, that Dana (age 14) and Kevin (age 11) were doing well in school and were both playing sports, and that I was coaching them and still playing myself as well.

Ann had left college when we were married in 1968. We had promised her parents she would someday return to school and get her degree. By our 20-year reunion, Ann had graduated from the University of Cincinnati with her degree in Accounting. However, she loved math and was so good at explaining it to others, she chose to manage the math tutoring program at a branch campus of her alma mater instead of pursuing an accounting career.

I was still working for P&G and had moved from Manufacturing to Research and Development, the career change that prompted our move to Cincinnati.

By the 20-year reunion, classmate and friend, Marc Tenzer, had become my stepbrother. Marc had lost his dad, and I had lost my mom; both dying much too early in their lives and ours. Yet his mother and my father had found each other. We missed our parents who had died, but could both sincerely say, "I'm OK now."

By 1994

Gorbachev-glastnost-perestroika
Achille Lauro-Leon Klinghoffer
Rock Hudson-AIDS
Nintendo video games
Oliver North; Iran-Contra
Robert Bork
Prozac
NAFTA
PanAm 103-Lockerbie
Global Warming
Ayatollah Khomeini-Salmon Rushdie-Satanic Verses
Tiananmen Square
Berlin Wall-German reunification
Oprah
Fatal Attraction-Rain Man

Exxon Valdez-Prince William Sound
San Francisco earthquake-7.1
Virtual reality
Navritalova/Evert to Graf/Seles
Becker/Lendl to Sampras/Agassi
Persian Gulf War
Seinfeld-The Simpsons
Hubble Space Telescope
Apartheid repealed-President Mandela
Cold War ended-President Yeltsin
Anita Hill-Clarence Thomas
Pee Wee Herman
Rodney King
Branch Davidian Complex-Waco
World Trade Center bombing (the first)
Nancy Kerrigan-Tonya Harding
Sarajevo
O.J. Simpson-Lance Ito-Johnnie Cochran
Internet Protocols
Spamming

Soul Mates

Our 30-year reunion was the second to take place over a Thanksgiving weekend, November 25-27, 1994. The weekend timing was ideal because many out-of-St. Louis classmates planned to come home for the holiday, and a reunion allowed them to be with both family and classmates in a single trip.

Nearly 200 classmates and about 130 guests were in for a great weekend. On Friday evening we returned to the site of WigWam. Saturday night was the big dinner-dance at the Stouffer Concourse Hotel near the St. Louis airport. Sunday morning was a brunch in the high school cafeteria to which families were invited.

My daughter, Dana, was born in Northeastern Pennsylvania, grew up in Cincinnati, and went to college at Washington University in St. Louis. While in St. Louis, she fell in love with University City, which borders Washington U's campus. When she graduated, she moved to U City and, at the time of my 30-year reunion, lived in an apartment only a couple of blocks from my high school. For the reunion brunch on Sunday morning, Ann and I picked up our son, Kevin, who was attending Washington University. We parked in front of Dana's apartment, and the four of us walked to school—just like the old days.

A few classmates were treated to a bonus reunion event, which was held on Saturday afternoon. Second-baseman Steve Novack took the lead to organize a reunion of our 1963 state championship baseball team for teammates from all classes. Despite the class reunion weekend being for 1964 graduates, teammates from the classes of '63 and '65 also made arrangements to come to the baseball reunion.

Very few teammates were missing. Classmate and team equipment manager, David Nemon, copied, enlarged, and posted newspaper clippings. Coach Henry Buffa was there. Phil Shanker, who was a year behind us, flew in from California just for the baseball team reunion. Ken Holtzman, who had finished his major league career as the winningest Jewish pitcher of all time (yes, he won more games than Hall-of-Famer Sandy Koufax), was there. Spouses and children were there. And many of the parents, who had supported us throughout the years and especially in that championship season, were there.

The remainder of the weekend was a treat as well. But it was also a time to reflect, because, by 1994, 15 of our classmates had passed away. We mourned those who had died and sorely missed the many others who did not or could not make it to the reunion. For those who were there, the weekend brought together teammates, classmates, and soul mates.

Just Plain Folks

Everyone had a story to tell. As a sampling, by 1994, members of the class had had plenty of opportunity to do some impressive and unusual things. Larry Klein had been the traveling secretary for Vincent Bugliosi, who, as Los Angeles County Deputy District Attorney, prosecuted Charles Manson.

Richard Van Allen had been on a TV show with Ray Bradbury, had flown in NASA's zero-gravity training aircraft, and had worked on the Voyager-2 Project, the spacecraft that had flown past Jupiter, Saturn, Uranus, and Neptune. He would go on to work on the Strategic Defense Initiative, sometimes called "Star Wars." Richard then took a break from space to head a team that developed a new method for cataract surgery.

Jim Katzman was the co-founder of Tandem Computers, holder of over 20 US and international patents, and the 1993 winner of the Koret Leadership Prize, awarded to the person "who most notably fulfills Jewish leadership potential."

Janet Lever had co-hosted "Women on Sex" on the Playboy Channel and was co-author of the "Sex & Health" column for Glamour magazine.

Nikki Nakano Hara was happy for some things she had not done. She traveled to Japan and did not cause any international incidents, and she was still 4' 10" but had not become a jockey.

When it came down to it, by 1994, most of us were just plain folks who were continuing to grow families, grow careers, and just get by. Just plain folks.

Donald Scheffing was a scoutmaster.

Ann Seidel enjoyed tennis, reading, and TV.

Slight and mild Rhonda Andrew Appel had earned her karate brown belt.

Marsha Klibansky Soshnik boasted the only regulation shuffleboard court in Creve Coeur, a St. Louis suburb.

Ellen Glazier was a Hospice volunteer.

Several were cancer survivors.

Some had quit smoking; some had not.

Bob Cooper had taken up country-western dancing and was now teaching it.

Sallie Cohen Craig was taking flying lessons.

Harvey Citerman had become a marathoner and was using his races to raise money for charity.

Carol Haseltine Bergman was on the Craig School PTA Board, a member of the St. Louis Track Club, and the president of her bowling league.

A number of classmates were divorced—not surprising, because by 1994, more than one-third of baby boomers had been divorced.

Some had remarried; some had not.

Some were much heavier than we would have guessed—some much lighter. Many (of the guys) were balding.

Teachers, housewives, doctors, engineers, lawyers, computer geeks, accountants, massage therapists, volunteers, clothing designers, barbers.

Runners, readers, tennis players, TV watchers, political activists, pro-choice, pro-life, Democrats, Republicans, in good health, ill, physical fitness fanatics, swimmers, bicyclists, international travelers, golfers, musicians, needle-pointers, writers.

Just plain folks.

Embracing 50

Our 10-year and 20-year reunions in 1974 and 1984, respectively, were wonderful—our 30-year reunion was even more special. No one wanted to say good-bye. Before Saturday night had ended, we knew we needed to get together before another ten years went by. Someone suggested that since we were all going to be turning 50 together in only a couple of years—why not have a joint 50th birthday party. Decision made; we would gather again in 1996.

Two years later, Elaine Levin Unell created a birthday logo that captured us perfectly—an Indian losing his feathers and hugging a 50 as tightly as he could. Her caption and the theme for the birthday party was, "U City Class of '64 Baby Boomers Embracing 50."

"U City Class of '64 Baby Boomers Embrace 50"
Logo for Class 50th Birthday Party created by Elaine Levin Unell

Were we all happy we were turning 50? No. But we were turning 50 together. Nearly 100 classmates celebrated our Birthday Bash in the building that had once housed WigWam.

Classmate Gary Presley followed a traditional education and career path. He received his Bachelors Degree from Southeast Missouri State and his Masters Degree from Southern Illinois University-Edwardsville. He became a psychologist and worked for several school districts. Later he worked at other things, including being the Regional Manager for Castrol Oil Company.

But in his soul, Gary Presley, who shares more than a name with "The King," is a musician. As a teenager, he spent time and was musically inspired in Memphis, having had the opportunity to be present at live recording sessions for Isaac Hayes and "Booker T and the MGs."

Gary started his professional music career with classmates Lynn Newport and Mark Feldman in a band called "The Campus Three." He began writing pop tunes and was asked to record an audition tape for a local studio. Gary grew musically and went on to play in major venues in the St. Louis area, Casa Loma, the Admiral, the Chase Hotel, and most of the country clubs.

Being a guitarist in St. Louis in that era, Gary found every opportunity to listen to Ike Turner play in person, being more interested in Ike and his guitar gear than in Tina Turner. One evening Gary was at an Ike and Tina performance at the Club Imperial with fellow U City guitar player, Larry Weisberg. They found themselves stage-side next to Tina—Larry asked her to dance and she accepted. Gary still regrets being too shy to have followed suit.

Gary is busier with his music since retiring from his mainstream career. He plays with musical partner John Pyatt as part of the group "Sounds Unlimited." Gary and John, who have been playing together for four decades, are the house band at "Cookies, Jazz, and More" in St. Louis. Through this gig, Gary has had the opportunity to play with a number of high-caliber musicians who have stopped by to jam—among them and most memorable was legendary trumpet player, Maynard Ferguson.

Our class 50th birthday party was made even more special, when on Saturday night, June 29, 1996, classmate Gary Presley brought his bass guitar and his band, and we danced to their music.

The planning committee provided picture frames that read,

"UC Baby Boomers Embrace 50." Someone took Polaroid pictures (remember them?), and we put them in our frames. To this day, Ann and I have the picture and frame displayed in our family room.

In the Birthday Bash booklet, Debbie Brownstein Zetcher posted a poem by an unknown author.

The Golden Years are here at last

I cannot see
I cannot pee
I cannot chew
I cannot screw

My memory shrinks
My hearing stinks
No sense of smell
I look like hell

The Golden Years have come at last

The Golden Years can kiss my ass!

While, thankfully, the poem was premature in many ways, it did make the point that things had changed and were going to change even more.

By 2004

Rwanda, Bosnia, Croatia, Chechnya, Hutu-Tutsi
Rock and Roll Hall of Fame
Sheep clones-Dolly
Yitzhak Rabin assassination
#7
Mad cow disease
Unabomber
TWA Flight #800
Heavens Gate cult suicides

Murrah Building-Timothy McVay
Harry Potter-J.K. Rowling
Titanic-11 Academy Awards
Monica Lewinsky-impeachment
Viagra
Y2K
Columbine
JFK, Jr.
The Blair Witch Project
Human Genome Project
Melissa, Chernobyl-computer viruses
Elian Gonzalez
Hanging chads
The Williams sisters
Survivor
Slobodan Milosovic
Anthrax
Randy Johnson-Curt Schilling
Enron
Stem cells
Sonny-Flo Jo-Jerry Garcia-Mother Teresa-Ray Charles
Ted Williams-cryogenics
Yasir Arafat-Mahmoud Abbas
Gray Davis-Arnold Schwarzenegger
Tsunami
Gay marriages
Google
Michael Moore-*Fahrenheit 9/11*
Mel Gibson-*The Passion of the Christ*
Water on Mars?
Taliban-Afghanistan-al-Qaeda
9/11
The War on Terror
WMD-The War in Iraq-Abu Ghraib

Touching Your Heart

By 2004, I had been retired for two years and had settled into a comfortable life of grandparenthood, volunteer work, traveling to play baseball around the country and around the world, a bit of private consulting, daily trips to the gym, recreational reading, crossword puzzles, and traveling to visit family and sightsee.

Ann had also retired from managing the mathematics tutoring lab at the Raymond Walters Branch of the University of Cincinnati. She had also been doing private math tutoring in our home for years. When we run into her past students from across 23 years of tutoring, Ann introduces me to them and then asks about their families, especially their children, by name. The former students invariably let me know how much of a positive impact Ann had on their academic lives and their lives in general. It is as if she were both math tutor and social worker. I am very proud of what she accomplished and the difference she made in people's lives.

Ann and I quickly found in retirement that connections with the people we care about were critical to our happiness. These included family, the senior baseball community, our respective high school classes, our former work colleagues, friends both in and out of town, and the people with whom we do our volunteer work.

It is no surprise, therefore, that we were looking forward to my 40-year reunion and to hers two years later. We were expecting the reunion weekend of the University City Class of 1964 to be exceptional. It was.

We had already begun to get a taste of the reunion a year early, because Neal Handler had an idea and turned it into a reality. Handler Happy Hours began in 2003. Many St. Louis classmates and anyone who was visiting from out of town met on the first Thursday of every month at Rick's Café, a local watering hole.

Attendance typically ranged from 20 to 35. On the Thursday before the 40-year reunion weekend, there were so many people, it was hard to move or hear. Handler Happy Hours continued after the reunion—there had been about 40 of the monthly affairs when they wound down in 2006. I suspect them to be revived at some point.

The 40-year reunion did not take place over Thanksgiving weekend because fewer classmates were returning to St. Louis for the holiday. By this event, many classmates' parents had passed away or moved away from St. Louis, such that the holiday was less of a reason to return to the area.

More than 200 classmates and about 100 significant others converged on the high school on Friday evening, October 8, 2004 for a party in the gym. The informal affair gave us a chance to both catch up with each other and to tour the school. Many had not been in the building for 40 years. Classmates especially wanted to see the Hall of Fame corridor.

Our Saturday night dinner dance was held at Harrah's Casino banquet facility just outside of St. Louis. Many stayed overnight at Harrah's as a way to extend the party into the wee hours and, for some, to take advantage of the casino.

For the Saturday event, classmate Morrie Mayer created a masterpiece to match what Tim Arnold had produced 20 years earlier. Morrie is not only a high school classmate but also my AEPi college fraternity brother. He and classmate Nancy Rosenberg are married and live in Houston, Texas, where Morrie runs a business called "Bytes of Life" (www.bytesoflife.com). The business's tag line is "Capturing Your Memories...Touching Your Heart."

That Saturday night, Morrie touched our hearts when he showed his creation, *UC64—A Blast from the Past.* Every classmate left the party with a copy of the DVD.

Morrie produced a moving retrospective of our senior year with research help from Mickey Leon Sandmel and Elaine Levin Unell. The presentation started with the video clip of Walter Cronkite, close to tears, announcing that JFK had died. It went on to Ed Sullivan introducing the Beatles for their February 1964 Sunday evening appearance to the screams of the teenage girls in the audience.

Morrie then took us on a video and musical tour of our senior-year lives, moving through our alma mater being played by our high school band, historical clips, photos from high school, radio DJ's, movies, American Bandstand and other TV shows, restaurant menus, Mohammed Ali defeating St. Louisan Sonny Liston, Stan Musial retiring, sock hops, swim meets, team pictures, cheerleaders, Stephen Kowarsky performing our Senior Song (his creation), and on and on. When we thought the experience could be no more moving than it had been, Morrie presented his "In Memoriam" segment and brought us to tears.

Magical

There were many other memorable aspects of our 40-year reunion weekend. Californian Anne O'Brien and St. Louisan Neal Handler, both who came to the reunion divorced, danced, sang, and partied together all weekend. Shortly thereafter, Anne moved back to St. Louis to live with Neal.

Neal Handler and Anne O'Brien after
singing to the class at the 40-year reunion

Helene London Rothman was in a wheel chair recovering from a stroke but still joined her husband, Marty, and everyone on the dance floor.

With over 200 classmates at the weekend events, seeing everyone we wanted to see and finding the time to catch up was not easy. Adrienne Nadler Hirschfeld ran into Francine Fox Cooper just before midnight on Saturday and said to her, "Did you just get here?" No, she had been there the whole evening.

Ron Brown had not been to any of the previous reunions or to the 50th birthday party. Because of deep feelings of insecurity, Ron had viewed high school as the worst years of his life and could not imagine wanting to reconnect with classmates. However, prior to the 40-year reunion, Ron joined-up with classmates living in Cincinnati and became one of the planners of a Cincinnati mini-reunion that drew participants from around the Midwest. Ron found himself so enamored with the Cincinnati experience; he was compelled to attend the upcoming class reunion. Following the reunion, Ron captured how he felt about it in just one word, "Magical."

On Friday evening, I brought my catcher's mitt, my fielder's glove, and a new baseball. After having a good chance to get in my greetings and hugs, I found classmates Steve Novack and Ronnie Neeter and Ira Bergman (class of '65), who is married to classmate Carol Haseltine Bergman. Steve, Ronnie, and Ira had all played varsity baseball. When I told them about the gloves and ball, they quickly nodded their heads. After a trip to my car and a few minutes to clear classmates out of the way, we were playing catch in the gym; the first time we had done that in over 40 years.

Terry Mitze came to the reunion, and it was a delight to see him. He still had that engaging twinkle in his eyes, but he looked gaunt, and he carried a jacket with him because he got cold easily. I remember thinking this may have been because he had lived so long in Saint Thomas in the US Virgin Islands.

When we lost Terry to cancer a year later, Tom Norman wrote, "I was thinking about Terry today and have it that he had a gift of making every friend of his think he was their best friend...Terry had a great gift and was a great gift...A spirit like Terry's doesn't die, that is how I have it."

Reconnections at the reunion were running rampant. Elaine Levin had not seen her girlhood friend, Marcia Millner, for a very long time. They had been neighbors as little girls and played together virtually every day. Through junior high and high school, however, Elaine and Marcia had drifted apart.

Elaine knew that Marcia would be coming to the reunion, and looked for but could not find her. She had, however, noticed a stunning woman, whom she did not recognize, and assumed she was the wife of a classmate. Shortly thereafter, someone tapped Elaine on the shoulder. As Elaine turned, she was face-to-face with the woman she had seen earlier. "Hi Elaine, it's me, Marcia."

When they stopped hugging, they developed a plan for which they recruited Marsha Klibansky and Delores Finkelstein, who were also neighborhood playmates. On the Monday morning following the reunion weekend, the "little girls;" Marcia, who lived in San Diego; Delores, who lived in Fort Worth; Marsha and Elaine, who both still lived in St. Louis; met for brunch. They then literally took a "stroll down memory lane" as they walked the streets of their old neighborhood, even knocking on the doors of their former homes. At Elaine's and Marsha's girlhood houses, the current owners invited the group in for tours.

They ended the day with a heartfelt visit to Elaine's mom in the nursing home. Marsha even brought with her a bib that Elaine's mom had crocheted for Marsha when she was a baby.

This girlhood friendship went a long way back and was rekindled on this very special Monday in October 2004. The visit to Elaine's mom validated the yearbook quip chosen for Marcia Millner: "You have not lived a perfect day unless you have done something for someone Who will never be able to repay you."

While there had been other reunions, mini-reunions, monthly dinners and happy hours, and a shared birthday party, there was something more intense about the reconnections being made during the 40-year reunion weekend, both at and outside the planned events. It was as if the longer we were out of school, the closer we were becoming. The reasons the class was so close seemed to be strengthening.

A group of girlfriends had their first slumber party since high school. A group went jogging together in Forest Park, the municipal park in St. Louis that housed the 1904 World's Fair. Groups of people were finding each other and taking pictures; elementary school classes, the junior high school football team, those who had become college fraternity brothers, former boyfriend-girlfriend pairs, and the one-time high school football backfield. Some brought their senior yearbooks and asked classmates to sign them again next to the original.

Perhaps more importantly, connecting was not limited to old high school groups. What cliques that existed had evaporated—what posturing was being done during school and the early reunions had stopped—what concerns we had about who had been in the "popular" groups or who had been one of the "jocks" had been left behind. We were all members of the University City High School Class of 1964, were proud of it, and were thrilled to reestablish and strengthen friendships, as well as to make new ones that did not exist four-plus decades earlier.

Perhaps Sue Corman Slater said it best of her school friends Nancy Rosenberg, Sharon Marcus, Sharon Lee, Barb Goldstein, Diane Gordon, and Jan Goldberg: "Being with old friends and talking about the good old days and catching up on the time since high school is the best part of reunions and mini reunions! There is nothing like old friends. You may not have seen them in 30 or 40 years, but you pick up like it was yesterday! When you have lost your sight like I have and cannot see your friends anymore, it is nice that it does not matter to them. To them, you are still the same fun girl you were 40 years ago!"

Rethink Middle Age

The reunion weekend was electric. Our shared 50th birthday party had been a success. Mini-reunions around the country had become the norm. We were connected electronically on a daily basis. We were on a high and looking for the next time we could get together. The obvious answer was a 60th birthday party.

Classmate Harold Sanger is President of AMC Tile Supply, a distributor of ceramic tile products in St. Louis. Shortly before our 60th birthday party, he had opened a beautiful and spacious showroom and was kind enough to offer the space to the class for our event.

Gary Singer, Lenny Koblenz, Dee Leabman Koblenz, Harold Sanger,
and Kay Rudolph at the class 60th birthday party

Classmate Zara Haimo, who lives in Palo Alto, California, where she is happily retired, raising her three children, traveling a lot, and enjoying life, put turning 60 into perspective.

Zara wrote to the class, "I'm pretty sure I am the youngest member of the class of '64 and the last to cross the 60th birthday line, so we are all now in our 60s. When I was in the rush of being 16 and trying to figure everything out, I had no clue that I would ever live this long or experience any of the things I have so far. Remember never trusting anyone over 30? Are we now at the point where we shouldn't trust anyone over 90? I used to think middle age happened at 40 and one became old at 60—my grandparents were in their 60s when I was a kid and were definitely very old then. Wasn't my mother already old at 60? In retrospect, I'm ashamed I had that thought as she was very active and an intrepid world traveler until Parkinson's caught up with her in her 80s. Given all the things I do now that I couldn't do even at 50, it may be time for me to rethink what being middle aged or old means."

Nearly 100 classmates and a number of spouses converged on Harold's showroom to celebrate 60 together. Although the party was only a single evening event, classmates traveled from around the country to be there.

Arleen White Bly came to the party late after making sure her husband, Howard, who was ill and in the hospital, was settled for the night. She was not sure whether she was going to come, as her role as caretaker through Howard's illness had been so draining. Arleen finally decided to come, because she felt that she would gain strength from being with longtime friends who cared about her so much. She was right.

Reach for the Stars

We attended University City High School in the early 60s and set out on a journey in which human history, personal history, and class history intertwined. We are now in our early 60s, molded into what we have become by shared culture, personal experiences, and life lessons learned.

A welcomed perspective on who we were and who we have become was offered by Sylvia Slotkin, classmate Joanna's mother. Sylvia wrote to represent our parents, more specifically our mothers. At this stage of our lives, many of us have lost at least one of our parents. As part of our extended family, Sylvia stepped in on their behalf.

In an introductory note, Sylvia, who has a great sense of humor and of self and is blind, typed, "Dear Alan: I thought one of the mothers of the class of 1964 should say at least 'hello.' I have no idea what I typed or even if it came out on the sheet. But I felt like saying it…"

What she typed not only came out on the sheet; it came into our hearts.

"Dear Children:

"This is a letter from your mother. Only one of you belonged to me, but all of your mothers watched you grow up with much pride and pleasure and much wringing of hands. We protested only mildly when you spoke endlessly on the telephone with your friends. We covered our ears when you played your records loud enough to be heard in the next county. We watched and listened to your screaming over the Beatles. And we sat and mourned the loss of your young President. Some of you did a lot of folk dancing. Some of you ironed your hair on the ironing board. And some of you came home screaming excitedly, 'Ma, Danny kicked me today in school. Does that mean he likes me?' And my job as a mother was to reassure you that it did mean he liked you…

"And you grew up to be a wonderful generation of bright responsible people. But to your mothers we still remember the scared, worried, shy, eager young people who grew up to be the wonderful men and women you are today.

"We loved you then and we love you now. And we're glad we hatched you…

"Mama"

This is from the same wise woman who advised her teenage daughter, Joanna, "Reach for the stars; you'll grow a long arm."

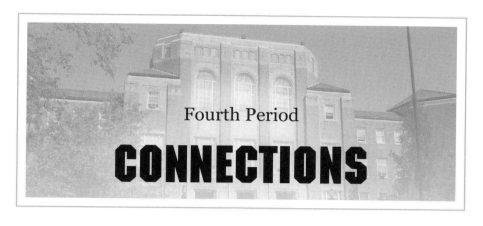

Fourth Period

CONNECTIONS

*"Piglet sidled up to Pooh from behind. 'Pooh!' he whispered.
'Yes, Piglet?' 'Nothing,' said Piglet, taking Pooh's paw.
'I just wanted to be sure of you.'"*

A. A. Milne

---

*"Every person, all the events of your life are there because you have
drawn them there. What you choose to do with them is up to you."*

Richard Bach

Mark Stuart Glickman

*"The man that lives and laughs
well must surely do well."*

Steve: *"Ilene and I wouldn't miss one of these reunions for the
world."*

Marla: *"People aren't just waiting for the reunions. They're getting
together all over the country every chance they get, often
with people they weren't even close to in high school.   It's
like mini-reunions."*

Judy: *"I haven't had a chance to travel much, but I feel connected
anyway through the Yahoo! Group that Les Berger
started."*

Anne: *"What I enjoy is that I'm not just spending time with the people I ran with in high school. It's certainly good to see old friends, but it feels really nice to make a new one with a classmate."*

Mark: *"The five of us are a great example. We weren't all that close in high school. That is except for the summer before our senior year when Judy and I went steady. I can still remember how you looked with my ring on a chain around your neck."*

Judy: *"That was a great time, Mark."*

Anne: *"You're a real romantic, Glick."*

Mark: *"There's a lot more than high school romances that bring us together and keep us close between reunions."*

Steve: *"Yeah, we've all been trying to describe what it is that makes us want to stay connected like we do."*

Judy: *"There has to be more than one reason. Maybe some day we'll figure it out."*

Marla: *"Someone probably will, and I wouldn't be surprised if they do before I get anyone to meet me under the clock."*

Classic, Classy, Class Reunion

Classmate Jill Friedman Chapin, who lives in Santa Monica, California, is retired from her career as a guidance assistant at a local middle school. During her tenure, she developed a concern that parents were abdicating their responsibility as primary caretakers. Consistent with Jill's approach to deal with issues head on, she authored the bilingual book, *If You Have Kids, Then Be A Parent!*

Jill also wrote a children's book, *My Magic Bubble*, to help young people deal with bullying. More recently, she co-authored a book with Jennifer Aumais. *Fly on the Wall* is hilarious and sometimes raunchy. It is an account of Jennifer's life with her husband and two of his closest friends, who had to move in with them shortly after their honeymoon. Jill and Jennifer are still trying to get it published.

Jill now focuses on her role as social observer and commentator, writing articles with social conscience for *The Fog City Journal*. She is also an active contributor to our class Yahoo! Group and delights in how it continues to bring us together.

On March 26, 2006, a couple of years after our 40-year reunion, one of Jill's essays was published in *The Canyon News*, the paper for which she was writing at the time. The essay provides a perfect segue between our post-high school history and a more detailed look at how and why many of us enjoy being so closely connected. The essay is entitled, "A Classic, Classy, Class Reunion." Jill wrote:

"What makes a reunion both classic and classy? Is it long-lost friends, acquaintances and near strangers meeting up again to discover how much they are united by common memories? Is it where dozens of friendships are created or rekindled with a depth that simply could not have been possible in high school? Is it where superficiality and boastfulness are checked at the door—all that enters is a warmth and unconditional appreciation for those with whom we were raised, and with whom we are delighted to realize how much we share in our common history? Is it the knowledge of life's challenges beyond the big game and a date for the prom to a deeper awareness of the fragility of life and a newfound, profound sense of gratefulness that all of us in attendance are - well, all here?

"I can only speak for my fortieth high school reunion, a class of over six hundred in the Midwest, where a large percentage are now scattered across the country and a few around the world. A class in which about five percent are scattered through the heavens, having left us far too soon. At my reunion, however, I felt as close to those who were gone as I felt to those who were there. They were given a tribute that put a humanity to their photos displayed on a screen and, for that brief moment, we were the entire class of 1964.

"Which may make you wonder why I am writing about a reunion that occurred a couple of years ago. The answer is simply that the reunion is not yet over, and evidence is mounting that it may never end. Why? Because mini-reunions are taking place across the country. Some take a train from St Louis to Chicago to share memories and a Cardinals/Cub game. Cincinnati, New York, San Francisco, San Diego, Houston, Los Angeles, Kansas City, Austin, and dozens of other cities find alumni who make plans to gather and gab. And they are evolving from stories of the good ole days to current events in our lives that keep us fresh, interested, and interesting.

"But how did this all come about? How can so many people from so many places find out who lives where and plan an event like this? Isn't this daunting and ultimately not worth all the effort that it would take to plan such a convoluted rendezvous?

"Yes, unless you were lucky enough to have a classmate like we do, who, a year before the reunion, took the time to set up a web site for our class. He invited us to speak openly and freely, first to fill everyone in on the last forty years, and then to just see where it goes. The site took on a life of its own. People began to talk about old times, places, teachers. Then it would move on to current events, feelings, or favorite books, lots and lots of political opinions, jokes galore, and more. Some would get upset at the politics or the onslaught of too many jokes. We were all gently reminded of that nifty "delete" key, and everyone calmed down.

"The mini-reunions took flight because it was easy to set a time and place to meet. RSVPs were unnecessary. A classmate might post online that he would be in Philadelphia and anyone who wanted to see him should meet at a certain restaurant at a designated time. There was always a gathering, and they had the proof with pictures of the reunion posted to our site.

"That's how I came to have an impromptu dinner with four classmates. One was captain of the cheerleaders (who I discovered lives down the street from me), one was in the "popular" crowd, another was my elementary school friend, and another was my longtime, ongoing high school friend. So there we were, eating and chatting as though we had not missed a day in each other's lives in forty years.

"And so it goes, all over the country, all the time. And much of the credit goes to that one guy who cared enough to set up the internet connection that led to a most personal connection among our classmates.

"Thank you, Les Berger. Your name is the very definition of a classic, classy, class reunion."

Jill Elaine Friedman

"Such a brown inner light
From eyelids out broke
You looked at her silence
And fancied she spoke."

Welcome to the UCity 1964 Group

On December 17, 2002 at 12:31pm (St. Louis time), Leslie Berger sent a message to every classmate for whom he had an e-mail address. The message announced the start of a Yahoo! Group entitled "UCity 1964." His simple yet visionary message read, "Welcome to the UCity 1964 group. If you are in contact with any former classmates, please ask them to join the group. The more classmates who use the group the more fun everyone will have here."

It took about a year for classmates to find the group and begin active messaging. Eventually nearly 225 classmates would join. Between January and February 2004, the monthly message count jumped from 19 to 157 and continued to grow. In September 2004, the month before our 40-year reunion, there were 889 messages sent, almost 30 per day.

On December 17, 2007, the group's fifth anniversary, Carol Enger Canis sent message 10,909—we had averaged almost 2200 per year or six per day over the five years.

The September 2004 record message count was shattered when in September and October 2008, political fever hit the class as the presidential campaign intensified. Over those two months, there were 2405 messages, about 40 per day.

By Election Day, November 4, 2008, the message count was nearing 16,500, but did not stop there. The postings continue to mount.

These numbers are only an accounting of those messages posted to the site. Many prompt and even solicit private e-mail discussions outside the group, adding tens of thousands additional connections.

The energy of the group varies over time as does the subject matter. Classmates share personal information, send photos of family and mini-reunions, evoke memories, argue politics, tell jokes, ask for advice, give advice (some asked for, some not), announce the birth of grandchildren, search for lost classmates, and cover countless other topics. Some classmates are active contributors, while others monitor the group and only comment occasionally; an activity called "lurking." But, there is no doubt that the Yahoo! Group is key to our connectedness.

A good example of how messages build on each other started

with a string of seemingly-innocuous postings that led to a profound place. The subject of the message string was, "World's Greatest Joke." Eddie Friedman, an attorney in Chicago, wrote, "Two hunters go into the woods. One is from Czechoslovakia and one is from Poland. They come across two bears in the woods. A male bear and a female bear. They fire but miss. The male bear attacks the man from Czechoslovakia and eats him. The female bear attacks the man from Poland but he gets away. He runs into town and everyone says to him, 'Where is your friend?' He says, 'The Czech is in the male.'"

One could hear a collective electronic groan, but the messaging went on.

More than a week later, Hank Schneider, a clinical social worker in Columbia, Missouri, wrote, "Here's another way this site has made a difference. Recently a longtime friend died, and yesterday I spoke at his memorial service. My friend was well known for his humor, especially puns. I ended my talk with Ed Friedman's 'world's best joke' ('The Czech is in the male'). It received a wonderful response—a loud groan mixed with laughter. My friend would have loved it."

Hank concluded with, "Thanks, Ed. And thanks to Les and all who add to our group site."

That is not to say that all of the messaging is positive and well received. As with any on-line communications group, there are times when the give and take gets testy. We went through such a time in mid-2008.

Ellen Smith Rich lives in Dallas, Texas, where she is an early childhood special educator and memory box artist. After a particularly pointed political conversation, Ellen posted a message with the subject of "Good-Bye." Ellen wrote, "It was great seeing some of you at the 40th, but I joined this list to keep in contact, not put up with all the 'stuff' that has been flying around…Wish you all well…"

What followed was a healthy debate about what was acceptable for the group. Karen Paulsen Bauch responded from her home in Winnipeg, Manitoba. Her posting about Ellen's good-bye and others' perspectives addressed the issue.

In part, Karen wrote, "We can't be in much of a relationship with one another if we are afraid to be honest, and it does seem that the people writing are just saying how it looks to them; I don't think they're trying to offend anyone. Isn't this how we grow? Nobody has all the answers, and I for one really learn from hearing both sides—check and balance. Now of course some people are more comfortable when words are chosen carefully and tactfully, and others are fine with bluntness."

Karen continued, "As I age, I become more comfortable with bluntness, because then at least the intended meaning is clear, and because sometimes people are not so good at 'tactful,' which then can feel more offensive then 'blunt.' We are living in an exciting but frightening time—so much possibility for improvement, and so much possibility for tragedy. Collectively we can make a difference, so don't we need to talk about things?"

She concluded, "I rarely post messages, but I do read what is written and feel very enriched by the communications of this group, arguments included, and perhaps especially."

Shortly thereafter we heard from Ellen again, "Well, as you can see, I am back...couldn't stay away...Yes, it is true that everyone is entitled to their opinions, and we should all be encouraged to share our views here. There is room for everyone. I do not, however, think we should be mean-spirited to those whose views differ from our own. I will now go back to lurking."

We were stronger as a communications group and as a class for Ellen's challenge and the subsequent conversation. Thank you Ellen, Karen, and all the classmates who are connected through the group.

And as Jill and Hank wrote, "Thank you, Les."

Top Ten Reasons

Leslie Berger's introduction of the Yahoo! Group has clearly been instrumental to keeping a large percentage of our class closely connected. But there has to be much more than that. Other classes have initiated electronic community groups, but with little ongoing activity. Many classes have reunions, but with little contact in between. I can only conclude that there are fundamental reasons the University City High School Class of 1964 is predisposed to take advantage of the opportunity Leslie afforded us.

What follows are my top ten reasons our class has remained close. The list is not a menu from which to choose. Rather, for us, each reason is applicable, and each one complements the others. These are the reasons, as Jill wrote, that many of us are together "as though we had not missed a day in each other's lives in forty years."

Here is a brief description of my top ten reasons, followed by more details about each.

#10. Technology: In 1964, technology as we know it today was in its infancy. A long distance phone call was expensive enough to be considered a discretionary household budget item. The high school had just converted to a more accurate grade recording system, something called a "magnetic brain," by which teachers made marks on IBM cards that were sent to a data processing center to be read and recorded onto magnetic tapes. Now we have personal computers, wireless networks, PDAs, Yahoo! Groups, Google, e-mail, aircards, Twitter, unlimited long-distance calling minutes, Skype, text messaging, and access to information and to each other at the click of a mouse or press of a speed-dial key on a cell phone.

#9. Need for Belonging: In his 1954 book, *Motivation and Personality*, Abraham Maslow identified a hierarchy of human needs that must be satisfied before an individual can reach his or her full potential. One is what Maslow calls "the belongingness and love need." We belonged to our high school class and graduated together. We then went our separate ways, built families, and joined other communities, organizations, and institutions. As we grow older and retire, our relationships are changing. For many of us, still being connected to or reconnecting with our high school class is fundamental to helping meet our personal need for belonging.

#8. Common Culture: While our life experiences have been diverse, we are bonded by a common culture. We emerged from a virtually all-white, largely Jewish, middle-class community that expected and demanded we be well-educated. That shared culture allows us to comfortably and readily maintain and reestablish relationships, even though we are together less frequently than we would like.

#7. Memories: As we share a common culture, so do we share a common memory—the people, places, events, and emotions we experienced collectively. Even when flawed, memories evoke that long-ago. Even when selective, memories developed together bring us together.

#6. Maturity: Measured by the decades between class reunions, we have continually reduced social competition and posturing. Age and life's lessons have humbled and mellowed us. We have become much less judgmental and much more accepting, thereby enabling us to more readily connect, even with those with whom we may not have been close in school.

#5. Happiness: Happiness is an elusive concept, difficult to define. Yet by one man's definition, we had every opportunity to be happy being part of the class when in high school and have every right to be happy to be part of it today. Happiness is being a valued member of a valued community.

#4. Means/Mobility: We grew up in middle-class families. Travel, even for vacations, was typically modest; a car trip to Chicago or maybe as far away as Washington, DC. In general, we have grown economically, thanks in large part to our collective level of education and the work ethic passed on by our parents and grandparents. We have had a travel experience far greater than we could have imagined in the early 60s. As a result, we have the means and willingness to travel to see each other at reunions, at mini-reunions, and on class cruises.

#3. We Care: Unfortunately, we have learned through experience that classmates sometimes need our support. Fortunately, we have also learned we are a caring community that is both willing and able to mobilize to help. Being connected affords us access to help and the opportunity to pitch in when needed.

#2. Personal Initiative: Leslie Berger took the initiative to begin the Yahoo! Group. He is one of many classmates who are not only connected but who step up to enable the rest of us to be so. Mickey Leon Sandmel, Judy Inger Shanfeld, Ron and Elaine Levin Unell, and others take the initiative to make reunions happen. Morrie Mayer and Tim Arnold captured and shared video memories. Jill Friedman Chapin, Alan Resnick, Steven Karty, Don Pearline, Carol Enger Canis, Jerry Weiner, Paula Glovinsky Sigel, Mark Gants, Barb Glick Koch, and many others stir the e-mail pot to prompt class participation. Oh, and there is a guy who has taken the initiative to write a book about the class and make it a class project.

#1. Pride: We are proud of whom we have become collectively and individually. We are proud of our desire to be close to each other. We are proud to be the University City High School Class of 1964.

Reason #10: Technology
Hugo

In 1964, the concept of computers was the farthest thing from our minds. Even technology progress while we were in college was not much greater when compared to where we are today.

I started engineering classes with a slide rule hanging from my belt and was excited about my first "powerful" $100+ Texas Instruments calculator that added, subtracted, multiplied, divided, and was even advanced enough to calculate square roots at the press of a button. Of course, this was only when you plugged it in to avoid the problems with virtually no battery life.

We began learning about computer programming using punch cards, had to get in the queue to run our card stack through the processor, and then hoped that the cards would not jam during our run.

There was a single dial telephone at our fraternity house shared by 35 residents. We were on the honor system to log our long distance calls. For privacy, we could pull the phone with its long extension cord into a closet.

One of my college fraternity brothers is high school classmate Marshall Faintich. Marshall is brilliant. While the rest of us mere mortals were struggling to memorize important formulae for tests, he would derive them from first principles when he needed them.

Marshall earned his BS Degree in Applied Mathematics and went on to earn his Masters and PhD in Astronomy (Orbital Mechanics) from the University of Illinois. Although he cannot share many details, he moved on to a career that included his involvement with the development of GPS (Global Positioning Satellite) technology.

It was no surprise that it was Marshall who utilized comparatively simple, yet powerful, technology and his personal initiative to electronically locate and contact Hugo Ostropolsky, our senior-year foreign exchange student from Argentina. Marshall did so with the intent of not only reconnecting Hugo with our class but to invite Hugo to our 40-year reunion. On March 9, 2004, he posted a message on our Yahoo! Group entitled, "I FOUND HUGO!"

Hugo Luis Ostropolsky

"The friendship between you and me will not compare to a chain; for that the rains might rust, or the falling tree might break."

Marshall passed along a note from Hugo, whose warmth and fond memories shone through any issues he may have with English. Hugo's note read, "My good Friend Marshall:

"Today when I did open my mail, I received your mail. I'm very much pleased to hear from you. I'm the same guy who was in US during the school year '63-'64.

"Many times I wanted to hear from my old mates. It was very sad not to keep in touch during these 40 years...

"I'll make you a brief update of what happen to me after I left U City. I became a lawyer, and had private practice in my City of Mendoza. After the cruel dictatorship until 1983 I became the Attorney General for my State of Mendoza for 4 years. Although I was like a State Supreme Court Judge, became tired and did resign to return to my private practice. I was married in 1972 and have 3 kids. Two boys and a girl. My eldest is General Manager of Cancer Clinics in Dominican Republic. His is married. My second boy is an Architect finishing his Master Degree in the University of Pamplona in Spain. He is staying there for a while. And my daughter is an Engineer and is now waiting for a baby, my first granddaughter. Up now I'm working as the representative of my State of Mendoza in Buenos Aires 1,100 kms. from home, where I flight every week.

"Please let me know when will be the get together, because I am eager to meet you all again. I'll do my best to come and see you. Please lets get in touch from now on."

We had reconnected with a distant member of the University City Class of 1964.

Hugo began to make plans to join us at the reunion later that year. Unfortunately, travel restrictions imposed after September 11, 2001 made it impossible for him to get his visa in time. It would have been spectacular had Hugo Luis Ostropolsky of Mendoza, Argentina been able to be in University City, Missouri again on October 8, 2004. But being thousands of miles and four decades apart was no longer a reason to be out of touch.

What we now view as simple technology, the Internet, search engines, and e-mail, enabled Marshall to find Hugo. It allowed us to connect with him long distance in real time. All of this would have been impossible and, for most of us, unimaginable when we graduated, because the first e-mail was not introduced until 1972 nor broadly applied until well after that. The same technology that found and connected Hugo helps us find and support each other every day.

Here are excerpts from an update Hugo sent to me on May 23, 2008.

"Since I mailed to my friends before, a few things happened. I had a heart operation...but after 14 months I had to be reoperated because the valve was untying. I've decided not to work anymore and stay at home enjoying the privileges of my family especially my grandsons (2) and granddaughters (2).

"Technically I'm not retired but I do not want to go on with my work as a lawyer. I am taking care of my private business and of course playing a lot of golf. I am a pretty bad player. I have 32 of handicap. But have a lot of friends and enjoy being with them.

"I remember with love all the time I spent with you there in U City High. Sincerely, Hugo Luis Ostropolsky"

Hugo, we remember you and, through technology, will remain connected.

Reason #9: Need for Belonging
Completely Enriched

We belong or have belonged to families, work groups, synagogues, churches, volunteer organizations, bridge groups, golf foursomes, dinner clubs, baseball teams, support groups, book clubs, the audience that watches *American Idol*, college sororities or fraternities, and on and on and on. Belonging feels good.

In his book *Motivation and Productivity*, Abraham Maslow describes what has become to be known as the "hierarchy of needs." As we satisfy our more basic human needs, like making sure we have enough to eat and that we are safe and secure, we can move up the hierarchy to satisfy higher-order needs. At the top of the hierarchy pyramid is self-actualization, becoming all that we can be. In the middle of the pyramid is our need to belong and be loved.

Maslow wrote, "...there will emerge the love and affection and belongingness needs... Now the person will feel keenly, as never before, the absence of friends, or a sweetheart, or a wife, or children. He will hunger for affectionate relations with people in general, namely, for a group or family, and he will strive intensely to achieve this goal."

In essence, each of us has belonged to the University City graduating class of 1964 since we joined it sometime during our progression from elementary school to junior high to high school. However, as our lives have unfolded, many of us have a need to belong that is increasingly intense and is manifesting itself with a new level of engagement. What has happened over the years that has increased our desire to actively belong to the class?

We have belonged to families in which our parents and grandparents and aunts and uncles provided us unconditional love. We are now in our 60s—our grandparents are gone—for many of us, one or both parents are gone. Others of us can see when that will happen all too soon. While the term is not generally used for mature adults, we are or about to become "orphans."

We reared our children, and for most of us, they are out of

the house. It is a good thing that we have helped them become independent. Many of our children have started families and have made us grandparents, for some many times over. Despite the joy of seeing our children doing well on their own, the reality is that they are no longer with us at home.

We are beginning to retire from our careers that, for so many years, defined us. "What do you do?"

"I work for Procter & Gamble."

I belonged to the company, my business unit, my work team. Then on May 2, 2002, I retired and no longer belonged.

Some of us, regrettably, have lost spouses to divorce or death.

Some have moved frequently, never having established long-term local relationships.

As we age, therefore, we confront the reality that many of those things in our lives that helped us meet our need to belong are no longer available. Why not reach out for a community that is ready to provide unconditional love—a community made up of others wanting the same thing—a community, for so many other reasons, that is predisposed to want to be closely connected?

Not everyone had a warm, positive high school experience at U City. For some, that has not precluded reaching out and reconnecting with classmates.

Adrienne Nadler Hirschfeld recalls feeling disenfranchised at school. Already feeling that way in her sophomore year, she developed an eating disorder, made even more difficult because, at the time, the malady was not yet commonly understood or even acknowledged. She lost 20 pounds.

The issue persisted for about 18 months during which the school called Adrienne's parents twice, concerned about her weight loss, but no one knew what to do. Thankfully, Adrienne had the inner strength to recover on her own. By her senior year, she became somewhat more active at school, including going on the class trip to Washington, DC. She still found it difficult to make new friends.

Despite feeling distant for much of her high school career, Adrienne currently appreciates the feeling of connectedness of the class of '64. She wrote, "I do very much love to read the website and I feel my life has been completely enriched by the saga of '64. Aside from the friends and neighbors with whom I currently associate, I am lucky to have this group of friends who I also know and love and who give me a sense of security that they will always be there for me and always be supportive...I love everyone today much more than in school. It's a special club and we're all members."

Adrienne is connected to our high school class, and she wants to remain that way. She has attended every reunion and the class 50th and 60th birthday parties.

Adrienne belongs. We all do.

Laya Firestone Seghi earned her BA in History and her Masters in Social Work from Washington University. She now lives in Miami Beach, where she is a licensed psychotherapist and certified bodytalk practitioner. In her spare time, Laya enjoys swimming, poetry, yoga, nature, and dancing. She and husband, Tom, have three children and five grandchildren. (www.layaseghi.com)

Laya Firestone

"Be not ashamed to be what you are;
be ashamed to be what you are not."

Laya's high school experience was one in which she sought and found a place to belong, albeit, as she describes, "out of the mainstream." Laya tells her story in an essay entitled "A Minority Voice."

"Curiosity about our 40th reunion prompted me to go online and read the U City '64 Yahoo entries. Regardless of whether I had felt part of the high school experience or not - the three years our class spent together gave us a shared history, a common bond. We each had particular experiences and unique perspective. But looking back after more than 40 years, the essence of the intervening years made our shared experiences much more pronounced to me than our differences.

"What a different perspective from the one I had as a 14 year old entering U City High for the first time in the fall of 1961! After the sheltered world of the Epstein Hebrew Academy where I attended through ninth grade, graduating with less than ten classmates, the cavernous corridors of U City High seemed like another world. As the only one of six children in my family to attend public school, I had no reference point, no clue of what to expect from or how to adapt to my new surroundings.

"In my Orthodox elementary school, the theme of our religious uniqueness was emphasized. We were not like 'the OTHER peoples' – but set apart by our Kosher diet, Sabbath and holiday observance, and the written and oral teachings of the Torah that dictated guidelines for the most minute detail of daily living. At U City High I found myself for seven hours a day in the midst of these 'OTHER' people. As I look back now, it's easy to realize that relative to the rest of the world, these 'Other' people were really not that much different than me. The vast majority of the class was Jewish, even if not of my strict Orthodox variety background.

"Nevertheless, from finding my way to and around the school, to sitting in classes of 30 students, to taking 'physical education' or eating in a large cafeteria serving non-kosher food, I was in a constant state of adjustment. I wasn't in a foreign country speaking a foreign language, but I may as well have been. The English language, the books, teachers and homework assignments were all familiar, but the public school culture was not—student assemblies with rallies for sports teams, elections for homecoming kings and queens, school dances and after-school activities, 'teased' hair styles, cashmere sweaters and weekend dating—these were all well beyond my scope.

"In retrospect, considering my conditioning, it was natural for me to fall into one of the school's sub-cultures. I found myself drawn to Vicky Sleator, a girl in my sophomore English class. She had long, blond hair and a green book bag—something about her intrigued me. Soon we connected for brief conversations, exchanging basic information about ourselves or notes about homework assignments from class.

"Then I would notice her in a hallway or the cafeteria or in the auditorium during an assembly. At times I saw her talking or laughing with a group of friends, both male and female. Most of them wore dark turtleneck shirts or sweaters and the same style of book bag – a thick green canvas mailbag used by postal carriers - slung over their shoulders or in a diagonal across their chests.

"Unlike the majority of girls at school, the girls in this group showed little interest in hairstyles, clothes, or makeup. The green baggers were indifferent to fashion; yet shared the traits of exceptional scholarship or creativity, a passion for the arts, or involvement in select school groups like the Pen-in-Hand Club, International Folk Dancing, or social action causes.

"As I was introduced to this 'green bag' crowd, my fascination for Vicky spread to the group, including her older brother Billy, who was one of the school's musical prodigies.

"Many gravitated to the group because of their philosophical or intellectual leanings or special artistic talents. Others were attracted because their social awkwardness isolated them from the mainstream or because they were disinterested in the norm of fashions, sports, and social networks. In general, the 'green baggers' were high achieving students, many of them 'Merit Scholars,' destined to attend Ivy League schools and become a new intellectual elite, or to 'drop out' and become hippies, social activists, or live otherwise eccentric lives.

"It was back in the early 60's, before Vietnam and the ensuing social unrest were even on the radar of the collective conscious. Civil rights, drugs and gender issues were not yet the hot topics they would soon become. Our high school was a microcosm of our community about ready to explode. We were a white, middle-class school with ethical values and respect for education, and the green baggers represented a bohemian alternative within that culture, rather than something alien from outside. While the green bag was a symbol of non-conformity for those who wore it, we were just as naturally prone to conforming to our group's ethic as any other group member to theirs. Yet we were in the first wave of our generation to register the hint of times yet to come.

"In 1964, the year of our high school graduation, Bob Dylan's song 'The Times They Are A-Changin' was released. 'Come gather around people wherever you roam' opened his prophesy about the years that lay ahead. Listening to the words again now and reflecting on the intervening decades, it's hard not to feel nostalgia for the innocence of our youth.

"When we graduated, regardless of our high school affiliations, we soon stepped more deeply into the story of our own personal lives and into the unstoppable social, political, and economic revolutions that were to come. With our individual stories came the unrelenting change that brought each of us love or lack, achievement and loss, pain and possibly joy. And while living our own lives, even now, the times continue to change as we partake in our collective experience as a nation and as a global family.

"As I reflect on my high school days as a 'green bagger,' the old adage 'plus ca change, plus c'est la meme chose' comes to mind. In the midst of accelerating change around us, certain constants remain. I continue to stand apart from the mainstream, as I always have. Just as the 'green bagger' that I once was, I also count myself among those that question authority and the status quo. As a class, our reunion in person or in cyberspace validates our earliest common memories and also offers a healing change of perspective. After all these years, we can allow ourselves the recognition that as different as we were and are, the space and time we shared together gives us a unique bond that transcends our differences. This awareness seems to me the ingredient that has made the U City Class of '64 such a remarkable community. Hail, Hail!!"

Laya belongs. We all do.

Reason #8: Common Culture
Strong and Cohesive

In his 1987 book, *Cultural Literacy: What Every American Needs to Know*, E. D. Hirsch explores culture in general and argues that the strength and cohesiveness of any society is predicated on a common understanding of its background knowledge.

I am confident that Hirsch would agree that the culture of University City's class of 1964 is exceptionally strong and cohesive as, one could argue, is the culture of early baby boomers in general. As noted, our class was all-white, had a large Jewish contingent, came from predominately middle-class roots, and was well educated. As early baby boomers, we shared a common background, growing up with the same TV shows, movies, music, and current events.

Our class also shared the local St. Louis and school culture—sports teams, news stories, restaurants, social events, activities, and on and on. It is no surprise, therefore, that when classmates get together, the connection is virtually instantaneous.

Classmates Fran Fox Cooper, Dave Goodman, Ron Brown, Arleen Inger, and I all lived in Cincinnati in 2004. Prompted by the upcoming 40-year reunion and messages on the Yahoo! Group, with

Ron's lead, we decided to get together as a group for the first time.

While Arleen and I had run into each other a couple of times over the years, this was a group of people who, in general, did not even know the others lived in Cincinnati. Fran and Ron had only recently moved to town. Additionally, this was not a group of classmates who were especially close in high school. We knew of each other but ran in different circles. Despite all of that, we felt compelled to reconnect and, along with spouses and significant others, that is what we did.

After a couple of very enjoyable dinners together, we decided to host a Cincinnati mini-reunion. We planned for a weekend prior to the 40-year class reunion and let the class know that anyone wanting to join us was welcome. We had a great time planning the event and an even better time once it arrived.

We were joined by out-of-town classmates Harry Bunn, Howard Danzig, Ron and Elaine Levin Unell, and Leslie Berger and his wife Judy. Again, those attending were not necessarily close in high school. Yet, we spent virtually an entire weekend together as if we were at a family reunion.

Ten classmates, each having led separate lives since graduation, yet each of us steeped in the culture of our class, our upbringing, and our times. Reconnecting was easy, valued, and nourishing. Our strong and cohesive background allowed us to fit into each other's lives again.

Hirsch gives an example of how culture works. He asks readers to picture a person walking down the street in Boston wearing a suit and carrying a briefcase, apparently a local businessman. The man stops someone and asks for directions to a certain building. The directions are provided with just a few words and motions.

Now picture a person walking down the same street in Boston, this time donned in tourist attire, carrying a street map, a camera hanging around his neck. Again, he stops someone to ask for directions. This time the directions are given with elaborate references to landmarks, street names, and other basic Boston information.

Why the difference? The direction-giver in the second case could not assume the tourist had the same background information about Boston as the local businessman, so he felt compelled to provide much more detailed explanations.

When classmates reconnect, we can assume common background information and, therefore, a strong and cohesive cultural base. This makes the conversation easy and the reconnection comfortable.

Our common culture predisposes us to remain close to each other after all these years.

Reason #7: Memories
Soda Fountains to Monkeys

On January 7, 2008, Sue Corman Slater posted a seemingly innocuous message to the Yahoo! Group. The subject was "Soda." The message read, "I have noticed that the same flavor of soda can taste different in different cities. I think it could be the water used in producing it. Diet lime Coke tasted different in Florida than it did here in St. Louis."

Don Pearline, who had once worked for Coca-Cola, responded with a technical explanation. One could not have predicted that those two messages would lead to January 2008 becoming one of our top messaging months with 626 postings. What caused this outpouring of sharing?

After a number of other messages about soda, including some about the old soda fountains, Tom Norman specifically mentioned the soda fountain at Glazer's Drug Store, a neighborhood establishment in University City. Tom's memory opened the flood gates. For the remainder of the month we shared memories of tonsils being removed, Elvis Presley, and local Department Stores (Famous-Barr, Stix Baer and Fuller, Scruggs Vandervoort and Barney; none of which still exist).

We remembered Smokey barbeque sauce at Redwood, carhops, and local five-and-dimes (Neisners, Newberry's, and Woolworth; none of which still exist).

Jukeboxes (E-7 for "Twistin' the Night Away"), Velvet Freeze ice cream, and "f'narking" at the big birdcage at the St. Louis Zoo (screaming "f'nark" near the birdcage sent all of the birds into a frenzy—we were very mature).

Doing somersaults and cartwheels (a number of 60+ year old classmates actually reported trying to do these when the topic came up, some successfully), Dean Martin and "That's Amore," downtown pool halls (losing money to Rudolph Wanderone, also known as New

York Fats and the inspiration for Jackie Gleason's role as Minnesota Fats), and the Forest Park Highlands Amusement Park.

In the midst of the flood of memories, Arleen White Bly broke in to report that she had heard our West Coast classmates were experiencing what was reported to be the "Storm of the Decade." While our concerns continued until we heard from all those classmates that they were safe, Arleen lightened the moment when she shared, "My son Brad lives in San Francisco and said he is rounding up two of every animal, but can't find a second platypus."

We remembered elementary schools, saving and redeeming Top Value and S&H Green Stamps, local bakeries (Komen's) and candy stores (Mavrakos), Fatman's shoeshine parlor, and Bounce-a-Bit Trampoline Park.

"Boy-girl" parties, *The Creature from the Black Lagoon*, hula hoops, The Riviera swimming pool, skating rinks, playgrounds, movie theaters (Varsity, Tivoli, Pageant, Ambassador, Victory, Beverly), the Olympic Drive-In Theater, double features, childhood friends, and friends lost.

Three classmates also remembered that they had pet monkeys while growing up. Soda fountains to monkeys—go figure.

It became clear through this very active messaging month that the outpouring of memories helped solidify our connectedness and, in fact, brought us closer together. The same thing occurs during reunions, mini-reunions, and anytime members of the class have an opportunity to share memories.

Research has shown that memories are associated with our emotions and, fortunately, pleasant emotions are usually remembered more reliably than unpleasant ones. Who would not want to recall events associated with times they enjoyed, especially if they could do it with the same people with whom they first made the memory?

Reason #6: Maturity
If I Only Knew Then What I Know Now

A group of St. Louis-based classmates has been getting together for dinner at a different local restaurant every couple of months since the 30-year reunion. Within this group resides the core of the wonderfully energetic committee that has planned our reunions and our shared birthday parties.

When Ann and I retired in 2001 and 2002, respectively, we began to visit St. Louis more frequently to see our daughter, Dana, and her husband, Vince, who had given us even more incentive to visit. Their first child, Jordan, was born on December 5, 2001.

On one St. Louis trip, we were visiting high school friends, Ron and Elaine Levin Unell. They told us the dinner group would be getting together while we would still be in town. We decided to go.

Ann and I showed up at The Cheshire Inn, an old high school haunt near Ann's girlhood home, expecting to sit with the Unells and to catch up with others who we had not seen for some time. We walked up to the long tables that had been assembled for the group and saw that all of the places were taken except for two pairs, but not together such that we could sit with Elaine and Ron, who had not yet arrived.

We walked around the tables introducing and reintroducing ourselves to classmates and significant others. Then we settled into our chairs. I found myself seated across from Maureen Wasserman.

Maureen and I had been classmates at Daniel Boone Elementary School, Brittany Junior High, and U City High School, and we had each been to all of the previous class reunions and our shared class 50th birthday party, but had likely not spoken 25 words to each other in all of that time. I am not sure of the reason for that—perhaps we just ran in different circles. Was there not the opportunity? Did I not look for the opportunity? Was I just too insecure to step outside of my comfort zone of friends?

Maureen Beth Wasserman

*"She who has patience shall have
what she will."*

I am ashamed to say that when I sat down across from Maureen that evening, I was playing old tapes in my head—we were not close during or after high school—we have nothing in common—it is going to be a long evening—what would we possibly talk about?

Three hours later, Maureen and I stopped talking and only did so because everyone else was getting up to leave. I found the conversation with her so compelling that I focused on her the entire evening.

Maureen had earned a BS in Secondary Education in Mathematics from the University of Missouri. Instead of going into teaching, she had become a program analyst for the Federal Reserve Bank. She had lived in Kansas City, Charleston (West Virginia), Chicago, and Phoenix before returning to St. Louis. Although Maureen was looking forward to even more travel because she had recently retired, she had already been to Mexico, Ireland, Scotland, Hawaii, and Nassau.

Twenty years earlier, Maureen had taken up painting and had become an active member and leader of the St. Louis Gateway Tole Society (tole painting is a decorative folk art on tin and wooden objects). She was also deeply interested in other crafts and hoping retirement would give her the time to further develop those talents as well.

As Ann and I drove home to Cincinnati, I reflected on my evening with Maureen Wasserman. If I am honest with myself, I would realize there was a time when I was immature enough that I would not have gone out of my way to talk to Maureen. I may have even gone out of my way not to talk to her. I would not have felt badly about that at the time, but I do now.

Maureen is an accomplished, energetic, interesting, engaging woman with one of the world's great smiles. I know that now but never gave myself a chance to know it earlier. During our conversation over dinner, I learned a lot about Maureen, but I learned more about myself.

Over four-plus decades, our class has collectively matured. Connections and even friendships are being made that would have seemed unlikely in our school years.

Thank you, Maureen, for being a great teacher. I look forward to that hug we have each time we get together. Maybe I am maturing—maybe our class is maturing—one would hope so—it is about time.

If I only knew then what I know now.

Reason #5: Happiness
The Happiness Trilogy

What is happiness? Poets, lyricists, philosophers, psychologists, Charles Schultz, and the rest of humanity have been trying to answer this question—forever.

"But what is happiness but the simple harmony between man and the life he leads?" Albert Camus

"Happiness belongs to the self-sufficient." Aristotle

"Happiness comes mainly from our own attitude, rather than from external factors. If your own mental attitude is correct, even if you remain in an hostile atmosphere, you feel happy." The Dalai Lama

"Independence is happiness." Susan B. Anthony

"Happiness is as a butterfly which, when pursued, is always beyond our grasp, but which if you will sit down quietly, may alight upon you." Nathaniel Hawthorne

"Happiness is nothing more than good health and bad memory." Albert Schweitzer

"Happiness is when what you think, what you say, and what you do are in harmony." Mohandas K. Gandhi

"Happiness is a warm puppy." Charles Schultz

Happiness will, and perhaps should, mean something different to each of us. I have found a happiness definition that makes sense to me. It applies to life in general, even though it was developed in a business context, referring to the happiness of a workforce and the positive effect that has on productivity.

Roger Martin is the dean of the Rotman School of Management at the University of Toronto. BusinessWeek has called Martin one of the ten most influential business professors in the world. In 2005, he wrote an article for the *Rotman Magazine* entitled, "The Power of Happiness." He lays out the case for why happy employees make productive employees and posits, "Nobody can tell a person that he or she is, or should be, happy. Happiness is an entirely subjective feeling of well-being."

Martin goes on to report that Tom Tyler, eminent social justice scholar, has shown, "Individuals develop their sense of identity from feeling pride in their place in their relevant community and respect for the stature of that community."

From these and other concepts, Martin developed his "Happiness Trilogy." Happiness, he argues, occurs when all three components of his model are in place—(1) when an individual is a valued member of a community (2) that is both valued by the individual and (3) valued by others outside the community.

There were some classmates who did not have a happy high school experience. However, the opportunity to be happy at U City in the early 60s was exemplary as measured by the three components of the "Happiness Trilogy." The school was valued by the local community and recognized by others as a benchmark of academic, athletic, and arts achievement. The student body valued the school and knew we were part of something special.

Importantly, we had every opportunity to be valued at the school, whether through academics, athletics, activities, or the arts. As students at University City High School in the early 1960s, we were valued members of a valued community.

We are also valued members of a valued community today. Classmates are treated with respect and, one might say, unconditional love. We value the group as a whole because it nurtures us and, when needed, supports us. And, as measured by my own experience, when we share how close our class is with those from other classes and other high schools, the response is consistent—one of surprise and longing for something similar for their class.

We had every right to be happy in high school and have every right to be happy now as we remain connected and valued members of a valued community.

Reason #4: Means/Mobility
Closed the Place Down

Using the Yahoo! Group, personal e-mails, and telephone calls to stay connected is wonderful. But none of those replace seeing each other face-to-face. Fortunately, many have the means and mobility to do so.

Five high school classmates, who had not all been together since high school 44 years earlier, met in Frisco, Colorado for a long weekend in June 2008. This was but one of the many U City '64 mini-reunions that take place frequently around the country.

Classmates Steve and Ilene Weinstein Novack live in Chicago most of the year but have a second home in Frisco. The Novacks invited the other classmates and their spouses for the long weekend.

The other classmates were Marc Tenzer, my stepbrother, Marc Golubock, my best friend growing up, and me. Marc and Elaine Tenzer live in St. Louis, Marc and Susan Golubock live in Phoenix, and Ann and I live in Cincinnati. On that weekend, we lived in Frisco.

Alan Spector, Marc Tenzer, Ilene Weinstein Novack, Steve Novack, Marc Golubock
on the Novack's back deck in Frisco, Colorado

Not only did the five classmates and respective spouses get together, but we actually lived in the same house for four days. A problem? No—it was as if we had been living together as family all these years. Our interests were diverse, prompting compelling conversation, but it was what we had in common that ruled the day.

We hiked and toured and ate and talked. Sports were definitely part of the conversation. Marc Golubock, Steve, and I were three of the four infielders on our high school varsity baseball team. Marc Tenzer and Steve played varsity high school basketball and went on to the University of Missouri-St. Louis (UMSL) to play college ball together.

We recalled a great experience when I was doing the play-by-play of basketball games for the school radio station at the University of Missouri-Rolla. Rolla played UMSL my senior year, giving me the opportunity to announce a game in which my two close high school friends were playing, albeit for the opposing team.

Just two weeks after we left Frisco and only a few miles down the road in Breckenridge, Colorado, there was another U City '64 mini-reunion. Classmate Marvin Tofle and his wife, Ruth, from Columbia, Missouri, and classmates Howard Danzig and his wife, Myrna, and Ellen Polinsky Cohen, living in St. Louis, visited Randy Goldenhersh over the fourth-of-July weekend.

At both Colorado mini-reunions, our shared school experience and culture made the weekends comfortable and energizing—not unlike when classmate Sue Corman Slater and her husband Larry went to Houston for a family bar mitzvah. Sue contacted Houston classmates, and they gathered at an Italian restaurant—Lenny and Dee Leabman Koblenz, Morrie and Nancy Rosenberg Mayer, and David and Suzie Nemon joined Sue and Larry (only Larry had not attended U City).

The class shared in the camaraderie of the evening when Sue later reported, "...we ate great Italian food, had wonderful conversations and everyone said they were glad that I had put it together. We would have sat in the restaurant until 1:00 in the morning talking, but the piano stopped playing, the violin played a goodnight song, the air conditioning was turned off, and the lights started dimming, so we closed the place down."

Frisco, Houston, Cincinnati, Croton-on-Hudson (New York), San Francisco, Breckenridge, New York City, Norwalk (Connecticut), Miami, Chicago, West Palm Beach, Winnipeg, Dana Point (California), Las Vegas, Davie (Florida), and other places have been the sites of University City High School Class of '64 mini-reunions. In St. Louis, it seems like anytime there is an out-of-towner coming in, someone gets the word out, and a mini-reunion is in the making.

Beginning on Labor Day 2008, face-to-face connections between reunions have no longer been limited to the regional get-togethers. Eleven classmates and nine significant others sailed out of New York City on what we referred to as the "first annual class cruise." We cruised to Saint John, New Brunswick and to Halifax, Nova Scotia and spent two days at sea. But it did not really matter where we went—what mattered was that we went there together. Someone said, "You could have put us in a row boat in the middle of the ocean, and we would have had a great time."

Cruisers traveled from Texas, Connecticut, Ohio, and Missouri. Some got to New York City early and went sightseeing together. Classmate Tim Arnold and his wife, Diane (U City '62), despite not being able to join us on the cruise, invited the group to their lovely home overlooking the Hudson River north of the city to spend the afternoon before we set sail.

On the ship, we partied, ate, danced, sang Karaoke, ate, attended shows, played bingo, ate, worked out in the gym, hit the casino, drank, relaxed in the hot tub, ate, went on excursions, and, oh, did I mention—ate. Despite all of these activities and more, what we did mostly was to hug and reminisce and laugh and cry and just enjoy being together.

As a bonus, we were contacted by the Associate Art Auctioneer on board and personally invited to a champagne art auction. Why the personal invitation? The ship staffer, Scott Pokres, received an e-mail from his mother, Ilene Sokolik Pokres, telling him to look for us. Ilene is a member of the University City High School Class of 1964—small world.

Another bonus class connection was made in Halifax. When we docked, Joanna Slotkin Baymiller called classmate Suzanne Biernbaum Funnell, who is an Associate Professor at the Nova Scotia College of Art & Design. They made the arrangements and a number of the cruisers spent time with Suzanne throughout the day. We added a Halifax mini-reunion to our cruise itinerary.

This was not the first Canadian mini-reunion. Don Platt, his wife, Michele, and their son, Nikita, were passing through Winnipeg, learned that Karen Paulsen Bauch lived there, and got in touch. Karen reported the Platts, "...came for supper...we didn't even know each other in high school, and probably don't even have all that much in common, but it didn't matter—we had so much fun."

Karen Ann Paulsen

*"Sunshine in her hair;
starlight in her eyes
and goodness in her heart."*

Karen is no stranger to mini-reunions. She and her husband, Richard, have gathered with classmates Jill Friedman Chapin, Marsha Weltman, Linda Thaw Kayland-Chretin, and Alan Resnick and their spouses in California; and classmates Mark Glickman, Judy Garber Ellsley, Barb Glick Koch, and me with our spouses in Davie, Florida. Living almost 100 miles north of the US border has not kept Karen separated from the class.

It is highly likely there will be other class cruises. We began making plans for future trips even before disembarking from this one. Ellen Polinsky Cohen captured how we all felt when she wrote upon returning home, "It will be hard to express this trip to anyone else; it was the feeling in the air."

These chances for classmates to reconnect around the country would not be possible were it not for the means and mobility many of us have. Discretionary travel was not an option for most of us when we were growing up. Our parents were in jobs that provided neither the income level nor vacation time needed to travel.

And travel was more difficult—cars were much less reliable and air travel was not as readily available. My first commercial plane trip was when I flew from St. Louis to Wilkes-Barre, Pennsylvania for my P&G company recruiting trip as a college junior. By contrast, our daughter, Dana, was on a plane before she was one. When she was six and Kevin was four, they flew together, but without us, from Cincinnati to St. Louis to be picked up by grandparents. Our grandson, Jacob, has been on four airplane trips before his first birthday, with his parents of course.

Our educations have generally allowed us to build careers that have given us the means to travel more readily than we could have imagined. It feels like nothing to get on an airplane or in a car and travel to a mini-reunion, reunion, or cruise.

At this stage in our lives, many of us are retired or in work situations that give us more time flexibility than when we were younger. For example, by the time of our Frisco, Colorado mini-reunion, Marc Golubock, Ilene, and I were retired. Steve did some work while in Colorado, but did so using his laptop and cell phone. Marc Tenzer owns his own business and was able to make arrangements to be gone even though he and Elaine would be traveling to Israel for ten days just a week later.

Also important, as Jill Friedman Chapin pointed out, it is easy to make mini-reunion arrangements through our Yahoo! Group and e-mail.

So, in general, we have the funds, the time, the availability of transportation, the ease of planning, and the physical capability. We have the means and mobility to stay close.

Reason #3: We Care
Stand Up Guy

Jerry Weiner is one of those people that you would be proud to call a friend. Why? Because Jerry unselfishly does what friends are supposed to do. And you do not even need to be his close friend to get special treatment.

On Sunday, December 10, 2006, our class received a message from Sue Corman Slater. Although Sue moved to another school district prior to graduation, she continues to feel an affinity for the U City Class of 1964, and we are glad to count her among our connected minions. Don Singer, Neal Harris, and Dee Leabman Koblenz are other examples of classmates who started with us at U City, who did not graduate with us, who declared themselves to still be part of the class, and who we still gladly call our own.

Sue is a remarkable woman. She is a travel agent and wedding planner who had been losing her sight for 25 years—she is now totally blind. Sue uses special software, a voice synthesizer, a Braille printer, and other technological aids. She manages the daily challenges of her business and life with the full support of her loving husband, Larry.

Her message, in part, read, "My son's wedding was last week in Marble Falls, Texas. We had my 86 year old mom with us. My mom started feeling bad and we took her to urgent care and she was taken by ambulance with pneumonia to the hospital in Austin, Texas, 90 minutes away. She has been in the hospital since then and I do not know how long I will be here. If I can get to Houston, I have my family there and I can stay with them while she is in rehab getting strong enough to fly back to St. Louis. Meanwhile, I am in a hotel room, which is a fortune. Taking her by ambulance to Houston would cost ten thousand dollars. I sure could use some help. Thanks for any suggestions."

Her classmates went into action. Within the day, the following took place.

Carol Enger Canis (St. Louis, Missouri) wrote reminding the class that we had only recently contributed to help another classmate who needed some support and asking should we not do the same here.

Alan Resnick (Culver City, California) wrote he recalled Tim Arnold, who coordinated the previous collection, had indicated there were funds remaining.

This is where Jerry Weiner, who lives in Austin, got involved. Jerry called Sue and provided a detailed report to the class about her status and needs. He established himself as the class's point of contact and proceeded to coordinate the activities in Austin.

Tim (Croton-on-Hudson, New York) confirmed that there were funds available and wrote, "Of course we're there for Sue best we can be. Jerry, thanks for being a stand up guy."

Jerry shared Sue's mother's name, provided to him by Janice Goldberg White (Saranac Lake, New York) and the address of the medical center.

Carol wrote, "Les (Les Berger, St. Louis) just called me and he said he will take over and send the checks to Sue as they come in. Jerry Weiner is there in Austin doing what he can do to help. This is starting to feel like a Christmas/Chanukah story of Good Will. I think the class of 1964 is amazing. I will send a check to Les and others have e-mailed me, personally, that they would help."

Les reported that a committee has been active to deal with this type of classmate need and will work together to help. They are Arleen Inger (Cincinnati), Paula Glovinsky Sigel (St. Louis), Ellen Smith Rich (Dallas), and Tim Arnold.

The following morning Jerry Weiner wrote, "I don't know what Sue needs most from us now. Moral support from us might be high on her needs list. She has lodgings, a friend to drive her around, medical care for her mother, kinfolk standing by in Houston, a sensible plan, and high morale. She has me to call for backup and assistance, 24-7. I first met Sue at a party at her house. She was totally gracious and charming. Now she needs a friend in Austin, and here I am."

One day later, Jerry wrote, "Today I visited Sue at St. David's Hospital...I treated Sue to a lavish lunch at one of Austin's best neighborhood restaurants...the effect on her morale was uplifting and our conversation turned light-hearted. Sue is facing the challenge with strength and courage and a reasonable plan of action. Thankfully she is not facing it alone."

Less than a month later, on January 2, 2007, Jerry Weiner wrote,

"My sympathy goes out to Sue Corman Slater...on the death of (her) mother."

Tim was right. Jerry is a stand up guy. And the University City Class of 1964 is a stand up group.

On July 9, 2007, after sending a very gracious and lengthy thank you to the class earlier in the year, Sue wrote, "I have just finished paying back the money into the U City class of 64 fund. I just want to let everyone know how much your support and words of comfort meant to me while I was in Austin and Houston. The money really helped me out with all of the unexpected expenses I had then. Again, thank you so much. I am so lucky to be a part of such a caring and loving group of people!"

Classmate Janice Goldberg White captured it when she said simply, but profoundly, "We are us and we care about each other."

Reason #2: Personal Initiative
Shapes in the Clouds

We grew up on the playgrounds, in the streets, on the ball fields, in the front yards, and in the back alleys of University City. While we had some organized activities, our primary source of amusement was each other. Each of us was within walking distance of a local playground and within biking distance of many more. Importantly, it was a time when parents sent us out to play; by ourselves; all day. The result is that we learned to create, to play together, to manage without adults and without prescribed rules—we learned to take initiative at an early age.

As I wrote in my first book, *Baseball: Never Too Old to Play "The" Game*, "Being happily within walking distance of school playgrounds and parks with baseball diamonds, even before age seven we were beginning to meet friends to play. Throughout our youth, the neighborhood boys and I spent all day, every possible day, when weather permitted and sometimes when it did not, playing some game with a bat and ball. Sometimes we made it home for lunch; we were typically late for dinner. Regrettably, it is different today but, thankfully, our parents were not concerned for our safety when we left the house in the morning with a bat over our shoulder, our glove dangling from our bike or belt, and a ball stuffed into a pocket or the bike's saddle bags (yes, we really did have saddle bags).

"On the way to the playground or park, we stopped at the homes of the usual suspects and accumulated players on the way. When we got to the park, we would discover who else came from other neighborhoods and count noses. Depending on the number of players, we would decide what game to play. Seldom did we have enough for two full nine-man teams. But if we were close, say seven on seven, we could adjust and play a full game of baseball. Two outfielders versus three and the at-bat team providing the catcher would suffice.

"If we did not have enough for two 'full' teams, we would start playing Indian ball, rounds, hit the bat, step ball, wall ball, run-down, bottle cap ball, cork ball, or other games. Then, on no particular schedule, we would change games throughout the day just for variety or because the number of players changed as kids came and went."

For me, the game frequently had a bat and ball involved, but activities were diverse and carefree. There were games of tag and hide-and-go-seek that were played over four square blocks. There was lying on our backs on hot summer St. Louis days sucking on popsicles and finding shapes of animals or castles or cartoon characters or whatever in the clouds. There was playing hopscotch and swinging as high as we could on the playground equipment trying to go all the way over the top.

The choices were endless, and we were making the choices. It took our personal initiative to collect our friends, pick an activity, decide on the rules, pick the teams, referee the game, change activities throughout the day, deal with injured playmates, compromise when there were arguments, get back home in time, and get up the next day to do it all over again.

It took that same personal initiative to go off to college, to build families and careers, and to take the steps to connect and reconnect with classmates. Leslie Berger took the initiative to begin the Yahoo! Group. Mickey Leon Sandmel took the initiative to lead reunion planning. Tim Arnold took the initiative to create a video of our time in the 60s for our 20-year reunion and Morrie Mayer did the same to create the DVD for our 40th. It took personal initiative for the group of classmates in Cincinnati to plan a mini-reunion and invite classmates to join us for a weekend. It takes initiative for Jill Friedman Chapin to care deeply about social issues and share her thoughts with the class and for Alan Resnick to do the same on political issues.

The list goes on. Every day, someone takes the personal initiative he or she developed so many years ago and reaches out to classmates.

Reason #1: Pride
Where Did You Go to High School?

The high school reunion is at the primal core of connectedness. Some classes have reunions every five years; some, like ours, every ten. Some are skipped because there is no one willing to take on the planning role. Some classes never have reunions.

My friend, Mary Carlson, Rossford High School class of 1965, comes from a small school (graduating classes between 50 and 125) in a small town (Rossford, Ohio—population around 3000 in 1965). For the first 30 years after graduation, her class held reunions every five years. Because of dwindling attendance, they decided to join with every Rossford class that graduated in the 1960s to combine reunions. The first of these multi-graduating-year events drew upwards of 300 alumni.

In general, classes find times and places to come together on some regular basis, reintroducing people to their school, their classmates, and the pride they have in each.

In *Baseball: Never Too Old to Play "The" Game*, I wrote, "...St. Louis, a city in which one is identified by his or her high school. Here is a typical conversation between two people who meet and discover they both grew up in St. Louis.

'Where are you from?'

'I live in Boston now, but I grew up in St. Louis.'

'Me too, but I live in Cincinnati now.'

'That's great, where did you go to high school?'"

The Beach Boys rallied our generation around our respective schools when they recorded "Be True to Your School" in September 1963. The song opened,

> *When some loud braggart tries to put you down*
> *And says his school is great*
> *I tell him right away*

Now what's the matter buddy
Ain't you heard of my school
It's number one in the state
(Hey, hey Take It Away! Get that ball and Fight!)

So be true to your school
Just like you would to your girl or guy
Be true to your school now
And let your colors fly
Be true to your school

For our 40-year reunion, Elaine Levin Unell wrote the poem, "Where Did You Go...?" She captured the essence of the pride we have for our school, for our class, and of our coming together.

Young lives touch, mingle
Gather in circles under a clock
Share joys, sorrows, news of the day
Pass each other in halls
Sit and study together in classrooms
Watch and participate
In sports, plays, dances
Share an impressionable time of life

Wonder, doubt, excitement, fear
Determination, anxiety, love, pain
Togetherness, loneliness, friendship, abandonment
Strength, weakness, pride, arrogance
Confidence, insecurity, hope
Spirit, esteem, POTENTIAL
Little did we know the relevance
Of emotions and experiences shared

Forty years later
Separated by miles, time, direction, life
We are drawn together by a unique bond
Details and issues of the past are blurred and faded
But a feeling from deep within our souls stirs
A kinship with those who can answer
That oft teased "typical St. Louis" question,

"Where did you go to high school?"
Aren't you proud to answer?

"University City High, 1964"

We were and are proud and happy to be members of the University City High School Class of 1964. We have the technology, a strong common culture, the means and mobility, and the maturity to easily connect with classmates. We value our memories and take the initiative to stay connected so we can happily share them together. We care about each other in a profound way. Our high school experience and the times and place in which we grew up predisposed us to seek each other out and remain committed to each other four-plus decades later.

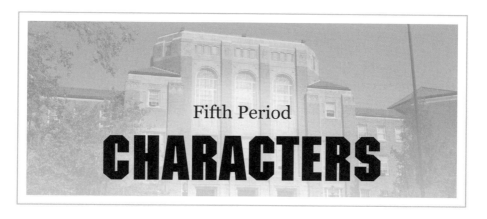

Fifth Period
CHARACTERS

"What you leave behind is not what is engraved into stone monuments, but what is woven into the lives of others."

Pericles

"Praising what is lost makes the remembrance dear."

William Shakespeare

Marla Faye Schukar

"Friends mean a fortune; meet a millionaire."

Mark: *"You mentioned Terry Mitze—I saw him right before I ran into you all. He didn't look well."*

Anne: *"I hope he's OK. He is one of the truly memorable characters of the class; one of a long list."*

Mark: *"You can think about characters in a lot of ways—the funny ones, like Tofle, Danzig, and Rathert. We had our share."*

Steve: *"There are those who exhibited character—as you said, '...a long list...'"*

Marla: *"And there are the characters who help keep us together in special ways, like Mickey, Les, Elaine, and Ron. And you,*

Judy. You've been deeply involved in reunion planning. Thanks for handling all of the money to help make this happen."

Judy: *"A labor of love."*

Steve: *"When I think about class characters, I can't help but think about all of those we've lost along the way—Joe Oshins and Bill Fuchs and Sheila Arnold and Vicky Sleator and so many others. I remember Ellen Glazer—when we were in the sixth grade, she was picked first for every sports team, even before the boys. That girl could play!"*

Anne: *"The list is too long, but I guess that's how this whole thing works."*

Mark: *"Marla, I remember your brother, Steve. He was the freest spirit I've ever known and was the spirit of our class. We loved him."*

Judy: *"Amen to that."*

Marla: *"Thank you. You know Steve and Terry were very close— maybe Mitze will meet me under the clock."*

Contribution and Leadership

Identify any random group of 600 high school graduates from across the country and across the years. When they are in their early 60s, try to select a few who accurately represent the entire group.

Your task would be nearly impossible—each of the 600 would have gone on from high school to different colleges or not have gone at all; to different careers or none at all; to different branches of the military or not at all; to different geographies. They would have built different families or none at all; would have traveled around the world, around the country, or around their hometown; and would have been influenced by friends, family, religious beliefs, public figures, culture, personal experiences, and historical events. They would have followed different life plans or no plans at all. They would have made their luck or had none at all. They would have remained healthy or had either minor or major health issues. Some would be living long lives—some would have already died.

To make your selection of group representatives a little easier, limit the 600 graduates to being from the same high school, one with a relatively homogeneous population and from a relatively strong and shared culture, and from the same year. While this group would have much more in common than the first more random group, all of the diverse influences that affected their lives after high school would still apply.

This was my dilemma as I set out to choose high school classmates who would appropriately represent the University City High School Class of 1964. How did I select those people whose profiles you are about to experience? I further simplified the selection criteria—choosing classmates based solely on their contribution to, and leadership in, helping the rest of us stay connected.

Here are the stories of Michele "Mickey" Leon Sandmel, Leslie Berger, Elaine Levin Unell, and Ron Unell.

Mickey
Nothing's Stopping Me

Michele Leon

*"Laughter, like time,
has no limits."*

After graduation, the closeness of any high school class is, in many ways, defined by its reunions. The energy created at these relatively infrequent events is a major determinant as to how intensely a class will stay connected between reunions.

For the University City Class of 1964, our reunions and our shared birthday parties have been immaculately planned, precisely executed, well attended, dynamic, loving, and just plain fun. While the collective spirit of the class at large has a lot to do with the success of reunions, it also takes a dedicated committee to make the event happen.

Class spirit—necessary; dedicated committee—necessary; however, whether in a business, volunteer organization, or sports team, or any time a group of people come together to get something done, the key to success is leadership.

Michele "Mickey" Leon Sandmel is our leader.

Unlike many who moved into the community later, Mickey attended University City Schools all the way from kindergarten through high school graduation. She was born Michele Liebowitz, but her family changed their name to Leon when she was one. Born in the city of St. Louis only a couple of miles from what would become the site of the St. Louis arch, Mickey moved with her family the 12 miles to U City when she was five. She now lives in Chesterfield, a St. Louis suburb, 25 miles and a lifetime from the inner city.

In U City, she lived on Seville, a street parallel to Fullerton, where I grew up. Our backyards shared an alley only a few houses apart. Recall when I moved there in the third grade, we encountered a farm, horses, unpaved streets, and a lack of sidewalks. Mickey got there three years before I did, when our elementary school, Daniel Boone, had yet to be built and her street was a dead end—it was opened by the time I showed up.

Mickey's mother still lives in the house on Seville almost six decades later. Unfortunately, Mickey lost her father 25 years ago. She has fond memories of her dad. He was a baseball fan, who loved the Cardinals and instilled a love of the game in Mickey, who passed it along to her children. She and her oldest son, Ben, attended opening day Cardinals' games for years.

Her father was a traveling salesman throughout Southern Missouri, Southern Illinois, and Northern Arkansas, selling what are called "shoe findings." As Mickey describes it, "He sold everything about shoes except the shoes themselves."

The Liebowitz/Leon family journey that brought Mickey to University City is another example of the many disparate family stories that created our high school class. Mickey's dad went to school in Detroit and was a salesman for a number of companies before settling in St. Louis. Her mom grew up and went to high school in Los Angeles. Their migration brought Mickey to our high school class and to reunion planning leadership. And we are the better for both.

Mickey's parents were not supportive of her continuing education after high school. She nevertheless acquired a passion for education that has been a core principle of her life. I would like to think the educational environment at the University City schools served to nurture her passion.

She began night classes at the University of Missouri-St. Louis just after high school graduation. When Shelley, her husband, was stationed at Fort Riley, Kansas and then deployed to Vietnam, Mickey stayed and took classes at Kansas State while working for a university professor. When Shelley was discharged, they returned to St. Louis where Mickey completed her degree. While it took 11 years, Mickey earned her degree in Sociology from the University of Missouri-St. Louis. Throughout her extended college career, Mickey continued to work full or part time. Her personal motto was and is, "Nothing's stopping me."

Shelley (U City '59) and Mickey reared three strong, independent children, each of whom, not surprisingly, is well educated. Ben has a Masters in Sports Management from Western Illinois. Karin did her undergraduate work at the University of Tulsa and received her Masters from Harvard and her PhD in Special Education from Vanderbilt. Josh, the youngest, attained his degree in Culinary Arts Management from UNLV.

After the children left the nest well prepared for life, Mickey's passion took her back to the classroom as a student and a teacher. She takes every class she can find time for and studied Russian, Spanish, and Cooking. Because she missed her Bat Mitzvah as a young teenager, Mickey decided to study Hebrew and, in her 50s, went through the ceremony with grade-school friend and classmate, Sharon Broad Safron.

Mickey has aspirations of returning to the University of Missouri-St. Louis to seek her Masters in an English-as-a-Second-Language (ESL) program. Her interest derives from her family having housed foreign exchange students and from Mickey's evening volunteer work as an ESL teacher in her local school district. She has also attained her certification as a substitute teacher and is often called by the school district to fill in, somehow managing to do all of this while still working a full schedule.

Unfortunately, Mickey's time over the years has not all been spent on her labors of love, her family, her work, her education, and her volunteer efforts. She has struggled through some very serious health issues, including major operations and emergency room visits, one which Mickey refers to as "a real *ER* experience."

Thankfully, with everything else Mickey has accomplished and dealt with, she has found the time to offer herself to her classmates as well. We see Mickey as the person who is singly most responsible for the success of our reunions. She modestly tells the story differently, attributing the success of the events to dedicated committee members and to those classmates who have attended. But we all know better. Sure, others help. But Mickey's willingness and energy to take the lead is what really makes everything happen.

She does not do it for the glory, although we are glad to heap that upon her. She does it because she loves it. She enjoys doing what she calls "big things" and seeing something "come out of the chaos." Mickey sees her reunion planning leadership as an opportunity to reconnect and, frequently, to connect for the first time with interesting classmates with whom she shares the common bonds of high school.

Before our 40-year reunion, she and committee-member Kay Kruvand Watts personally called everyone for whom they had contact information, about 90% of nearly 600 classmates. These conversations and connecting at the reunions are, in large part, what keeps Mickey going. She is a people person who says the connections are her "opportunity to meet and talk to so many cool people."

Michele Leon Sandmel values her family, education, doing big things, and the traditions of our high school class. And we value her. Her values are emblematic of our generation, our culture, and our class. She represents who we are and leads us when we need it most.

Nothing is stopping her.

Leslie
Never Hide Your Light

Leslie Berger

*"Sincerity and truth are the basis
for every virtue."*

Les Berger had a pleasant enough elementary school experience. He transferred to Daniel Boone School in the third grade when his family moved from the city of St. Louis to their home on Trenton Avenue in University City. Les was an only child, but was surrounded in both of his childhood neighborhoods by those who would become high school classmates. In St. Louis, neighbors included future classmates Don Pearline and Andrea Kolker. In University City, neighbors were Steve Novack, Mike Resnick, Jackie Weinreb, Sharon Broad, Ellen Glazer, Maureen Wasserman, Dan Martorelli, and again, Andrea Kolker.

His school experience turned sour, however, when Les moved on from Daniel Boone to Brittany Junior High School. He has two distinct, both unhappy, memories of Brittany. One is that his now-good friend Alan Resnick beat him up in junior high. Neither recalls the reason for the beating, although Les sarcastically says today it happened because, "Alan was a schmuck, and I say that with all the love in my heart."

He recalls the only satisfaction he got from the incident was that Alan broke his thumb on Les's head.

The other junior high memory made him feel "out of place." He vividly remembers being called hurtful names and feeling so badly about it that he would run home after school, hide in his room, and cry. These feelings served to shape his high school experience as well. While he heard the names less frequently, Les Berger did not feel good about high school. In fact, his exact words are, "I hated high school."

On his 16th birthday, Les got his first car and used it to "escape" by spending more time with students from neighboring high schools with whom he was more comfortable.

Les was not voted the 1964 University City senior most likely to succeed, most popular, or most anything. And, now in his 60s, Leslie is an average-looking not-in-your-face kind of guy, who carries a lot of weight and has been slowed by two strokes.

So why select Leslie Berger to profile in this section of the book? Simple—if there were a vote today, he would be among the most beloved members of the U City class of 1964. And, importantly, he no longer needs to escape. In fact, he sincerely loves the class as a whole and the classmates as individuals. Leslie Berger is, in many ways, the glue that holds us together.

His journey from escapee to trustee began when a number of life challenges confronted Leslie about the same time. In 2002, he suffered a heart attack and his first stroke, which affected his gait and severely limited his eyesight. Among other issues, he was neither able to drive nor to work—Leslie retired.

Just two months later, Leslie's mother passed away, his father having passed away in 1965. Perhaps you noted that I began this section referring to him as Les and now as Leslie. Throughout his school life, we called him Les—that is how we knew him. However, his mother called him Leslie. When she died, in her honor, he asked to be called Leslie. The transition is by no means complete, but we are trying.

Having been limited by the stroke and having lost his mom, Leslie found two things to be true. One was that he was spending many hours in front of the computer, as he had little else to do.

Leslie had been involved with computers when many of us had yet to hear of them. As Leslie's son was growing up, Eric had an innate interest in computers, so Leslie and he would spend hours together tearing apart and rebuilding hardware and understanding software. Leslie notes that the computer-based relationship worked until Eric was about ten, when he flew by Leslie in knowledge and interest and has not looked back since. Eric refers to his dad as the "glitch between the seat and the keyboard." He also says that his dad frequently gets the "ID-Ten-T" error message, which spelled out is I-D-I-O-T. For us, Leslie's computer skills are just fine.

The other truth was that, despite the support he received from Judy, Leslie's love-of-his-life wife, and their children, Michael and Eric, Leslie felt "lonely." He felt a need for a greater belonging.

A classmate friend urged him to "just put yourself out there" to get more connected with other classmates. Leslie, despite the memories of his school experience, counted on the common history and culture from which the class came and said to himself, "Why not?"

He had some previous experience with web-based discussion groups and decided to begin one to bring the class closer together. In large part, the Yahoo! Group was also about bringing Leslie closer to the class from which he had been estranged—that is exactly what has happened.

An indication of how we value Leslie and all the things he does to bring us together was a moving incident at our 40-year reunion. Ron and Elaine Levin Unell, the master/mistress of ceremonies, were giving out token gifts to thank all of those who helped make the weekend possible. All involved were recognized with meaningful applause. When Leslie's name was announced and as he slowly walked to the front of the room, those gathered, more than 200 of his classmates and many significant others, rose spontaneously and gave him an extended standing ovation. Leslie describes this moment of moments with deep emotion and the hint of tears.

Leslie's first-generation-American father was an entrepreneur, owning several businesses at the same time, a salvage/auto parts yard, a plumbing supply store, a steel/iron distribution company, and a trucking company. Leslie followed in his father's entrepreneurial footsteps as he held a number of jobs over the years, including working for himself and developing his own businesses. This was after he went to college in St. Louis for a semester, discovered he was only there because it seemed like the right next thing to do, and came to the conclusion he cared little for book education. Leslie has been one to learn more from life's lessons and from mentors along the way.

An early job was with a construction company that was building Mansion House, an upscale apartment building in downtown St. Louis. Leslie was helping surveyors lay out the site, when one day he stepped into a mud hole up to his knees. Because of the consistency of the mud, the only way they could get him out was to use a crane, strap him to a harness, and pull slowly. He believes that one of his work boots is still buried under Mansion House.

Leslie immediately told his boss that he was done with outdoor work and asked if there was a job for him inside. When the boss learned that Leslie had taken some engineering drawing courses in high school, he assigned Leslie to help the engineers document their designs. After only a few days, Leslie found the process by which the engineers were completing drawings, getting them to the home office, and accessing them to be very cumbersome.

He recommended a more efficient process that was immediately accepted. The boss was so pleased after seeing the new process operate simply and effectively, he awarded Leslie a $50 bonus—not bad for someone making $60 per week. Upon handing him the bonus check, the boss told Leslie he was a great example of a favorite saying, "Don't hide your light under a basket." Leslie has remembered that saying and life lesson to this day.

Leslie met Judy Goldberg in the mid 1960s through classmate and friend Don Pearline. Don's girlfriend brought Judy along on a visit to Don's house when Leslie was there. After Don's girlfriend and Judy left, Leslie turned to Don and said, "I'm going to marry her."

It took some time for Leslie to convince Judy to even go out with him. When she finally agreed to a first date, he went to her house to pick her up. Judy introduced her mother to Leslie, who, even though he was meeting Mrs. Goldberg for the first time, responded, "Hi, Mom. Get used to me calling you that. I'm going to marry your daughter."

Leslie has now called her "Mom" for more than four decades.

Judy continues to work at a long, successful career with the Special School District in St. Louis. She is at all of our events, somewhat because she is Leslie's driver, but mostly because we love it when she is there.

She has also traveled extensively with Leslie, who does more for the class than administer our Yahoo! Group. Judy and he travel the country seeing classmates and prompting mini-reunions. They have been to several places in California, staying once with Alan Resnick (the guy who beat him up in junior high) and once with Judy Elbom Cameron. This visit prompted a large West Coast reunion. They have visited with Kay Rudolph in Chicago, with Ronnie Blumoff in San Antonio, with Marshall Faintich in Nellysford, Virginia. They joined the Las Vegas get-together and drove from St. Louis to join us at our Cincinnati mini-reunion. And the list goes on.

Leslie is not content to rest on his laurels or to accept the current level of connectedness of the class. He envisions and is working toward a time when every classmate is connected in some way. He is making personal contact with as many classmates as he can to encourage their participation. He is promoting mini-reunions, fostering the newly developed tradition of class cruises, and constantly looking for ways to even further energize and grow our electronic community. Leslie also took the lead to plan a 45-year reunion, the first of every five-year versus 10-year events.

Starting out with a poor school experience has not stood in the way of Leslie Berger being an important character in the University City Class of 1964. Despite Eric's derision of his dad's computer literacy, we know that Leslie has used his computer skills along with his vision, initiative, and persistence to make a difference in our lives.

He is definitely not one to hide his light under a basket.

Elaine and Ron
It's the High School Thing

Elaine Sue Levin

*"An effervescent personality
Bubbling from a stream of
friendship and happiness."*

Among those who married within the class are Ilene Weinstein and Steve Novack, Marsha Ahmann and David Arthur, Joyce Arky and Tom Lewin, and Nancy Rosenberg and Morrie Mayer. These couples found each other in high school.

Another of our married classmate couples took almost three decades after high school graduation and part of a lifetime of personal growth and learning to find each other. They then took another two years to figure out they should be, could be, and would be life partners.

Elaine Levin was born in University City and lived in the same home throughout her school life. Ron Unell was born in the city of St. Louis and, unlike virtually all of his classmates, never actually lived in University City. When Ron was in the fifth grade, his family moved to a corner of the community of Vinita Park, which was close enough to U City's Daniel Boone Elementary School for him to be assigned there.

After attending different junior high schools, Elaine's and Ron's lives finally converged at U City High. Both of them refer to their high school experience as being social. Ron did well academically, but most of his memories are of very close friends, a wide circle of good friends, social events, and sports—he played sophomore baseball and varsity golf. Elaine feels that "at some point I absorbed some education," but also mostly remembers the social part of high school. Looking back, Elaine is astonished that her mother allowed her to go out so much, stay out so late, and even do so on weeknights. Her high school diary is replete with the names of boys who called and asked her out. Unfortunately, Ron was not one of them.

While Elaine and Ron shared friends and knew each other in high school, they were not close. Each then went on to attend and earn their degrees from the University of Missouri, where they also did not connect. Only later were they surprised to discover that for two of their four years at Mizzou, they had lived in the same apartment complex.

Elaine earned her undergraduate degree in elementary education while Ron's degree was in accounting. Both went on to professions for which they had studied. Elaine, who later earned her Masters, became a kindergarten teacher; taught at one school for several years; took a year hiatus to reassess her career choice; rededicated herself to teaching; and changed to a new school district, where she taught kindergarten, first grade, and, ultimately, her school's gifted program. During her 33-year career, Elaine's only time off from teaching, other than her one-year hiatus, was maternity leave for the birth of each of her two daughters, Angela and Robin. Elaine retired in 2002.

Ron began working with a Big-8 accounting firm, decided corporate politics were not for him, moved to a small firm, decided that working for someone else was not for him, hung out his own shingle, and successfully grew his firm for 30 years. He enjoyed every day at work as he built and nurtured personal relationships with his clients, some of whom were high school classmates. Ron retired in 2008.

Along with attending U City High and Mizzou and living in the same apartment complex for two years, there were two other things Elaine and Ron had in common that turned out to be important to bringing them together in 1991. They had both married and divorced, and both were very good friends with high school classmate Phil Kogan.

Elaine married at the age of 24 and thought she was in love, but found that she and her husband did not share the same basic values. She hoped that as the marriage matured, these values would come together, but that was not to be. Elaine was very unhappy. It was at this point she was fortunate to receive some insightful and timely advice from an unexpected source, the first of two such times this would occur on her path to find her real life partner.

Elaine's daughter, Angela, had a friend whose mother had been divorced. Elaine had the foresight to ask the mother how she knew it had been time to make the big decision to seek the divorce. The woman told Elaine, "When you feel more alone together than when you are by yourself."

Elaine could relate to the advice and took action. Her marriage, which had lasted ten years, was over.

Ron married his high school sweetheart, who he met on a train ride to a Jewish youth group convention in Kansas City. Over the 23 years of their marriage, they grew apart because, Ron believes, they became different people than the ones who had fallen in young love. The marital problems were particularly devastating for Ron, who felt so emotionally oppressed he was hospitalized for five weeks. He came out of the hospital feeling better and stronger and, at age 44, moved out of his family home and in with his father and stepmother until his divorce was final a few months later.

About that time, Elaine was spending time with good friend Phil Kogan, who was between marriages. Phil would occasionally baby sit with Elaine's daughters when she went out on dates. When Elaine would return from such an evening, Phil, who owned a printing business, would greet her with, "Well should I start printing wedding invitations?"

But none of Elaine's dates had led anywhere near to a yes answer to that question.

It was Phil who told Elaine that Ron Unell had recently been divorced and asked if she would like Ron to call her. She said sure, if he wanted to. Phil let Ron know, and he called the next day.

Ron came to pick Elaine up for their first date. He had not seen her since high school where they had not been close, so he was pleasantly surprised when Elaine opened the door and greeted him with a big warm hug. Elaine says that the hug was spontaneous, like greeting any of her old high school acquaintances. It was an immediate feeling of the warmth and bond of a shared past. She now refers to the moment as, "It's the high school thing."

When Ron dropped Elaine off later that evening, he walked back to the car thinking, "I could be married to her—this could work."

They dated steadily for more than a year, but Elaine found herself not feeling as strongly about Ron as she thought she should. Despite a healthy degree of skepticism, Elaine occasionally visited psychics. One of them provided Elaine with her second unexpected piece of insightful and timely advice. The psychic told Elaine that she was resisting letting a special someone into her life because of past "losses and hurtful experiences." She suggested that the next time Elaine was with this someone, she should say to herself, "I will not accept these fears."

Elaine did just that and found a weight lifted. Her feelings deepened, and classmates Elaine Levin and Ron Unell were engaged several months later—any skepticism regarding psychics was gone.

Ron and Elaine are convinced that Phil Kogan, who passed away not long after their wedding, stayed alive long enough to give his friends a lasting gift—each other. Oh, and by the way, Phil printed their wedding invitations.

Ronald E. Unell

"For this is wisdom;
to love, to live
To take what Fate
could possibly give."

Elaine and Ron have become active members of the reunion planning committee and the official mistress and master of ceremonies for the formal program at the 30-year and 40-year reunions.

They have the ability to command everyone's attention while not detracting from the focus of the event; are entertaining without being the center of attention; and add to the comfortable and warm feeling while also keeping the program running like clockwork. In general, the Unells bring balance to the reunions in the same way they bring balance to their lives and to the lives of those who know them.

The Unells, however, are much more to the class than planning committee members and mistress/master of ceremonies. They have attended regional mini-reunions, went on the "first annual class cruise," go to virtually every dinner with the St. Louis group that gets together every couple of months, and are frequent contributors to the class Yahoo! Group (well, Elaine is—maybe now that Ron is retired, he will be as well).

It is clear that Elaine and Ron have found their life partners. They are bonded by love, caring for their blended family, a large group of special friends, and their commitment to our high school class. Perhaps they are also bonded by the most important thing—golf. Elaine began playing after marrying Ron. They are, to put it mildly, fanatics. They are on the golf courses in St. Louis every chance they get and travel with their clubs, playing around the country.

Regardless of what bonds them together, the University City High School Class of 1964 is more tightly bonded because of Elaine and Ron Unell.

It's the high school thing.

Soul-Shards

Phil Kogan

"His worth is warrant for his welcome."

In his book, *I Am A Strange Loop*, Douglas Hofstadter describes a conversation with his mother as she was holding a picture of his father, who had passed away 15 years earlier. In despair, Hofstadter's mother decried the lack of meaning of the photograph—it was only "a flat piece of paper with dark spots on it here and there."

Hofstadter thought for awhile and then said, "In the living room we have a book of the Chopin etudes for piano. All of its pages are just pieces of paper with dark marks on them, just as two-dimensional and flat and foldable as the photograph of Dad—and yet, think of the powerful effect that they have had on people all over the world for 150 years now."

He further explained that the sheet music has, over the years, given untold thousands "partial access...to the experience of living inside the head, or rather the soul, of Frederic Chopin.

"The marks on those sheets of paper are no less than soul-shards, scattered remnants of the shattered soul of Frederic Chopin. Each of those strange geometries of notes has a unique power to bring back to life, inside our brains, some tiny fragment of the internal experiences of another human being—his sufferings, his joys, his deepest passions and tensions—and we thereby know, at least in part, what it was like to be that human being, and many people feel intense love for him. In just as potent a fashion, looking at the photograph of Dad brings back, to us who knew him intimately, the clearest memory of his smile and his gentleness, activates inside our living brains some of the most central representations of him that survive in us, makes little fragments of his soul dance again, but in the medium of brains other than his own. Like the score to a Chopin etude, that photograph is a soul-shard of someone departed, and it is something we should cherish as long as we live."

We have lost an ever-increasing number of classmates, each of them characters that walked the halls of University City High School in the early 1960s and who have left behind soul-shards for us to cherish as long as we live.

M. J.
Lest We Forget

M. J. Savoy

"There is no man but may make his own paradise."

At a time when most of us were in the middle of our college careers and beginning to form a vision of our futures, classmate M.J. Savoy was deployed to Vietnam. He went for the shortest of tours; killed in a mysterious plane crash on his first day. M.J.'s body was never recovered. MIA means something.

Classmate David Pactor wrote to me, "MJ was a quiet boy, not active in sports or clubs or groups or cliques. He was a quiet boy in a noisy school. He did not stand out in school—perhaps he will stand out now in your book. Perhaps we can remember him now. A son and a friend and a soldier taken away never to be returned for a decent burial. It saddens me greatly to recall his short life."

David continued, "As a tribute, I went to the Vietnam Wall, traced his name, and gave the framed piece to the high school as a remembrance, lest we forget and not thank him and acknowledge him for this sacrifice."

David captured how we feel about M.J. But, perhaps no words can tell M.J.'s all-too-brief story more simply and profoundly than those that appear on the Vietnam Memorial Website.

M J SAVOY

AN - E3 - Navy - Reserve

Length of service 0 years
His tour began on Jun 17, 1966
Casualty was on Jun 17, 1966
In OFFSHORE, MILITARY REGION 2, SOUTH VIETNAM
Non-Hostile, died missing, FIXED WING - CREW
AIR LOSS, CRASH AT SEA
Body was not recovered

Panel 08E - Line 58

Neal
Lift My Spirit

Hyman Neal Harris

"Happiness is not a station you arrive at, but a manner of traveling."

Hyman Neal Harris was neither the most active nor most athletic member of our high school class. If fact, he did not actually graduate with us. Hy, as he was known in high school, was a few credits short and finished his degree later to graduate with the class of 1965.

Yet Neal, as he preferred to be known more recently, in many ways became a central part of the ongoing psyche of our class. Though burdened with medical issues, chief among them being diabetes, Neal's quick and engaging smile and his almost daily e-mailing of humor, some good-much bad, kept the class in good spirits.

We lost Neal on October 19, 2007, a week before his 61st birthday. Tributes poured in from classmates around the country, and some in St. Louis attended his memorial service.

Jerry Weiner wrote the following tribute to Neal, one of many shared among classmates.

"I phoned him in the hospital before he started dialysis. He sounded worried. I tried to cheer him up and soon we were cracking jokes and laughing. I said goodbye with encouragement that the dialysis would heal him. I never imagined it would fail him.

"When I met him in 1958, he was Hyman or Hy. Even then he was mirth personified. He was in my cabin at Camp White Cloud, when the 6th grades of Daniel Boone and McKnight were merged for a week. His boisterousness was infectious. During an afternoon rest period he persuaded Mike Bornstein (who has also passed away) to bounce him around on the mattress of Hy's upper bunk from Mike's lower bunk. Hy was hefty but Mike was strong and after a few bounces Hy fell through the screen window and down about 6 feet into some bushes. Uninjured. Laughing. Mr. Walker, my teacher, stormed into our cabin and blustered and threatened Hy into silence. Hy was unfazed. A minute after Mr. Walker left, he had us laughing again.

"I saw Neal for the last time in the Spring of 2005 while I was vacationing in St. Louis. He was using his middle name then. We dined a few times. We both were divorced, with beautiful grown-up daughters. I had a long-time sweetheart, and he still was looking for one. We both had close brushes with death. I understood the joys and sorrows of his life and he understood mine. But he still had the same infectious mirth. And he posted his jokes and funny graphics to UC64 almost daily.

"Last Wednesday morning (I did not note the exact time) I had an ominous feeling about Neal. For several days I'd waited for Leslie to email that Neal's surgery was successful. But on Wednesday morning an awful thought suddenly entered my mind: 'Neal is about to let go of his life.' I tried to deny it, and told myself, 'No, he has to hang on for a while longer to see his grandson born.' Then came the rebuttal, 'He can't hang on any longer. He's too sick, too weak, too much in pain. His body is failing and his spirit is letting go of it.' I put the awful thought out of my mind and resumed hoping for the best. But late that night I read Leslie's email about Neal's cardiac arrest during breakfast. Somehow I'd known it when it happened that morning. That night I thought Neal might be gone already, medical resuscitation notwithstanding. And now he is gone.

"I miss him. But whenever I need to lift my spirit, I will remember Hyman Neal Harris."

Susie
Her Wisdom and Her Laughter

Susan Marlene Schechter

"Is it too small a thing to have enjoy'd the sun, to have light in the spring, to have loved, to have thought, to have done?"

Her family, her friends, the national social services community, and our class lost Susie Schechter in February 2004.

Susie was very active in high school—student council, yearbook, Pep Club, Girls Athletic Association, Student Disciplinary Committee, Model United Nations, prom committee, and more. She was among the brightest of classmates, earning honors each year and receiving a National Merit Letter her senior year.

Her high school friends remember her as "pretty, smart, and fun;" as "reasoning on a higher level;" and as "upbeat and bubbly, tall, slender, and graceful, a good athlete, and with a little ditzy side."

I remember her as one of those people who light up a room.

Despite her involvement, intelligence, and ease among friends, there was little indication during high school that Susie would become one of the finest examples of the social conscience of our class, a nationally-respected leader in the fight against domestic violence.

She earned her Bachelor's Degree from Washington University in

St. Louis and her Master's Degree in Social Work from the University of Illinois in Chicago.

Susie built a career in which her capability, compassion, and tireless efforts led to many meaningful contributions to the cause of ending violence against women and children. While her focus was on helping those in need rather than on personal gain, Susie was widely recognized for her program development, expertise, and writing.

In 1986, she founded the first program in the country to address child abuse in families that were also affected by partner violence. She called it AWAKE, Advocacy for Women & Kids in Emergencies. The program is still active at Children's Hospital in Boston as well as having been implemented in other states.

During President Clinton's administration, Attorney General Janet Reno and Secretary of Health and Human Services Donna Shalala appointed Susie to the National Council on Violence Against Women.

Susie wrote two respected books, *Women and Male Violence: The Visions and Struggles of the Battered Women's Movement* (1982) and *When Love Goes Wrong* (co-authored with Ann Jones; 1992).

In 1999, she co-authored *Effective Intervention in Domestic Violence & Child Maltreatment Cases: Guidelines for Policy and Practice* (known as the "Greenbook"). It serves as a roadmap for child abuse and domestic violence professionals throughout the country who develop programs that serve children and their mothers.

In 2003, Susie received the National Association of Public Child Welfare Administration Award for Leadership, given to the person who best serves as a national leader to help child welfare agencies improve outcomes for children and their families.

Susie joined the University of Iowa faculty in 1991 as Clinical Professor in the School of Social Work. She lived in Iowa City with her husband, Allen Steinberg, Professor of History at Iowa, and their son, Zachary. In 2002, the University of Iowa, as part of its Celebration of Excellence Among Women, chose Susie to receive its Distinguished Achievement Award.

Susie appreciated the need for others to follow in her footsteps. In April 2003, shortly before she was diagnosed with cancer, she wrote, "As I work within the movement today, I am still amazed at what has been accomplished, surprised and disappointed by what we fail to foresee, and awed by the passion, pain, and renewal in the work of liberating women from tyranny and violence. Luckily for me, revelations continue. May they also continue for those who come next."

When Susie passed away, the Family Violence and Prevention Fund aptly established the Susan Schechter Leadership Development Fellowship to "honor the rich history of dedication, ingenuity, and compassion that are the hallmarks of the movement to end violence against women and children." The Leadership Development Fellows are among those who will follow in Susie's footsteps.

Susie Schechter lit up any room she walked into. She lit up people's lives, many who were very much in the dark. When Susie died, Susan Notkin, Director of the Center for Community Partnerships in Child Welfare said, "A light has gone out and we will miss her wisdom and her laughter, and mostly we will miss her."

Classmate Arleen White Bly recalls being on the yearbook staff and finding the quip that was to be used for Susie that "...at the time it described her perfectly...and she loved it."

Susan Marlene Schechter's quip was, "Is it too small a thing to have enjoy'd the sun, to have light in the spring, to have loved, to have thought, to have done?"

Arleen's 1964 choice of Susie's high school yearbook quip was perfect not just "at the time," but throughout Susie's life.

On Being Left Behind

Tim Arnold recalls an evening two decades ago that caused him to reflect on the relationship between the closeness of our class and the loss of classmates. He calls the recollection "On Being Left Behind."

"A most insistent realization is having to accept the loss of classmates who left us much too soon, incomprehensible gaps in our plans for reunions of, well, the living. It is perhaps this last irreconcilable truth that prods the shrinking circle that is our class of 1964, joins us back together, and helps produce a remarkable collection of reflections.

"I first became aware of this powerful notion one night some 20 years ago, when my telephone jangled me out of my suspended state of unrecognized opportunities ...

"It rang twice. The first time it was about 9:45; it was a woman I had seen just once in the past 26 years. That was at our 20-year high school reunion some six years earlier. Now she's trying to get together an east-coast version of another reunion and we chatted on about who we could track down close enough to New York to come and when and where to have it, and whether or not we should include everybody's kids, stuff like that. Anyway we'd talk again soon and wasn't it great to be putting all this together?

"Then around midnight the phone rang a second time. It was my daughter calling from St. Louis. Did I remember her friend Jeff Schukar's father, Steve, from U City? Well hell yes I remembered him. I was just talking to somebody in our high school class earlier tonight about a reunion. Well she had bad news, my daughter said. Steve had a heart attack a couple of days ago and he died.

"Oh sweet Jesus. It was as if the order and expectations and hopes of the night had suddenly and violently crashed into an unforeseen brick wall and dropped in a lifeless heap to the ground. I was dumbstruck.

"I had literally thought of Steve just yesterday, for the first time in forever. It was a mere moment in the middle of three miles on a treadmill. But there it was, vivid in its recollection. A fleeting note of high school nostalgia. It was one of those bleached-white sunny afternoons after school, and a bunch of us were in Steve's turquoise-blue and damned-near-new Chevy. A '62 Impala.

"A song on the radio earmarked this memory, like they do.

"'Hit the road, Jack ...' Ray Charles, the great Ray Charles.

"'... I guess if you say so, I'll have to pack my things and go. That's right ...'

"All the windows were down and nobody in Steve's car gave much of a damn about anything beyond that very moment, except maybe what the next song on the radio was going to be.

"That's all. That's what swam through my head only yesterday, all those pictures and emotions as I labored away on the treadmill, trying to put a few more nickels in my mortality bank.

"Steve was one of those hail-fellow hell yes kind of guys that everybody loved. Everybody. One of the guys. Hell I loved him even when he was stealing my girlfriend Ellen – before she even knew she was my girlfriend. He was funny, and cool. Wore kind of a slicked-back ducktail haircut a few years too long. One of those guys who just seemed to get it, and then laugh about whatever it was. He knew. He talked the walk – and he walked his talk, too.

"Why do all these things seem so damned clear to me now?

"I can also remember being in St. Louis twenty-something years ago and going to a Billy Joel concert with my first wife and some friends. And I'm cursing my way around the parking lot wondering where the hell I'm going to park when Schukar waves his flashlight at me out of the dark and the years and says, 'Right over here Arnold, you turkey.'

"He was one of the parking lot attendants. And I'm sure it was an extra gig after his day job.

"A couple of 'how the hell are ya's' and 'let's get togethers' and 'absolutelys' echo back into the night and the years. But we never did.

"That was the last time I saw Steve. But it wasn't the last time I thought about him.

"And now this nice, gentle 44-year old working stiff with a wife and two kids and great sense of humor was dead, gone, while some of the people he left behind are planning a fragment of a high-school reunion without him. And some of our children are trying to figure out how to get to college and grow up and survive and be loved and be safe long enough to enjoy it some. And not have heart attacks or otherwise get screwed out of about one-half of what's coming to you in life, by all rights.

"My daughter of 19 said that night she was convinced death was not something to fear, necessarily. She had been thinking about these things. That death is surely a prelude to something better.

"It's taken me another 20-plus years to believe it. And I believe it. I really do. But the terrible ache is for those of us who get left behind by those who depart much too early, much too suddenly to make any sense. We miss Steve. Steve does not miss us. His son has missed his father ever since, and will, until he dies too—just like I still miss my mother and father.

"Since then I've learned Steve Schukar never even graduated U City high school. Doesn't matter. Worse, he died nearly 20 years ago. Of course that matters along with the rest of the classmates we have lost. The rest of us—we've got roots, and years, and memories, and each other. We were thrown together by our parents, and the disparate and fascinating ways they arrived in the predominantly

Jewish suburb just next to the St. Louis city limits, and we experienced perhaps the most remarkable four years in our country's history, ripening from fresh, awkward teenagers into hopeful young adults. That was then, and this is now."

Stephen Charles Schukar

"To know him is to love him."

We Will Travel Together

We have lost Phil Kogan and M.J. Savoy and Neal Harris and Susie Schechter and Terry Mitze and Steve Schukar and too many others over four-plus decades.

They were a part of our lives as we navigated high school together. In many ways, they are part of our lives today. Each is a "soul-shard... (to) cherish as long as we live."

We cherish all our class characters. Each of us is one of those characters in a class that is greater than the sum of its classmates.

There is every reason to believe that Mickey Leon Sandmel, Leslie Berger, Ron and Elaine Levin Unell, and others will lead us to new levels of connectedness. Once again, we will travel together into our individual and collective futures, just as we did in June 1964. We carry those who have passed away with us. Some of us will be active and some not—some will stay connected and some not—some will lead and some will follow—regardless, we will travel together.

What will the future hold?

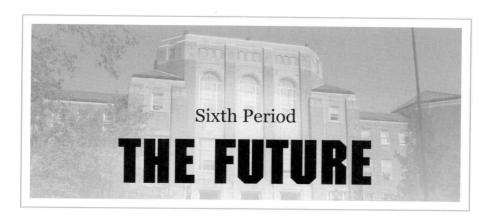

Sixth Period
THE FUTURE

*"Life is what happens to you
while you're busy making other plans."*
John Lennon

"One faces the future with one's past."
Pearl S. Buck

Steve Novack

*"U. City's spirit of cooperation
through competitiveness
and amiability."*

Mark: "So, do you think we'll be standing here ten years from now having the same conversation?"

Steve: "I just hope we're all healthy and fit and able to make the trip in ten years."

Marla: "Let's hope, but we don't have to wait that long to get together. We have our class 60th birthday party coming up in a couple of years."

Judy: "I think the conversation will have changed in ten years. We'll be almost 70—most of us will be retired and in a new phase of our lives."

Marla: *"We have a lot to offer. We'll have the time to give back to society what it has given us. I hope we're wise enough to take advantage of that."*

Anne: *"Oh, we will. We left high school with a strong social conscience and, based on what I hear classmates are already doing in their communities, I'm sure we'll make a difference."*

Mark: *"A difference in our communities and in our families—children, grandchildren, and someday great grandchildren; need to pass on our legacy."*

Judy: *"I know one thing will be true as we get older—that is, if we've learned anything from the past. If a classmate needs help, we'll mobilize and provide what help we can. And as we get older, more of us will need some kind of support. I'd predict we'll be there for each other."*

Anne: *"That's just another reason to stay connected."*

Steve: *"Not that you really needed to convince me, but I'm convinced. I hope even more classmates—you know, those who haven't stayed as close—reconnect as time goes on."*

Mark: *"Speaking of staying connected, I have about 200 more people to hug and talk to this weekend. So I better get started. I love you all."*

Marla: *"Speaking of love—Anne, would you please go keep my husband busy for awhile. I'm going to go find Terry Mitze and drag him under the clock. I may not get another chance—ever."*

A Great Balancing Act

When we graduated in 1964, we were prepared for our futures but filled with uncertainty. We knew the basic path we were about to travel, but knew little of what we would encounter along the way—steep hills, sharp curves, unexpected bumps, strong winds, and dead ends. We knew little of the partners with whom we would travel, and we knew little of nor thought much about our destination.

Four-plus decades later we have a new path to navigate or, perhaps, it is merely an extension of the same one. We understand the basics of what is ahead of us, but, again, the specifics are uncertain. Fortunately, we go forward with a more well-developed skill set to handle whatever we encounter than the one we had leaving school. We are also more in touch with the final destination although classmates disagree to some extent on that.

What might our path look like? We will be retiring from careers and redefining ourselves as we enter this new phase of our lives. We will be using our new-found time to give back to our communities, develop new hobbies, and pursue old ones. We will be concerned about our health and fitness and doing what we can to manage both. We will be attending to families that are expanding across generations and geographies, hopefully passing along the values and wisdom we received from our parents and grandparents.

The top ten reasons to remain close will only intensify with time. We will stay connected and look for ways to become even more so, bringing into the fold those who have not been as close over the years. We will care about each other. We will support each other and recognize the need to do so will be greater every year.

We will lose classmates and mourn them together. Despite what we know will be some tough times ahead, we will be stronger as a group knowing that we are a group. We continue to travel the path together to better deal with the steep hills, sharp curves, high bumps, strong winds, and dead ends.

Dr. Seuss could very well have been thinking about us and what we would experience on our path when he wrote *Oh, the Places You'll Go*. He starts by telling the reader,

> *"Congratulations!*
> *Today is your day.*
> *You're off to Great Places!*
> *You're off and away!"*

After describing, in Dr. Seuss manner, what we may encounter along the way to our "Great Places," we are told,

> *"You'll get mixed up, of course,*
> *as you already know.*
> *You'll get mixed up*
> *with many strange birds as you go.*

So be sure when you step.
Step with care and great tact
and remember that Life's
a Great Balancing Act."

Three Questions

In May 2002, I was fortunate to have the opportunity to retire from a 33-year career with The Procter & Gamble Company. While I was considering the retirement decision, I interviewed P&G colleagues who were also thinking about it and many who had already retired. I wanted to know what factors were important to them while making their decision. From those who had already retired, I also wanted to know what they had learned from their actual experience compared to their expectations.

During that time period, I ran into Peter Graham, a former boss, who had retired a number of years earlier. You may recall him as the one who taught me about there being "only two decisions in your life that of are any real consequence."

Peter and I caught up for awhile, and he asked if I was considering retirement. When I told him I was working on the decision, he told me his decision was really easy—it came down to answering three questions, and when the answer to each of the three questions was "yes," it was time for him to retire. The questions are:

Do you have enough?

Will you have enough to do?

Have you had enough?

Although developing the answer to each of these questions required a great deal of thought, he was right—the questions brought focus to my retirement decision.

Ann, who has an accounting degree from the University of Cincinnati, and I were able to run the financial calculations to answer the first question, "Yes." We then consulted a financial planner to confirm our conclusion.

The answer to having enough to do was also, "Yes." I had a meaningful list of things in which I was interested. Among them were spending more time with grandchildren and other family members and more time in the gym, traveling more, researching

Ann's and my family tree, becoming a personal trainer with the intent of volunteering my time with the elderly, and playing more baseball. In fact, I only half-jokingly told people, "Work was getting in the way of playing baseball, so I quit."

For me, the third question was the toughest. I enjoyed every day; well, almost every day; at P&G. It was a stimulating environment, and I was surrounded by intelligent, dedicated, collaborative people. Many P&Gers had become friends, and I felt I was still learning from my work and my colleagues. I had the opportunity to travel the globe as a Director of Worldwide Quality Assurance, meeting people and seeing sights in the 30-something countries I visited, many on a regular basis.

Despite the satisfaction I was still experiencing at P&G, I realized that just having started to think about retirement was a strong signal that I might have had enough. The attraction of life on the other side of retirement also helped me answer "Yes" to the final question.

When I shared these three questions with P&G colleague, Keith Lawrence, he offered the possibility of another question. Is your spouse ready to have you home full time? Happily, Ann and I could also answer this question with a "Yes."

Although I retired earlier than most of my classmates, they have been following me in greater numbers over these years. Certainly, by our 50-year reunion in 2014, virtually all will have retired. What we collectively and individually do with the opportunity of entering a new phase in our lives will, in large part, dictate the future of the University City High School Class of 1964.

Although making the retirement decision was liberating, some degree of anxiety accompanied it. For more than three decades, I had, in many ways, been defined by my career with P&G. It was time to redefine myself, which, happily, I found relatively easy to do.

Baseball, traveling, grandparenting, family trees, and physical fitness are still part of my plan. I chose, however, not to pursue the personal trainer idea. Instead, I have become a community volunteer, a private consultant to non-profit agencies as well as small and large companies, and an author. Perhaps what defines me is less about what I am doing, but more that I continually search for interesting, fun, and worthwhile things to do, manage to do them all, and enjoy most whatever I am doing at the time.

Perhaps a more stretching example of a person redefining himself in retirement is classmate Harry Bunn. As I am writing this section, Harry lives with his wife, Marsha London Bunn (U City '67; sister of classmate Helene London Rothman), in Indianapolis. He is retired from his position as a U.S. Customs and Border Protection National Finance Center Travel Section Chief. That mouthful sounds like a very left-brain job. So what might someone who has a job like that do in retirement?

It is obvious—Harry will move to Sedona, Arizona, change his name to Hari, and become a Medium/Psychic and Spiritual Advisor (www.hari-medium.com). Hari describes what he will do for his future clients as, "Provide information/guidance on how to handle situations you are in; connect you with a loved one that has 'crossed over,' help you on your spiritual path...work with spirit to perform Shaman drumming around your body which will make you feel better and at peace...discuss Universal/Natural Law to help you move towards a feeling of 'Heaven on Earth.'"

Harry became interested in and dabbled in such things as Tarot, numerology, Astrology, and the I Ching when he was in college. However, not until the mid-1990s did he seriously consider becoming a medium/psychic and spiritual advisor. In a conversation with a clairvoyant friend, he openly expressed the interest and, with that self-awareness, began studying and preparing for retirement.

Hari wrote, "To get ready for retirement is to take a serious look inside of yourself and identify what makes you happy/content with life and what you do...it is about finding out what you were really meant to do...retirement is where one goes to expand one's being/soul through doing what the heart desires."

Whether or not we subscribe to Hari's beliefs, we can follow his insightful advice about retirement.

How will each of us redefine ourselves? What will we do to further give back to our communities? What will our hobbies be? How will we manage aging? How well will we remain connected? What will our legacy be? The answers to these and other questions will mold our future.

Giving Back

An opportunity found me in March 2003. I had been retired for less than a year, when I received a call from Gibbs MacVeigh. He told me he was Chairman of the Board of a non-profit social services program in Cincinnati called Every Child Succeeds (ECS). He explained that MaryAnn Gale, a Vice-President at Procter & Gamble, was on the ECS Board and recommended that he talk with me about helping ECS achieve some of its objectives. We agreed to meet for lunch to talk more about it.

Gibbs brought Margaret Clark, the ECS Program Director, to lunch. She explained to me that ECS was a home visitation program for at-risk families having their first child. It was based on the understanding that the most important time in the formative years of a child's brain is from ages zero to three. In the absence of a home visiting intervention, children of at-risk families are themselves at a high risk of being underdeveloped socially, emotionally, and intellectually.

Gibbs then explained that ECS had made great progress over the several years it had been in existence but was finding it difficult to take its service delivery quality and its productivity to a new level. MaryAnn knew that I had worked on both of these results areas at P&G, and Gibbs asked if I could help.

The following week I joined home visitors, one a social worker and the other a nurse, as each conducted a session with one of her client families. I was hooked. These people were making an important difference in the lives of children and families and, by extension, in the development of the community. I have been working with ECS since then, am honored be on the Board and Executive Committee, and am proud to have received the Cincinnati United Way Leadership Impact Award for the work that I have done with the program.

My only regret about volunteering with ECS is that I had not found the social services community prior to retiring. There was no reason that I could not have been helpful while still working.

Since beginning my relationship with ECS, I have also worked with a number of social service agencies throughout the city. Then in early 2007, a new, different, and important opportunity came my way.

Dr. Victor Garcia is the Director of Trauma Services at Cincinnati Children's Hospital Medical Center. For years, Victor had been increasingly concerned about the trends of youth gunshot wounds with which he had, through his surgical responsibilities, very personal experience. The frequency of violence was increasing rapidly, and the average age of those being shot was decreasing.

Victor is particularly sensitive to the issue, because the victims are predominately African-American, as is he. Although he is a master at saving these young lives and putting the injured bodies back together, Victor concluded that he needed to do more. He began to search for an answer on how to stop the gun violence to prevent the shootings from ever taking place. For years he searched both the country and the literature for the answer and recruited others in the Cincinnati community to join him in making a difference.

Through his advocacy, persistence, study, and vision, Victor found and engaged Professor David Kennedy of the John Jay College of Criminal Justice in New York and convinced him to come to Cincinnati to help. David had developed an approach that had been demonstrated in Boston and other places to have dramatically reduced the homicide rate. With David's help, Victor was able to convince the Cincinnati City Council to fund and support the work.

He began to bring people and organizations together in a collaboration of all agencies of law enforcement at local, state, and federal levels; of social service agencies throughout the city; of influential members of the community; and of the Department of Criminal Justice at the University of Cincinnati. As he put his team together, Victor realized there were two problems for which he did not know how to proceed. One was that other cities had taken one to two years to implement David's methodology once the resources were in place. Victor did not want to wait that long. Every day of delay was another day of risk for young African-Americans and another day of fear in the community.

Secondly, a number of the cities that had successfully reduced their homicide rate saw their results deteriorate over time. How could Cincinnati both achieve results and, importantly, sustain them?

Because ECS offices are located at Children's Hospital, Victor heard about the work that I had been doing with that program. He spoke with ECS President Judy Van Ginkel, thought that I might be able to help, and contacted me. I am now a member of the "Cincinnati Initiative to Reduce Violence" (CIRV) Leadership Team.

We began our work in April 2007, and were operational by July, only four months compared to the one to two year timeframe we were working to avoid. As I write this section, we have been able to reduce homicides involving members of chronically violent groups, which account for about 75% of total homicides in the city. And, importantly, we have strategies in place to sustain and continually improve the results.

Professor Kennedy now cites Cincinnati as a benchmark implementation of his methodology, and our team is sharing our approach with other communities, states, and countries that are interested in reapplying it.

What is important here is not that I have been personally involved in these programs and their achievements. What is important is that my involvement is but one example of how there are critical needs in every community that can be met by those who have developed skills over the years of their lives and careers. Many classmates have been giving back to their communities throughout their lives. For the rest of us, retirement is the opportunity that will allow us to give back in ways that make a difference.

Lessons from Dad and Gimp

For those who know me or who read my first book, you know that physical fitness is very important to me. I am convinced that fitness is an essential building block for our quality of life and can have a significant impact on our health, especially as we age.

My father taught me many life lessons including one which he did so inadvertently. Dad was athletic throughout much of his life. He did not do aerobic exercise nor did he do strength and flexibility training, but he played softball, Indian ball, volleyball, or racquetball every chance he got, even into his 60s. He was a high-level bowler in St. Louis leagues, finally getting his 300 game on January 22, 1985, having just celebrated his 66th birthday.

Dad was an imposing man, six feet tall and weighing about 210, and he was strong. One weekend, he was visiting me at my college fraternity house. I do not recall how it got started—maybe I had been bragging about how strong he was—but soon there was a line of guys, and Dad was taking on all challengers in arm wrestling. He handled all comers but finally lost only because of having so many matches in a row.

Despite gaining some weight as he aged, Dad continued to be an imposing figure and to look strong even after he became less active. Bad knees and age kept him off of the playing fields. and he was doing nothing for personal fitness.

Then, at age 80, Dad was diagnosed with lung cancer, a product of smoking heavily since his early teens. Would physical fitness have fought off lung cancer? Not likely.

However, because Dad began his fight against the disease with little aerobic fitness or muscle strength, the course of the disease was much more difficult for him than it might have been. He weakened quickly, making life's routines much more difficult.

Observing Dad taught me a tough lesson. I have vowed never to allow my aerobic fitness or my strength and flexibility level to falter beyond the undeniable effects of the aging process itself.

Some of my classmates have settled into a good fitness and activity routine. Yet many others have settled into a routine of inactivity and poor physical fitness.

Classmate Dr. Richard Gimpelson, a gynecologist in St. Louis and former President of the American Association of Gynecologic Laparoscopists, has experienced both sides of the fitness choice. Before July 2003, Gimp carried 285 pounds on a short frame and characterized his lifestyle as "...years of abuse replete with milkshakes, hamburgers, French fries, and hot-fudge sundaes. I was a 'super-size' guy. I'd super-size orders for myself and my wife just so I could eat hers too. All my life, I was a quantity eater, not a quality eater. I could eat 30 White Castles or an entire pizza—no problem."

After July 2003, Gimp lost nearly 100 pounds on an 1800-calorie per day diet and began to exercise regularly. He appropriately started his exercise program slowly but now says, "If I don't work out at least four days a week, I'll feel guilty. I'll even park my car far away from my building and walk the stairs instead of taking the elevator—any excuse to do a little more."

What is the significance of July 2003? It was a heart attack and a prognosis from his cardiologist which Richard describes as, "He told me, 'You've had a heart attack. You have to exercise, lose weight, and change your diet, or you will die.' I think I needed that; if he had said, 'You might die,' I would have gone on the same way I had been."

Gimp learned his lesson and sharing it with his classmates taught us that we have the opportunity to make life changes before getting into trouble.

As we go forward, the quality of our lives will be affected by which side of this fitness/non-fitness decision we fall. This is not about running marathons or being a professional body builder. This is about basic fitness. Our level of health will not always be a choice—our level of fitness is always a choice.

Here is a crass commercial announcement, but one with the intent of giving you a simple, understandable approach to a basic fitness routine. See the "Extra Innings" section of my first book *Baseball: Never Too Old to Play "The" Game.*

Hopefully, as we head into our futures, we will do so having chosen to be as fit as we can. Our quality of life will depend on it.

Scares Me Beyond Belief

Historical events, political decisions, and cultural trends helped determine who we were during our high school years. They likewise helped shape who we have become over the past four-plus decades. How they will affect who we will become in the future is no exception.

No one can predict future events or trends. But there are some key societal issues that are crucial to our futures at this stage in our lives. One of the most important as we age is the accessibility, quality, and cost of health care. The issue is top-of-mind for many of us who have had a personal experience or have a child, other relative, or friend who is struggling meeting health care needs.

During the 2008 presidential campaign season, classmates were having an electronic discussion comparing the state of our national health care system to that of other countries. Arleen Inger helped personalize the issue when she wrote, "...as long as you have the money, you should be afforded the best in healthcare, yes? Approximately two years ago, I had a mild heart attack. Six months later, my echocardiogram was NORMAL. My insurance expired at the end of September 2007. The law in Ohio requires insurance companies to offer health coverage when your insurance expires from a group policy as mine did. I am marked for life! In other words, once a heart attack, always another heart attack. According to the 12 different insurance carriers to whom I applied for coverage, the best offer to date was $13,000/year in premiums with an $8,500 deductible prior to any insurance being considered.

"So, my classmates, I am one of the 47 million uninsured in this country. My state does not offer a high risk pool for individuals like me. Sorry, can't afford $21,500/year at this juncture. Scares me beyond belief. Before I can have any routine appointments with physicians, I have to ask the question of 'what is the cost for...?'

"My guess is that most of you have healthcare insurance through your employer or your businesses. Don't for a moment underestimate the value of your insurance. Until 2007, I had consistent health insurance beginning in 1969. Yet no one wants to hire a 61-year old accountant. My consulting business does not afford me that luxury. So, what do you propose for the uninsured in our country? Are either of the candidates offering viable options?"

As personal and governmental budgets tighten, the cost of healthcare continues to escalate, and early baby boomers move into retirement, the effect Arleen described will become even more impactful. Retirement decisions are being postponed. The quality of health care is being compromised. While some have good coverage through employers/businesses, many do not.

I am fortunate in that P&G has strong and affordable retiree health coverage. And I have the means to be a patient in a "boutique" doctor's practice. Here is how it works. For $1500 per year per person, Ann and I joined a private practice. We still pay our co-pays and insurance still covers its normal expenses, but for the annual fee we get very personalized service.

Our doctor, before he started this practice, had more than 2000 patients in his files. Now Ann and I are two of only about 400. He is on call 24x7 and actually once chastised us when we waited until after a weekend to call him about something. He is committed to be personally responsible for coordinating care among specialists if that is necessary. When I hurt my back playing baseball a couple of years ago, that is exactly what he did. He made sure I got into specialists' offices promptly and closely tracked my care, including with the physical therapist.

He proactively contacts patients when he learns new information that is relevant to our individual health status. Several times, he has called me to let me know the outcome of a recent study that pertains to my specific history. He also focuses on wellness. He has a nutritionist on staff, hosts presentations by experts on various health-related subjects, sponsors us in walks for health-related causes, and pays for our CPR certification.

Am I conflicted about this type of practice? You bet I am. This is how it should work for everyone. But that is not the case, and when it comes to the quality of my healthcare, I do not feel like making a statement by not joining his practice.

Just by virtue of aging, our health future will be uncertain. The weakness of the health management system in the country serves to magnify those uncertainties. There will be many societal and political issues that will directly and indirectly affect us, but perhaps healthcare will be first among them—another reason to maintain our physical fitness at a high level.

Pursuing Passions

As I was interviewing retired P&G colleagues while making my retirement decision, one question I asked was, "Has anything surprised you about retirement?"

I consistently heard two answers to this question. One retiree summed up the first surprise when he said, "I didn't know how tired I was when I was working, until I wasn't tired any more."

The other surprise was well articulated by another former colleague. He said, "I didn't anticipate the problem I'd have replacing the intellectual stimulation I got at work every day."

Now that I am retired, I can relate to both of these responses. I am getting seven to eight hours of sleep each night instead of five to six. And I am not averse to an occasional nap.

With regard to replacing the intellectual stimulation of work, I have found hobbies that meet the need. I read incessantly and work crossword and other puzzles every day. My volunteer work with non-profit agencies and social programs is intellectually stimulating, with many of the activities being very similar to what I was doing at work.

But most of my mental exercise comes from having made the commitment to become an author. In 2007, I completed, published, and marketed, *Baseball: Never Too Old to Play the Game.* You are reading book two, and I am choosing the topics for books three and four. This does not count the children's book for which I am still searching for a publisher.

All of these activities can be thought of as hobbies—the definition being "an interest pursued for pleasure and not as a main occupation."

Many classmates are also pursuing hobbies that are keeping them socially, physically, and mentally active. For those who have not yet settled on their passion to pursue, it will be important for their quality of life to find what interests them.

In my first book, I emphasized the advantage of identifying what we were passionate about when we were younger and then pursuing those passions throughout our life, especially in our senior years. Here is what I wrote.

"...to have a happy, successful retirement, each of us should be doing what we were passionate about when we were ten years old. The idea is that when we are ten, or thereabouts, we are old enough to choose to do what we really love to do, but not yet old enough to have been burdened by inhibitions, peer pressure, and all the other things that guide us away from our passions. Doing what we are passionate about should help make us happy, whether we are ten or 60. As simply put in the lyrics of Irene Cara's song 'What a Feeling' in the 1983 movie *Flashdance*, 'Take your passion and make it happen; what a feeling.'

"Logan Franklin is a retired publisher who maintains a web site for seniors called *Gray Iron Fitness*. In an article entitled, 'Rediscover Your Passion in Retirement,' Franklin wrote, 'Your interests probably are very different from mine. But somewhere in each of us the interests are there, only waiting to be rediscovered and released. One good way to uncover them is by looking backward to your childhood and adolescence. Recall the thoughts, activities and dreams that sent your imagination and spirit soaring. Those are your clues. Develop interests related to them and most people will experience a personal renaissance.'"

When Marshall Faintich was four years old, he came across an Israeli coin that had been minted only a couple of years earlier. He picked up the coin and saved it. He began a basic coin collection at the age of ten, and his interest in ancient coins was energized in 1984 when he visited the British Museum collection. He both collects and studies coins and in 2007, completed and published his book, *Astronomical Symbols on Ancient and Medieval Coins*. Marshall also maintains a website on the subject, www.symbolicmessengers.com.

By the way, he also still has that first Israeli coin, a ten prutot piece, nearly six decades later.

Marshall's hobbies have not been limited to coins. He began collecting stamps when he was eight and was keen about this hobby for more than 40 years. He has also become a dedicated nature photographer, having now taken photos of 132 bird species in his local Virginia area. Marshall periodically shares his magnificent photos with the class.

Steven Karty fell in love with amateur radio and electronics when he was in high school and still actively pursues both today. Steven recalls, "Back at U City, I wandered into Mr. Lanham's room one day during lunch period. He was one of my favorite teachers (Chemistry), and I was also in his Ham Radio Club. He greeted me with 'Hi, Steve. What's on your mind – besides sex and ham radio, of course?' I was unable to answer him. After all these years, I still haven't been able to come up with an answer."

Marc Golubock and I played tennis together when we were growing up—he still loves the game. What is a good way to measure his passion for the game? He is still playing—on two artificial hips.

My wife, Ann, is at Jazzercize every day we are in town and many days we are not, as she finds local programs when we are traveling. She belongs to an active bridge group, reads at least a book each week, and does puzzles, crosswords and sudoku, daily. She is at the center, with several others, of the development of her father's family tree that extends across the US and to Israel, England, and South Africa.

When Harold Sanger is not at home or at work, he is at City Hall. Local government is his favorite and most time consuming hobby. He has been elected to government boards, served as Mayor Pro Tempore, and chaired the Planning & Zoning Board. Harold also collects pocket watches, several which have been handed down through generations of his family, and drives and works on his '79 "T" Top Corvette.

Elaine Levin Unell—painting, creating pottery, reading, doing puzzles, playing Mahjongg and Scrabble, singing (has been performing with her local group for 36 years), exercising, photo editing, playing golf, volunteering for Gifted Resource Council programs, visiting with friends, laughing...not necessarily in that order...and always adding to the list

Judy Garber Ellsley—attending professional sports (Dolphins, Marlins, Panthers), dancing to the oldies, watching *American Idol* and reading *People Magazine*

David Nemon—singing songs from the 60s, building model cars, working on classic cars (full size ones—restoring a '57 Chevy, 283, 3-speed on the column)

Allan Markovitz—passed through a two-decade photography hobby, including hand coloring black and white photos for which he had a show in St. Louis; passed through Tai Chi; now it is "a 2005 Harley Fat Boy—custom paint, rims, and front end...even have the requisite tattoos"

Allan Markovitz and his customized Harley Fat Boy

Paula Glovinsky Sigel—collecting antique silver and other objects of art, archeology, gourmet cooking, oenology, and volunteering at the St. Louis Art Museum

Harry Bunn—bowling, reading, oil painting, exercising, and watching sci-fi programs and movies

Sue Corman Slater—travel, trivia, reading ("hearing my authors"), playing cards, anagrams, barber shop concerts, mystery nights, playing games online, museums, touring old houses and plantations, watching travel, food, and style networks and the *Law & Order* and *CSI* series

Mike Fleischmann—playing guitar, ukulele, recorder, piano, mandolin, and listening to music of all kinds; collecting sheet music including jazz, ragtime, ballads, and show tunes; collecting records with a focus on jazz from 1900-1930; collecting coins; photography, including creation of anaglyphs and cross-views; and doing puzzles

Leslie Berger—philatelist, numismatist, massage therapist, photographer, and Zadeh (Yiddish for grandpa)

Debbie Brownstein Pulley—gardening, raising orchids, cooking, reading, entertaining, decorating, traveling

Don Pearline—trying to solve the world's political problems, photography, history, reading, cooking

Arleen White Bly—acting in musical theater and straight plays, dancing, singing in a chorus, reading memoirs and historical fiction, family, walking, going to the theater, traveling, volunteering, enjoying art and music (Arleen says, "that's just the beginning!")

Janice Goldberg White—reading, watching soap operas, and trying to find more time for hobbies

Jim Grossman and his wife Jane spend more than six months each year in their RV traveling the country.

Ed Friedman is a Chicago attorney who grew up in an observant Jewish home then drifted away and became a Reform Jew when he was married at age 21. When his marriage unraveled twenty years later and he lost all of his tangible possessions, Ed began to search for something on a spiritual level. He returned to his observant roots, but did not feel as though he had reconnected until a very close relative passed away.

Self-reflection moved him toward a higher spiritual level and prompted him to begin studying the Talmud, the record of rabbinic discussions pertaining to Jewish law. His is not a minor commitment. Ed is part of a study group called "Daf Yomi," which means "a page a day." He studies every evening and is more than halfway through the seven years it will take to complete "the cycle," studying each of the 2711 pages of the Talmud. What happens when Ed completes "the cycle?" He will start all over again. Ed looks forward to going to study every evening after work. "Every night I can't wait to learn what the Talmud will say."

His studies meet the definition of the word "hobby." To Ed, the Talmud is a pleasure.

Our mental wellbeing will meaningfully affect our futures. Hobbies can help us achieve that wellbeing as they maintain our intellectual edge, enhance our socialization, meet our need to belong, help us become and stay physically fit, meet our spiritual needs, and help us help others. In our life's balancing act, pursuing our passions through our hobbies is an important component.

What were you passionate about when you were ten years old?

Legacy

One of our individual and collective responsibilities has been and will be to pass along our values and wisdom to succeeding generations. We began to do this when our children were born and continue as our children are having children.

While our legacy will be defined in part by what we will have accomplished, perhaps even more so it will be measured by the contributions of our children, grandchildren, and generations beyond.

Ann and I were married on August 25, 1968, just before my ninth and final college semester. She was 20; I was 22. Our daughter, Dana, was born in July 1970, making us parents at the ages of 22 and 24, respectively, and making our mothers and fathers grandparents in their mid-40s to early-50s.

Dana was 29 when she married Vince, who was 33. Their first child, Jordan, was born in December 2001, making Ann and me grandparents for the first time in our mid-50s. Their second, Aaron, was born in October 2004.

Our son, Kevin, born in January 1973 was married at age 33 to Lisa, age 27. Their first child, Jacob, was born in March 2008 when we were in our early 60s.

My mother passed away in 1976, and my father died at age 81, more than a year before his first great grandson was born and named after the two of them. Ann's mom and dad became great grandparents for the first time in their late 70s and early 80s, respectively.

Why share this genealogy? Well, for one reason, it gives me a chance to tell you more about my children and grandchildren.

But mostly I am using our genealogy as but one typical example of the trend in the average age of parents having their children. The Centers for Disease Control and Prevention reported in 2008 the average age of parents of first children was over 25, the highest all time. Also higher were birthrates among women ages 35 to 39 and those ages 40 to 44. This trend is, by extension, making grandparents and great grandparents at older ages.

Anna Yaffe Sauer and Debbie Brownstein Pulley were grandmothers by our 30-year reunion. It is not uncommon, however, for classmates, including Anna and Debbie as well, to be having grandchildren into our 60s.

As an example, as I was writing this section of the book, 62-year-old Marshall Faintich shared a chronic health condition he had been dealing with since he was 11 years old and urging us to get regular checkups. He finished his message with, "By the way, I became a grandpa for the first time early this morning—another reason to take good care of myself."

Shortly thereafter, Barb Rostenberg Sandmel sent pictures and wrote, "Here I am with my new granddaughter—Ariel Sandmel, born July 6, 2008, in sunny Santa Fe, NM to Jonathan and Katie Sandmel."

Classmate Don Platt may be stretching the trend to its extreme as he and his wife, Michele, adopted four-year-old Nikita from Russia in early 2004. Don is retired from a career in international helicopter sales and, with Michele, started a company called "AVNIK Defense Solutions," providing engineering and logistics to the government.

Where did the name AVNIK come from? AViation plus NIKita. Don and Michele are involved in their business, but are even more deeply involved in rearing Nikita.

There are two points to be made here. First, here we are four-plus decades after our graduation from high school, and we feel close enough to our classmates to want to share the good news of the birth of grandchildren and the adoption of children. I have not shared with you the congratulations that pour in to the new grandparents from all over the country. It is as if the class is a family, and lifecycle events are to be shared and celebrated.

Secondly, we are becoming grandparents at an older age than our parents did, and if the trends continue, we will become great-grandparents much later in life. For many, and perhaps most, of us, we will never know our great-grandchildren.

If our oldest grandson, Jordan, is married and has his children at the same age as did his mother, Ann and I will be great-grandparents at ages 82 and 84, respectively. Following the same logic, if our newest grandson, Jake, has his first child at the same age as his father did, he will make us great-grandparents at ages 95 and 97. While I look forward to all of that, there is much uncertainty involved.

The vast majority of us had the opportunity to pass along our values and wisdom to our children. And most of us have the opportunity to do the same with our grandchildren. I hope we have done and are doing a good job, because it will be up to them to pass our legacy along to future generations.

Importantly, what are those values? They are the ones passed on to us by our parents and grandparents. They are the values of family, education, a strong work ethic, integrity, community, loyalty, and compassion. Some may argue that these values are passé. I do not agree. They are everlasting and alive. It is our task to make sure they stay that way.

To the extent that we have the opportunity to directly instill in our great-grandchildren the same positive values, here is hoping that we do. To the extent that may not be possible, our future must include making the time to positively influence our children and grandchildren and, through them, our great-grandchildren and beyond. They will be our legacy.

No Brag, Just Fact

Our children are well along their road to being accomplished and to contributing to society. Our daughter Dana earned her Masters of Occupational Therapy at Washington University in St. Louis. She was progressing through her OT career and had gotten to the point where she was managing other therapists. That was until the Medicare regulations changed, limiting the number of therapy sessions available to patients.

Layoffs became the order of the day in the OT community. Although Dana retained her job, she no longer felt good about the quality of care she could provide given the limits placed on services.

Because Dana grew up with a social conscience, while she was building her OT career, she also made the time to volunteer at the Jewish Federation in St. Louis and had become a lay leader. About the time she was reevaluating her OT career, she learned that the Jewish Federation had an open staff position. Dana jumped at the opportunity, changed careers, and never looked back. She is now the Associate Director of Development at the Federation and continues to grow in her job. She is not only building a career, but is doing it in a profession that is helping many in need throughout her community and the world.

Our son, Kevin, earned his BS in Economics from Washington University in St. Louis and went on to work for Fidelity Investments in Boston. Kevin called one day after he had been working for several years. "Mom, Pop, I'm going to backpack around the world. What do you think?"

After a lot of questions to which he either had the answers or went to get them, we were fully supportive. He funded the trip himself, planned it all, and, with his friend, Billy Girasuolo, set out for a 13-month around-the-world adventure. Kevin's only restriction was that he had to be home in time to be cleaned up and groomed for his sister's wedding. What an experience!

Kevin returned to Fidelity Investments, decided he was not a big corporation kind of guy, and has been working for smaller companies ever since. He has continued to take on more responsibility and now works for FunMobile, a company headquartered in Hong Kong. Kevin is the Vice-President of Business Development and Carrier Relations, running the North American business and starting up businesses in other countries in the Americas.

Both Dana and Kevin are building careers and families. Importantly, they both have education, work ethic, integrity, and caring about others at the top of their priority lists.

Well, that was my chance to brag. I gave my classmates their chance, and here is just some of what I heard from them. In this context, "brag" is not meant to carry its negative connotation, but rather its meaning, "to speak with pride." Or as Will Sonnet, played by Walter Brennan in the late-60s TV show, *The Guns of Will Sonnet*, repeated frequently, "No brag, just fact."

Ellen Polinsky Cohen's son Brad has Tourette syndrome. While going through school, Brad was misunderstood by his teachers, who saw him as little more than disruptive. Along the way, he decided to become the teacher he never had. Against the odds, he earned his undergraduate degree, graduating Magna Cum Laude from Bradley University, and went on to earn a Masters and a Specialist Degree (an interim step toward his Doctorate) from Georgia State University. After receiving his certification to teach, he persistently searched for a job, found one after many rejections, and became the great teacher he knew he would be. Brad was awarded the "First Class Teacher of the Year Award" for the state of Georgia.

As if all that were not enough, Brad also wrote a widely-acclaimed book entitled, *Front of the Class: How Tourette Syndrome Made Me the Teacher I Never Had.* He donates all of the proceeds from the book to help others with Tourette syndrome. How widely acclaimed is Brad Cohen and his life story? He is asked to speak in advocacy for those with Tourette syndrome all over the country; he has appeared on *The Oprah Winfrey Show* to share his book and his insights; and the *Hallmark Hall of Fame* made Brad's life into a movie that aired on CBS in December 2008. Following the movie, Brad and his wife, Nancy, were invited by President Bush to join him at the White House for a Chanukah dinner. www.classperformance.com

Adrienne Nadler Hirschfeld's son, Matt, is a brilliant illustrator who lives in Los Angeles. He uses what is called vector art to draw caricatures, primarily those commissioned by celebrities and studios. Just after we all learned of the untimely death of Tim Russert, Adrienne shared one of Matt's illustrations, because some years earlier Matt had been commissioned to draw Russert. www.matthirschfeld.com

Karen Paulsen Bauch's daughter, Kristina, followed in her parents' footsteps, and then stepped out on her own. Karen and husband, Richard, play the violin and viola, respectively, for the Winnipeg Symphony Orchestra. Kristina began playing the violin when she was three, but also loved to dance. She has worked as a dancer and joined her parents for a couple of years as a violinist with the Winnipeg Symphony. Kristina has now combined her musical and dance talents with the dynamic group, "Barrage," which performs around the world. If you appreciate beautiful music and high-energy performance art, Kristina Bauch and "Barrage" are a must-see. Search "Barrage Violin" on YouTube and look for the blond. www.barrage.org

Very high on the priority list for Harold Sanger's family was understanding the need for a good education, extracting lessons both from the classroom and from life. At a young age, the Sanger children, Whitney, Stefanie, and Bryan, now in their late 20s and early 30s, learned about becoming involved in their community. From volunteering in Salvation Army soup kitchens in middle school to campaigning for candidates and causes they believed in through high school, college, and beyond, they have always stood up for those who could not stand up for themselves. The values that have defined their character and their academic accomplishments (among them they have four undergraduate and four postgraduate degrees) are the foundation upon which they are building their lives. Small wonder that Harold and his wife, Diane, are so proud.

Steven Karty's sons, Aaron and Sam, inherited the predilection for education that was brought to this country by their great grandparents, passed down to their grandparents, and instilled in their parents. Aaron received a BS in Chemistry and Biochemistry from the University of Virginia and a law degree from Temple University, while Sam earned a BS in Computer Engineering from Virginia Tech.

David Goodman's son, Darren, is an award-winning glassblower. Darren was inspired by his mother, Louise's (U City '65), glass collection, earned his Bachelors in Fine Arts in Glass from Bowling Green State University in 2003, and opened his independent studio in 2004, specializing in bowls, vases, and sculptured glass. www.DarrenGoodmanGlass.com

Barbara Rostenberg Sandmel's son, Jeremy, graduated Phi Beta Kappa with dual degrees in Music Technology and Computer Engineering. He now lives in San Mateo, California and is a senior project manager for Apple Computer. He is also Vice-President of a non-profit group that encourages individuals to develop new music and visual arts. www.newgalleryconcertseries.org Barbara's younger son, Jonathan, now lives in Santa Fe after earning his Journalism degree from the University of Missouri and his MFA in Painting from the University of New Mexico. He owns his own tech support company and has premiered a series of paintings entitled "Camouflage" with his brother's non-profit.

Janice Goldberg White's son, Joshua, has a Master's Degree in philosophy and a beautiful daughter. While Jan sees him working through a difficult marital issue, she also sees that he is a committed father. Joshua's experience with his daughter has helped him decide he wants to become an elementary school teacher where he can make a difference in the lives of young children. Jan's daughter, Rachel, followed her dream of becoming an actress, moved to Los Angeles, and had some small parts in *ER* and *Heroes* before coming to the conclusion she needed a more solid existence. She is returning to school to seek her Masters in Psychology with the goal of going on to a PhD. While both of her children are still in a state of transition in their mid-to-late 20s, Jan is proud of the way they are making decisions and committing themselves to their futures.

Judy Garber Ellsley's son, Rick, is recognized as one of the top-40 "up and coming" attorneys in South Florida and is one of the youngest attorneys to be nationally board certified. He earned his undergraduate and law degrees from the University of Florida, where he graduated Phi Beta Kappa and with honors from law school. Her daughter, Alise, works at the area's United Way and, despite being raised as a reform Jew, is now very active in the Orthodox community. Judy's pride comes through as she talks about her children and what they have accomplished, and her delight comes through when she talks about them having given her grandchildren.

The intent here is not to mention every classmate's children, although I would love to, because they are our greatest accomplishments. Rather, the intent is to share that, in general, our legacy is in good hands if measured by the lives our children are building. Some might be in transition and still "finding themselves," but with a basis of education, family values, work ethic, caring, and integrity, their foundation is strong, built on the shoulders of their grandparents and, proudly, their parents—that would be us.

It Takes a Village

Transitioning from work to retirement, giving back to our communities, staying healthy and fit, pursuing our hobbies, and passing on our legacy are some of what will consume the next phase of our lives. We hope not to face all of this alone—we hope that family and friends, among them our classmates, will be available to help. And we hope that we will be the family members and friends and classmates who will step up if needed.

The University City class of 1964 has created a culture of caring that helped Sue Slater when her mother became ill on their trip to Texas. Jerry Weiner and the class stepped up to help. There have been other incidents as well, and we have a fund and committee established to help as much as we can.

Sometimes support looks like financial help; sometimes it is other things. A classmate's husband suffered a brain aneurism, and she nearly lost him. Family and classmates rushed to provide logistical and moral support at a very difficult time. His recovery has been long but steady as has the support provided by the class.

A classmate's computer crashed. She was ill and did not have the resources to get another computer to stay connected to the class. We pitched in to supply funds, and a classmate delivered the computer and set it up. She was able to stay connected until she passed away.

Whenever there is a natural disaster or the threat of one anywhere, our first instinct is to determine which classmates may be affected, offer them our best wishes, let them know we are thinking of them, and then followup to ensure they are alright. We have been prompted by hurricanes in Florida and Texas, torrential rains, mudslides, and widespread fires in California, and tornados in the Midwest.

As I am writing this section, Hurricane Ike attacked Texas, roaring through and causing extensive damage in, among other places, Galveston and Houston. As we would with our own families, so did we quickly check on Morrie and Nancy Mayer, Lenny and Dee Koblenz, and David and Suzie Nemon. They had each lost power and tree limbs but were safe with little property damage.

Ike continued north then northeast and came through Cincinnati with winds still over 70 miles per hour. Five people died locally as a result of the storm, property damage was widespread, and power was lost in a historically high number of homes. As soon as she took stock of her own situation, classmate Arleen Inger called from across town to make sure we were alright. We were.

A classmate wrote that he needed advice, because his elderly aunt would likely need assisted living or nursing home care in the St. Louis area in a relatively short period of time. Stories of personal experiences, evaluations of facilities, questions to ask, and offers of help poured in. The classmate was not only able to then better help his aunt, but was also able to share the responses with other classmates with a similar need.

This next example may seem trivial compared to the others, but it merely shows what a tight community can do. We received a message from a classmate that his granddaughter was in a contest to be chosen to be the cutest toddler in St. Louis. He asked that we check out her picture on a website and, if we agreed, vote for her. Sure he was stacking the deck, but he had a group with which he could do so.

Support can be provided in many ways. We have provided classmates with moral support, financial support, logistical support, and the support that comes from just knowing there are people who care about you. Another form of support is the sharing of life lessons from which all can learn.

Brad Cohen shared his life experience with Tourette syndrome in his book and movie, *Front of the Class*. We not only learned about Brad's courage and persistence, but we also learned more about his mother, our classmate Ellen, than many of us already knew about this very special woman. Neither Brad nor Ellen would accept the nearsighted reactions to Brad's mannerisms—rather, they sought to understand, and then acted to build a beautiful life.

As their story unfolded before the class and the nation, we were moved and educated at the same time. Classmate Ken Brown was moved to the point of sharing his story with us as well.

Ken lives in Seattle with his wife, Ann, and is retired as the Director of Information Technology for a global engineering and construction company. Ken wrote, "I was recently asked to share my story with the class and I declined. But Ellen and her son, Brad's, story changed my mind. This last summer, I lost my leg to diabetes...As in Brad's case; the moral is to maintain a great attitude. Doctors and nurses will tell you how important that is for good healing. When my wife and I made the difficult decision for me to have the amputation, we also decided that we would keep a good attitude and keep our spirits high...We both are doing great, and my leg is nearly healed, and I will very soon be fitted for a prosthesis.

"What does my situation have to do with Ellen's son? Although our disabilities are different, there are many similarities. For example, although I lost my leg, they did not get my soul or spirit. You need to know when to ask for guidance and support. You learn that the human spirit can endure and adjust to almost anything. You have to laugh at your own situation, as laughter heals the heart as well as the body. Finally, you must persevere, even if the journey is long and hard. I believe that positive attitude trumps the rigors of losing a leg. I hope everyone remembers these lessons as you get older and face your own physical challenges."

These are life lessons from great teachers. They are lessons that are not easy to share, but in sharing them, Brad, Ellen, and Ken lifted us all on their shoulders.

It takes a village to raise a child. It also takes a village to support all of its inhabitants, especially as they age. As classmates, we are and will be close-knit inhabitants of the caring community that is our village.

Feel So at Home

We were close in high school because that is what we were supposed to be. We have been close over the decades since graduation because we wanted to be. And we are especially close now because of the top ten reasons. How close will we be in the future?

I belong to a writer's group that meets at Cincinnati's Joseph-Beth Booksellers, one of the rare remaining independent bookstores. Every Monday morning, promptly at 9:30am, we are called to order by our moderator, Vivian Kline.

Vivian was born in 1925 in an old brownstone house on the west side of Manhattan; literally born in the house. She graduated from Birch Wathen High School in the city and, since then, her class has been having a reunion every five years.

Vivian is creative in a number of dimensions. She has been an enameller for almost 55 years as evidenced by the pieces adorning the walls and shelves of her home. Vivian is on an enameling hiatus, however, as she is finishing writing a book that she has been working on (and off) for many years. Having become interested in the history of the Jubilee Singers from Fisk University, Vivian is chronicling their story. She is also writing a read-aloud work about her experience at and the people with whom she jointly ran a co-op art gallery in downtown Cincinnati for almost 20 years. While Vivian is unsure what the future of this piece will be, she is undeterred because it is the creative process that intrigues her.

Vivian previously wrote *Many Happy Returns: Recollections*

of a Great Grandmother, Grandmother, Mother and Daughter, a book that captures the perspective of her family's women across four generations. She and her late husband, Dan, self-published the book in 1998.

Vivian is energetic and curious. She plays tennis four days a week, travels extensively both nationally and abroad, and is a great storyteller. She is deeply interested in and distressed by current events and is, along with her children, involved in supporting the politicians they think will make a difference. And Vivian Kline is rarely seen without a small flower delicately placed over her right ear.

I was prompted to learn more about Vivian and her high school class one Monday morning after I read a piece I had written for the book and had received the insightful and constructive critique to be expected from the group. During an ensuing conversation about high school classes and reunions, Vivian quietly mentioned that she was about to attend her 65th.

She did attend as did nearly half of her graduating class. Even classmates who had not been heard from for decades were reconnecting. One gentleman said that, as he grew older, he had become much more interested in his past and wanted to be closer to the class.

Vivian believes her class is still close after 65 years because, "We came from such similar backgrounds and find it comfortable to be with people who have known us for so long."

A classmate of Vivian's, who now lives in Texas, expressed it differently when she said at their recent reunion, "I feel so at home."

I would like to think that my class will feel at home whenever and wherever we get together in the coming years. And I would like to think that we will connect frequently, not just electronically but also face-to-face. We will have reunions at least every ten years, the 50th, 60th, 70th, and beyond; plans are in place to begin having them every five years. We will share birthday parties, our 70th, 80th, 90th and beyond. We will have mini-reunions around the country and go on cruises together. Said another way, we will continue to do what we have always done.

Hopefully, as is true of Vivian's class, more classmates will feel the urge to reconnect, even if they have been out of touch for long periods of time.

Getting together will become more difficult physically. It may become more difficult for some financially. In any case, it will be our collective responsibility to make sure that we do what we can to overcome any barriers that individuals may have. But that is what we have always done.

We will lose more classmates, will mourn together, and will need to support each other to help deal with that eventuality. But, sadly, that is what we have always done.

Vivian Kline, her Birch Wathen High School Class of 1943, and other high school classes across the country that are older than we teach us the importance of remaining close. She and they teach us the importance of remaining fit and curious and interested and interesting. She and they teach us the importance of being creative and aware and engaged and compassionate. She and they teach us the importance of reaching out to those who have known us longest and to connect and reconnect with those who can help us understand our past.

Play tennis. Get involved in politics. Travel far and wide. Call a friend. Go to a reunion. Write a book. And—always wear a flower behind your ear.

The University City High School Class of 1964 has established a solid foundation over four-plus decades and has every reason to follow the example of those who are going before us. We have the opportunity to "feel so at home" for the rest of our lives.

A Modest Proposal

Feeling at home is a powerful concept. But where is home? Ann's parents recently moved out of the Clayton, Missouri house in which they lived for 57 years and into a senior living apartment facility called the "Brentmoor," which is in, of all places, University City. While they understandably delayed and even resisted the decision to move from their home, they are now very happy to have done so.

Ann calls the Brentmoor "a cruise ship on land." Meals are served in a dining room, with a happy hour every evening before dinner; there is an activity director who provides a diverse daily schedule of events; the apartments are roomy, well-maintained, and cleaned by the staff.

Perhaps most importantly, Ann's parents are surrounded by friends who understand their mutual situation and who care about and support each other. Many residents are longtime friends and chose the Brentmoor because of others they knew who already lived there.

Classmate Kay Rudolph's mother lives there as does Suzie (classmate David's wife) Nemon's parents. The Brentmoor is not the only senior living facility in the St. Louis area at which classmate's older relatives live. For example, my aunt Ethel "Tappy" Spector Harris (U City '34) and classmate's Joanna Slotkin Baymiller's mother, Sylvia, grace Crown Center, a stone's throw from the Brentmoor.

Here is my modest proposal. Instead of worrying about planning our 60th or 70th class reunion or our joint 90th birthday party, instead of fretting about how our classmates are doing, instead of traveling to regional mini-reunions when it becomes more difficult to do so, instead of sending someone an e-mail when you could just knock on their door—let us commandeer one of the senior living facilities, all move there, and have an ongoing reunion.

We thoroughly enjoyed our "first annual class cruise." Why not enjoy a perpetual cruise on land?

Certainly there are a lot of barriers to bringing this proposal to fruition. But why not start working on it? We may be surprised that the concept becomes much more comforting and viable as we grow older.

Someday there will be only two classmates left from the University City High School Class of 1964. Would it not be appropriate for them to meet for dinner in the Brentmoor's dining room every evening?

What might that conversation be like?

Care for the World

The theme of our senior yearbook, the *Dial*, is "Eternity." Classmates Shellie Klevens and Judy Fortus wrote a poem for the yearbook, and it was fittingly chosen to grace the last page. It is also fitting that the poem graces the last pages of the body of this book.

Michele Dee Klevens Ritterman is a psychotherapist, writer, and lecturer living in Berkeley, California. She wrote her first book, *Using*

Hypnosis in Family Therapy, in 1983—a classic in the field and still in print. Her second book is about human rights, dignity, and social justice, *Hope Under Siege: Terror and Family Support in Chile.* Its foreword was written by Isabel Allende. Her third is *Woman's Wisdom*, a book Shellie describes as "...helping the reader shift from a troubled to a useful state of mind." www.micheleritterman.com

Judith Ann Fortus Growe is a college librarian living in Vancouver, British Columbia, where she became a Canadian citizen in 2003. Judy, who was voted our "Smartest Senior," says she has "spent a lifetime learning that there is much more to her and to life than being an achiever (for one thing there is the joy of singing in a choir)."

Having recently been pushed to stare her mortality in the face, Judy says, "I'm doing my darndest to connect with people, with nature, with life."

Shellie's and Judy's poem is "Care for the World."

> *And the young will be taught about life.*
> *In order that they may better understand*
> > *and care for the world.*
> *And they will be taught by the wise, by the learned;*
> *The teachers will shape the minds of the young*
> *And thereby leave their deep mark in Eternity.*
>
> *If you wish to cast a rolling star through Eternity,*
> *Take from life what you can and give it all you*
> > *possess in return.*
>
> *Eternal is the need of man's spirit to express itself. . .*
> *his is a restless, yearning spirit.*
>
> *Who the winner and who the loser are soon forgotten*
> *It is all that we learn from the game that lives on*
> > *through Eternity.*
>
> *If one voice sings forth and is joined by others. . . each*
> *a part of the whole, yet each entire of itself. . . the*
> *sound created is the Eternal melody.*

Judy and Shellie still remember working on the poem together. Judy recently shared, "It feels good, all these years later, to still like what we wrote!"

Shellie added, "I have had it on my wall for a long time."

They created something meaningful and lasting; something for eternity.

There is a photograph in the yearbook above the poem. Classmates Jon Pollock (senior class President) and Sandy Cytron stand on the front steps symbolically looking back at the school for the last time. They could very well have been shown as looking out away from the school into their and our collective future.

Judy, Shellie, Jon, Sandy, and all of our classmates have now traveled four-plus decades into that future. We continue toward the vision the poem created. We have the opportunity to "better understand and care for (our) world," to teach others "and thereby leave (our) deep mark in Eternity," and to be "the sound created...the Eternal melody." We, the University City High School Class of 1964, now go into our next future—together.

Hail, Hail to U City High.

PHOTO GALLERY

"How old would you be if you didn't know how old you was?"
Satchel Paige

"The older they get the better they were when they were young."
Jim Bouton

*Debbie Brownstein Pulley, Marla Schukar Levinson, and Barbara Glick Koch
at the West Palm Beach mini-reunion*

Alan Resnick, Judy Elbom Cameron, Lynda Gold Shapira, Cheryl Robin Goldenberg, Elaine Katz Sobel, and Leslie Berger at Las Vegas mini-reunion

*Freshman (1960) football backfield at 40-year reunion— 75 pounds lighter
Ronnie Light (fullback), Myron Levinson (halfback),
Kenny Brown (halfback), Alan Spector (quarterback)*

Stephen Kowarsky playing at Carnegie Hall

Arleen Inger and Howard Danzig enjoying the Cincinnati mini-reunion

Classmates and then AEPi fraternity brothers at the University of Missouri-Rolla
Marshall Faintich, Alan Spector, Morrie Mayer

Tim Arnold, Diane Gebben Arnold (U City class of '62), Elaine Levin Unell, Ron Unell,
Sue Corman Slater, Leslie Berger, Alan Spector
at the Arnolds' home in Croton-on-Hudson, New York

Mike Fleischmann with Katie Couric at Today Show
2006 Holiday Party—Mike is a graphic designer/animator for NBC

Irene Langfeld Hirshfield and Ellen Polinsky Cohen with their sons,
Jordan Hirshfield and Brad Cohen
at Atlanta party for the Hallmark Hall of Fame movie of Brad's life, Front of the Class;
Jordan, Brad's close friend, was portrayed in film as Brad's roommate

"First Annual Class Cruise"
Seated: Tom Norman, Jahn Norman, Leslie Berger, Judy Berger,
Sue Corman Slater, Larry Slater
Standing: Elaine Levin Unell, David Pulley, Myrna Danzig, Debbie Brownstein Pulley,
Howard Danzig, Ellen Polinsky Cohen, Joanna Slotkin Baymiller, Ron Unell,
Marla Schukar Levinson, Suzie Nemon, David Nemon, Ann Spector,
Alan Spector, Robert Berkowitz

*Alice Schneider Powell, Susan Dulsky Hammer, Phyllis Lieberman Kamenetsky
at the class 60th birthday party*

*Senior year foreign exchange student Hugo Ostropolsky with his wife
and their face-painted grandchildren in Mendoza, Argentina*

*Neal Handler, Hank Schneider, Marvin Tofle, Gary Oxenhandler, Randy Goldenhersh,
Ron Pratzel, Richard "Dickie" Jacobs, and Lenny Rubenstein at the 40-year reunion*

Commencement Exercises

OF THE

UNIVERSITY CITY
SENIOR HIGH SCHOOL

JUNE TENTH

NINETEEN SIXTY-FOUR

6:30 O'CLOCK P.M.

AT THE

SENIOR HIGH SCHOOL STADIUM

PROGRAM

PROCESSIONAL—Pomp and Circumstance................Edward Elgar

University City High School Band
Richard Patterson, Class of 1964, Conductor

INVOCATION..Rabbi Julius Nodel

Shaare Emeth Temple

ADDRESS OF WELCOME.......................................Jon Pollock

BASSOON SOLO—Concerto for Bassoon—Rondo........................Mozart

Stephen Kowarsky
Kathleen Rudolph, Accompanist

ADDRESS—A Challenge of Choice.................................Richard Jacobs

Presentations of the Class to the President of the Board of Education

Dr. Mark A. Boyer, Principal

Awarding of Diplomas by the President of the Board of Education

Mr. Alfred J. Fleischer

THE ALMA MATER..The Class

RECESSIONAL—University Grand March
—Edwin Franko Goldman

University City High School Band
Mr. Roger W. Warner, Director

CLASS OFFICERS

President...Jon Pollock
Vice-President...Richard Seidel
Secretary...Joy Morros
Treasurer...Leslie Zuke

GRADUATES

Lawrence Werner Abrams	Scott Henry Baumgartner	Harvey Richard Blumoff
Marsha Jean Ahmann	Ronald Keith Bayer	Ronald Lee Blumoff
David Alexander Amitin	Jack Michael Becker	Timothy L. Boeschenstein
Frances Elizabeth Anderson	Judith Ann Becker	Alan Boime
Rhonda Lea Andrew	Pamela Lynn Becker	Michael Nathan Bornstein
Jeffrey Lynford Andrews	Todd Jay Bender	Mary Ann Boyd
Robert Lynn Aspach	Victoria Anne Benefield	Duncan S. Bradbury
Joyce T. Arky	Peter John Benitez	Susan Patricia Brant
Stanley Walter Arky	Eileen Janet Benson	Nina Mayeux Brewer
Henry Clair Armstrong III	Sandra Berg	Arthur Jerald Bricker
Sheila Lynn Arnold	Joel David Berick	Sharon Lynn Broad
Thomas E. Arnold, Jr.	John Berkowitz	Allen Mark Brockman
Samuel Jay Askuvich	Clifford Howard Bernath	Kenneth Alan Brown
Elliot Leonard Atlas	Susan S. Biegelsen	Ronald Bernard Brown
Victoria Ann AuBuchon	Brent E. Bierman	Deborah F. Brownstein
Michelle Elaine Bacott	Joanne Biernbaum	Lois Bukowsky
Leonard Mark Bain	Suzanne Biernbaum	Harry Bunn
Sherrye Lynn Baker	Linda Joyce Bixhorn	Jerry N. Buford
Jeff Bassin	Rita Blacka	William Warren Parker Burns
Rita Elaine Baucum	Richard Alan Blath	Gloria Elaine Bushman
Cheryl Lynn Bauer	Lynda Lee Blitz	Ronald E. Cann

William Franklin Cann, Jr.

Judith Capel

Lawrence Joe Carafiol

Jay L. Carl

Kathleen Ellen Carroll

Robert Neal Chapman, Jr.

Steven Chaskelson

Allan Byron Chazen

Susan Marilyn Choden

Diana Lee Christiansen

Harvey Citerman

James Howard Cohen

James Thurman Cohen

Judith Rae Cohen

Murray B. Cohen

Richard Alan Cohen

Robert Philip Cohen

Sanford Cohen

Kimble Albert Cohn

Sallie Jo Cohn

Susan Colletta

Linda Janet Collier

Daphne Jean Condaxis

John Louis Conlon

Robert Stanley Cooper

David S. Coven

Donna Maria Crall

Helene Frances Cuttler

Margo Ellen Cytron

Sandra Gail Cytron

Howard Jerome Danzig

Lawrence B. Davis

Neil B. Davis

Sandra Lee Davis

Marilyn Jane Davison

Robert Gleen Day

Mary E. Dennis

Jonathan Stewart Dewald

Mary Muckerman Dimond

Leslie Gail Disman

Dorothy Lorraine Dower

Frances C. Drebin

Susan Ann Dulsky

Frances Ann Ehrenreich

Beverly Sue Eisen

Carol Sue Eisenberg

Mark Ivan Eisenberg

Steven Ray Eisenberg

Judith Lynn Elbom

Joel Harvey Engel

Carol Bonnie Enger

Gale Beth Epstein

Stuart Jay Epstein

Marshall Barry Faintich

Allan Jeffrey Feinberg

Louise Susan Feinberg

Leslie Joan Feit

Mark Robert Feldman

Stanley Erwin Feldman

Richard David Fendelman

Michael Ferman

Alan Richard Fiddleman

Reva Fiddleman

Nadine Faith Field

Bernard Henry Finke

Dolores Ruth Finkelstein

Laya Firestone

Gary Jay Fischer

Sue Fischlowitz

Wilma Jean Fisher

Jeffrey Martin Fishman

Sherry Fishman

Isaac Meyer Flaks

Steven Michael Fleischmann

Alan Craig Fleishman

Judith Ann Fortus

Charles Harry Foster, Jr.

Mark Elliott Foster

Francine Marilyn Fox

Louis Michael Franklin

Marilyn E. Freund

James Lewis Frey

Edward D. Friedman

Jill Elaine Friedman

Jules S. Friedman

Mark Aric Friedman

Ross Allen Friedman

Sandra Kay Fry

William Joseph Fuchs

Bonnie Marsella Gale

Mark E. Gants

Judith Eileen Garber

Phyllis Ellen Garon

Jeffrey Marc Geist

Elaine Gers

Rose-Ellen Gers

Jay Lionel Gerstein

Theodore Olin Gest

Steven Edward Gilbert

Richard Joel Gimpelson

Ellen Sue Glazier

Barbara Jane Glick

Mark Stuart Glickman

Paula Glovinsky

Lois Sheela Gold

Lynda Frances Gold
Sidney Israel Gold
Janice Diane Goldberg
Marshall Goldberg
Ruth Sharon Goldberg
Larry Alan Goldenberg
Marsha Goldbenberg
Randy Stephen Goldenhersh
Charlyne Jane Goldman
Irene Beth Goldschmidt
Barbara Goldstein
Carol Mae Goldstein
Edward Mitchell Goldstein
Michael Gerald Goldstein
Alan Richard Golubock
Marc Barry Golubock
David Michael Goodman
Deborah Goodman
Diane Gordon
Terry Edward Goretti
Marvin D. Gorman
Mary Jo Gottlieb
Ronald M. Gould
Harriet Beth Grazman
Sharyn Wynne Greenberg
Joseph B. Greeson
Jean Marie Grefenkamp
Vicki Lynn Grieshaber
Faye Toby Grosman
James Michael Grossman
Paula Gutman
Bruce David Gutnik
Zara Tepper Haimo
Ann Katherine Hall
A. Dale Halsey

Elizabeth Anne Halstead
Theodore I. Hamburg
Alan Joel Handler
Neal Jay Handler
Carol Lynn Haseltine
Edward F. Haskell
Donald L. Haupt
Marilyn Geraldine Hechter
Joyce Christine Hefele
Donna Anne Heicher
Carol A. Heitner
Lawrence Heligman
Beverly Lynn Herrin
Anne Hexter
Dennis A. Hicks
Charles Himeles
Richard Hitt
Beverly Gay Hoffman
H. George Hofmann, Jr.
Ellen Sue Holtzman
William H. Hopkins
Sandra Edith Horwitz
Lesa Jane Horzmann
Marya Hubert
Carolyn Jane Hyatt
Alreen Sue Inger
Judith Elaine Inger
Carl David Inselberg
Gary S. Jacks
Diane Stephanie Jacobs
Richard Alan Jacobs
James Alan Jacobson
John Paul Jameton
Allen Fred Jolly
Tom G. Kallenberg

Harland Kalman
Allen J. Kanter
Alan Ray Kaplan
Phillip Karfeld
Steven Lance Karty
Elaine Rae Katz
Ronna Hope Katz
James Allen Katzman
Leslie Michael Kaufman
Lee Edward Kennon
Ronald Stuart Kessler
Annette Pittman King
Sandra Rae Klayman
Larry Michael Klein
Jack S. Kleinman
Michele Dee Klevens
Marsha D. Klibansky
Gary Wayne Knarr
Carl Steven Knobler
Leonard M. Koblenz
Philip W. Kogan
Andrea Jay Kolker
Joyce Eudice Kopperman
Philip Michael Kotter
Stephen Robert Kowarsky
Edward Kramer
Victor Carl Kremer
Jacqueline Ella Kremer
David Krombach
Harvey B. Krupin
Kathleen Ann Kruvand
Sheila Ann Kunin
Martin Charles Kurlander
Toni Kusmer
Marilyn Norma Labell

William F. Ladd

Faith Mariam Ladinsky

Kathleen Lally

Diane Rae Lamberg

Kenneth Land

Maureen Lander

David F. Lang

Thomas H. Langenberg

Irene C. Langfeld

Gloria Ann Lapin

James Peter Larson

William John Lawton

Anita Joyce Laycob

Louise Carol Lebowitz

Sharon Ann Lee

Yetty Leiba

Cynthia Ann Leigh

Michele Pearl Leon

Janet Rae Lever

Barry Jay Levin

Elaine Sue Levin

Marc Stephen Levin

Gail Harriet Levinson

Myron Jay Levinson

Anita Levitt

Carl Allan Levy

Jules Richard Levy

Thomas G. Lewin

Lawrence Lieberman

Phyllis Joan Lieberman

Frank Louis Liepman

Ronald Alan Light

Susanne Gloria Light

Ellen Fay Lilley

Ellen Jane Lincors

Leta Ray Lipman

Selina Frances Loeblein

Leonard William Lohnes

Ashley M. Loiterstein

Ronald Frank Londe

Helene Diane London

Harvey Alan Loomstein

Lois Lorberbaum

Carol Lynne Losse

Ellen Kaye Lowenstein

Emily G. Lowry

Herbert Steven Lugger

Shelby Anne Lycans

Harry Keith Lynch

Jerome Lee Madden

Manuel Y. Magence

Judith Mange

Susan Jane Mansbacher

Sharon H. Marcus

Sheldon Howard Marcus

Allan Barry Markovitz

Howard David Markus

Lynne Ruth Marshak

Morrie Mayer

Franklin Sharrocks McKeown

William Joseph McKeown

Elizabeth Ann Menz

John A. Mercurio

Daniel Lee Meyer

Robert K. Middleton, III

Jane Leslie Miller

Sandford Miller

Elizabeth B. Millner

Marcia Anne Millner

Brenda Phyllis Minkin

William Charles Minton

Donald Lee Mitchell

Michael Terry Mitze

Stephen Moran

Joy Sharon Morros

Stanley Kelley Moseley

William Guenther Myers

Adrienne Nadler

Sandra Lee Nagel

Nikki Nakano

Warren Stanley Nakisher

Ronald Jay Neeter

David Mark Nemon

Neal Neuman

Burton W. Newman

Lynn Gary Newport

Morris Newton

Larry Niemeyer

Thomas Daniel Norman

Sandra S. Novack

Steve Novack

Kathrine Louise Nymark

James Alfred Oakey

Anne Bates O'Brien

Nancy Darline Ochs

Reecie Pat Olian

Ralph Henry Orlovick

Joseph Oshins

Dora Osowski

Hugo Luis Ostropolsky

Larry E. Owen

Georgia Kaye Owens

Gary Morton Oxenhandler

David William Pactor

Lloyd Alex Palans

Sandy Pankewer	Carol Ann Reed	Leonard Mark Rubenstein
Kathleen Olivia Pasco	Dean Chandler Reese	Michael Gaylord Rubin
Richard Jerome Patterson	Reginald Maurice Reif	Michael Harry Rubin
Patricia Ann Paul	Faye Helen Reinschmidt	Sheila Rae Rubin
Karen Ann Paulsen	Marilyn Audrey Renth	Kathleen Rudolph
Rebecca Pearl	Barbara Judith Renzer	Sharon R. Ruffman
Donald Ira Pearline	James Jerrold Resnick	Norman Frederick Ruhl
Lawrence Harvey Peters	Michael Paul Resnick	Richard Theodore Safron
John Franklin Pickerel, Jr.	Robert Stephen Rich	Harold Jay Sanger
Marion Harvey Pines	Thomas Arthur Rich	Roger Louis Sarver
Max I. Pincus	Jeffrey Allen Rifkind	Ina Leigh Savan
Donald Lawrence Platt	Harry Israel Ringermacher	M. J. Savoy
Shelley Brent Plattner	Sandra Jean Ritchey	Arlene Clare Schachter
Sara Ellen Plax	James Cole Roberts	Susan Marlene Schechter
Stephen Ellis Plax	Jim Wayne Roberts	Donald George Scheffing
Natalie Plotkin	Cheryl Lee Robin	Bonita Joy Schenberg
William Jerald Poe	Linda Gayle Robinson	Karen Joyce Schenberg
Marsha Susan Poger	Barbara Ann Romero	Barbara Gail Scher
Alan Jay Pogorelsky	Lawrence Roodman	Alice Schneider
Ellen Jane Polinsky	Howard Eliot Rose	Harvey Alan Schneider
Jon Victor Pollock	Emily Etta Rosen	Henry David Schneider
Phillip Polsky	Lisa Adrian Rosen	Donna Lynn Schnidman
Carl Conrad Polster	Lee Alan Rosenberg	Richard Alan Schoen
Deborah Marlene Poore	Lois Arlene Rosenberg	Allan F. Schonhorn
Bette Portnoy	Nancy Jo Rosenberg	Steven Barry Schrier
Melvin Portnoy	Sandra Frances Rosenblum	Frank G. Schroeter
Christine Ann Pratt	Sandford Steven Rosenfeld	Alan Schukar
Ronald Barry Pratzal	Preston E. Roskin	Marla Faye Schukar
Gary D. Presley	Pamela Adele Rossner	Marilyn Sue Schulman
Ann Rachel Priwer	Barbara Lee Rostenberg	Roger A. Schwartz
Joyce Elaine Propps	Morris Martin Rothman	Sharon Kaye Schwartz
Elliot Michael Raizman	Stephen Otto Rothschild	Judith Helen Scolnik
Ian Dennis Rapport	Linda Ann Rotskoff	Robin Segal
Phyllis Beth Rashbaum	Sherman David Rotskoff	Ann Irene Seidel
Jane Loretta Rathert	Harriet Ilene Ruback	Richard Bruce Seidel

Stephen Seigel

Stephen Sol Seltzer

Donald Irvin Serot

Mary Ruth Sevedge

Alice Lee Shapiro

Aaron Mark Shatzman

Leonard Sherp

Martin M. Shulman

Ellen Silverstein

Gary Singer

Harriet Singer

Eugene Edward Slade

Vicky Sleator

Joanna Slotkin

Ellen A. Smith

Joan Ellen Smith

Warren Allen Smith

Samuel Sandy Sobelman

Ilene Marcia Sokolik

Debby Sonenschein

Janis Lea Sorkin

Alan Ritchie Spector

Jerome Maynard Spector

Michael B. Spector

Alan Bruce Spetner

Beverly Dea Spritz

Gail Spritz

John Edward Stanhope

Jules Paul Steimnitz

Louise Audrey Stein

Richard Sheldon Stein

Mark Steinback

Gail Leslie Steinberg

Maxine Steinberg

Donald C. Steinman

Norman Lewis Steinman

Peter Byron Stephans

Larry Steven Stern

Leonard E. Stone

LaVerne Sue Stoops

Philip B. Sturmfels

Michael B. Susman

Phyllis Svetsinsky

Phyllis Rae Taylor

Diana Teague

Marc Wayne Tenzer

Linda Elaine Thaw

Larry Wayne Tiemann

Russell Lee Timms

Marvin Tofle

Mary Ann Toll

Linda Joan Tonopolsky

Ronald Bruce Totarsky

Gregory Tsevis

Mark Richard Tucker

Phyllis Ann Tucker

Michael Jay Tullman

Mark Tulper

Marcia Sue Turner

James Anthony Turpiano

Carol Rae Tyner

Ron Unell

Richard E. Van Allen

Peggy Lee Van Der Tuin

Peter Brill Van Dyne

Richard L. Wagner

Harvey Nelson Wallace

Maureen Beth Wasserman

Thomas A Watters, Jr.

Audrey June Waxelman

Sheldon Ray Weinberg

Michael Edward Weinberger

Jerome Neil Weiner

Kenneth Mark Weingart

Jacqueline Helene Weinreb

David L. Weinstein

Ilene Devera Weinstein

Ruth Weitz

Marsha Sue Weltman

Arleen Sue White

Marianne Mallory Whorton

Charles Wiener

Myra Lynne Wiesenthal

Clarice Diana Wion

Edward Jay Wise

James David Wolf

Dennis Harlan Wolff

Judy Barbara Wolff

Barry Allen Wolkowitz

Richard Stephen Wortman

Judith Sherry Wraight

Mark Stanley Wylan

Anna Marlene Yaffe

Julie Anne Yates

Alan Neil Ziglin

Isaac Willard Zimbalist

Carol Lee Zimmerman

Gary Allen Zimmerman

William Eric Zimmerman

Donald O. Zuch

Leslie Craig Zuke

Deann Joy Zvibleman

Phyllis Elaine Zweig

About the Author

Alan Spector, born in 1946, is among the earliest of baby boomers. During third grade, his family moved from their apartment in St. Louis to their first house in suburban University City, linking Alan to 600 others who would become his high school classmates, many of whom would become lifelong friends.

Alan graduated from University City in 1964 and went on to earn his BS in Electrical Engineering. After college graduation, he went to work for Procter & Gamble, where, as a Director of Worldwide Quality Assurance, he retired in May 2002, after a 33-year career.

Alan is enjoying an enriching and diverse retirement. He still plays baseball, a lifelong passion, and wrote his first book about the experience. *Baseball: Never Too Old to Play "The" Game* was published in March 2007.

He is on the Board for Every Child Succeeds, a program for first-time, at-risk parents and their children. For this work, he received the United Way Impact Leadership Award. He also volunteers with the Cincinnati Initiative to Reduce Violence, targeted to significantly reduce the level of gun-related violence and homicides in the city.

Alan travels extensively with Ann, his wife of more than 40 years, visiting relatives, including their children and grandsons, and friends, including classmates all over the country; sightseeing; and playing baseball around the country and the world.

BOOKS BY ALAN SPECTOR

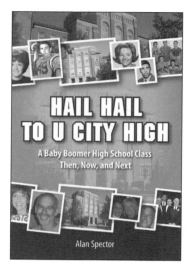

Hail Hail to U City High

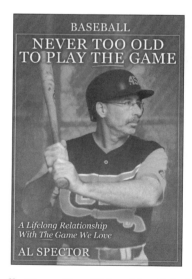

Baseball: Never Too Old to Play "The" Game

www.aaspector.com

Hail Hail to U City High

If you are a baby boomer, *Hail Hail to U City High* is your story. If you are a child or grandchild of a boomer, the book will help you understand your roots. Everyone reading *Hail Hail to U City High* will be able to relate their own friendships and experiences to those of Alan's classmates.

Baseball: Never Too Old To Play "The" Game

What were you passionate about when you were ten years old? Identify those passions and pursue them throughout your life, especially when you are older. *Baseball: Never Too Old to Play "The" Game* is a prime example of pursuing youthful passions as it captures the essence of continuing to play baseball while growing older at the same time, even into your 50s, 60s, 70s, and beyond.

These books are available directly from the author (signed) at BballNever2Old@aol.com OR from the publisher at www.cincybooks.com OR by sending this form to:

Cincinnati Book Publishers
217 W. 9th Street   Cincinnati, Ohio 45202

_____ *Hail Hail to U City High* $18.95 per book
                          **5 or more $16.95 per book

_____ *Baseball: Never Too Old To Play "The" Game* $18.95 per book
        **with purchase of *Hail Hail to U City High* $10.00 per book

_____ Total number of books

Postage & handling: $4.00 for 1 book and $2.00 for each additional book being shipped to the same address. Shipping to multiple addresses is $4.00 per book.

Book Subtotal $ _____

Postage & Handling $ _____

Sales Tax (Ohio only) $ _____ ($1.05/book)

Total Amount Due $ _____

For additional savings on purchases of ten (10) or more books, contact the author at BballNever2Old@aol.com.

Enclosed is my   o check o money order
Please charge my   o Visa   o MasterCard   o Discover   o American Express

Card # _____   Expiration date _____

Signature as on card _____

Name _____

Address _____

City _____   State _____   Zip ____